T0329227

Complete Guide to the

CITP Body of Knowledge

By **Tommie Singleton,** Ph.D., CPA.CITP, CISA, CGEIT, CMA

11151-378

Certified Information Technology Professional

Notice to Readers

Please note that the term "Dimension" used throughout the book is also be referred to as "Section" in other publications.

Complete Guide to the CITP Body of Knowledge Review Book is sponsored by the AICPA Certified Information Technology Professional (CITP) Credential Committee. Special Thanks to the following contributors:

CITP Credential Committee
(2010-2011)

James (Jim) Bourke – *Chair*
James (Jim) Boomer
William Ronald Box
Robert Fisher
Robert Green
Joel Lanz
Christopher Reimel
Chandni Sarawagi

CITP Review Task Force

James (Jim) Bourke
Robert Fisher
Robert Green
Mark Mayberry
Christopher Perry
Christopher Reimel
Chandni Sarawagi

AICPA Staff

Janis Parthun – Senior Technical Manager, Information Technology Division
Nancy Marc-Thrasybule – Manager, CITP Credential Program

Amy M. Plent – Publisher
Amy Krasnyanskaya – Senior Managing Editor
Martin Censor – Acquisitions Editor
Shandra Botts – Production Project Manager

1 2 3 4 5 6 7 8 9 0 PIP 1 9 8 7 6 5 4 3 2 1

ISBN: 978-0-87051-952-9

TABLE OF CONTENTS

RISK ASSESSMENT
Dimension 1

FRAUD CONSIDERATIONS
Dimension 2

INTERNAL CONTROL & INFORMATION TECHNOLOGY GENERAL CONTROLS

Dimension 3

EVALUATE, TEST, AND REPORT

Dimension 4

INFORMATION MANAGEMENT & BUSINESS INTELLIGENCE
Dimension 5

RISK ASSESSMENT

Dimension 1

The initial evaluation of risks that may impact the possibility of a material misstatement or the vulnerability of an organization's assets based on initial assumptions, research, and uncertainties.

LEARNING OBJECTIVES

1. To understand the types of risk assessment involved in a business entity and how they apply to IT and its relationship to financial reporting in particular, in identifying IT-related risks and the effectiveness of any controls to mitigate those risks, from a materiality constraint.
2. To understand the business environment and business processes, especially the risk IT itself brings to accounting information systems and financial reporting, and how to apply this knowledge. In public accounting, this application would involve IT-related engagements, especially the financial audit. In business and industry (B&I), it would involve managing those systems and processes effectively, as well as understanding the purposes, processes, and evidence the CPA/CITPs will be using in their engagements.
3. To understand and apply the audit risk model as defined in the risk-based standards: Inherent Risk (IR), Control Risk (CR), and the Risk of Material Misstatement (RMM). Relevant standards include Statement on Auditing Standards (SAS) No. 99, SAS No. 104–111 (RBA standards), Auditing Standard (AS) 5. Relevant models for risk include COSO, COBIT, and the P-D-C model.
4. To enhance one's understanding and evaluation of controls via walkthroughs.
5. To understand the most effective process of drafting a risk assessment report.

1.0 – INTRODUCTION

In recent years, all types of audits have become risk-based in their approaches. Standards by various professional organizations reflect this modern view that a risk-based audit is more effective than other approaches[1]. The American Institute of Certified Public Accountants (AICPA) spent years remodeling its financial statement audit approach which culminated in the risk-based standards issued in 2006, becoming effective in 2007. This approach for Certified Public Accountants (CPAs) in financial audits, and the focus on risk, is articulated by the following statement:

> *"The eight new Statements on Auditing Standards (SAS 104 through SAS 111) require both the auditor and the entity to rigorously assess the <u>risks</u> of material misstatement {RMM} of the financial statements and understand what the entity is doing to mitigate them."* [Refer to the AICPA/IT Executive Committee {ITEC} Discussion Paper]

These key standards affect both the financial audit and the role and responsibilities of the information technology (IT) auditor in a financial statement audit, and affects management and auditors in business and industry (B&I) as well. Exhibit 1.1 highlights the impact of these standards on Certified Information Technology Professionals (CITPs).

EXHIBIT 1.1: IMPACT OF STANDARDS ON CITPs	
SAS No. 99	Consideration of fraud risks, anti-fraud controls, and fraud auditing in financial audits (public accounting); and anti-fraud programs (B&I)
SAS No. 104-111	Considerations of IT in financial audits and RMM (public accounting); and IT risks, automated controls, and IT General Controls {ITGC} (B&I)
AS5	Same as Risk Standards, plus internal controls over financial reporting (ICFR), integrated audits, and Sarbanes-Oxley Act {SOX} §404 requirements

The risk-based approach (RBA) is key to the current financial audit and most other assurance services as well. Most agree it expands the role of the IT auditor in financial audits because of the need to assess risks associated with IT – beyond those traditional risks related to business processes, audit trail, etc. – and controls embedded in IT. Therefore, the IT auditor needs to identify the key relevant elements of systems and technologies in order to ensure that IT-related risks that exist in the entity are appropriately considered in the audit. These risks include concerns such as data integrity, data/systems/IT security, IT operational effectiveness, and systemized processes and controls.

This dimension of the CITP Body of Knowledge (BOK) focuses on the role and responsibilities of the CITP in both public accounting and B&I, and in applying the RBA to identify, evaluate, and mitigate relevant IT-related risks.

---

[1] Some examples include: AICPA, SAS No. 104–111; IIA, Attribute and Performance Standard #1220.A3; ISACA Audit Standard S11.

1.1 – TYPES OF RISK ASSESSMENT

Risk assessment in audits, security, and other areas should eventually roll up into the body of business risks at the enterprise level. That is, senior management of the enterprise should consider and assess the risks that exist in all areas and levels of the entity, including of course financial reporting, but also the IT function and its related activities.

Before breaking down risk assessment into the three primary areas of interest to CITPs, a review of a general risk assessment life cycle methodology is useful in helping the CITP to read, understand, review, and verify risk assessment reports from management. This approach, or a similar one, is also helpful in performing procedures related to risk assessment (e.g., risks of application controls, risks associated with IT general controls, and/or risks of any body of concerns related to the CITP's duties).

1.1.1 – Risk Assessment Life Cycle Methodology

Generally, the process to accomplish an effective risk assessment would include the following steps:[2]

1. RECOGNIZE
2. RATE
3. RANK
4. RESPOND
5. REPORT
6. REVIEW

1.1.1.1 – Recognize

The first step in a risk assessment is to use a formal, structured, effective process where the objective is to identify, as much as possible, the relevant, material risks that potentially could adversely affect the entity. For example, most entities could be adversely affected by competition or major changes in the demand for its product/service. But in most cases, the entity can also be adversely affected by some aspect of its systems, data, and/or technologies being used in business processes and/or communications, and the effect could be both relevant and material. It should be emphasized that the process should be one that is formal and structured. It is insufficient for a manager or management as a whole to have a thought process about what those risks might be without a thorough, formal, structured approach to a risk assessment. If it is not documented, it is of course not formalized, and probably not sufficiently structured.

This risk assessment process is constrained by the perspective and goal of the particular activity, whether it is external (e.g., financial audit) or internal (e.g., operational audits). Externally, the CITP will need to scope the risks to those that are in the IT space, have a relatively high RMM, and are associated with financial reporting processes, data, or reports. Internally, the CITP has different goals and is usually not constrained by these criteria.

Thus the external CITP needs to be cautious in putting IT risks into scope of an engagement. All entities have numerous IT risks in the IT space, some of which will be significant IR. But not all of the IT risks will end up in scope. For instance, there could be a significant IT risk (e.g., perimeter is weak regarding

[2] The steps provided herein are not based on any standard, guideline, or specific model but rather the author's attempt to provide steps consistent with risk assessment best practices in general. For example, there are some commonalities between this six-step process and the eight risk components of the COSO ERM model described in 1.1.2 below.

intrusions and unauthorized access to the network) where there is either no associated RMM (e.g., the financial systems are not connected to the Internet/Web server) or there is a compensating control, usually "downstream" from the point of risk (e.g., application controls and O/S controls are strong and there is a low residual risk that an unauthorized intruder can affect the financial reporting data or successfully access the financial applications). This goal is a balancing act that takes experience and care to make sure that all relevant IT risks are in scope, but that IT risks that do not in reality lead to the RMM are excluded. The internal CITP would likely include some of the IT risks the external CITP will exclude. In the example above, it is likely the B&I/internal CITP would include the perimeter risk in an audit or other activity.

1.1.1.2 – Rate

The next step is to assess the level of risk for each individual risk identified. That process usually begins with a rating of the significance of the impact for each risk identified. That significance could be as simple as high, medium, or low impact. It also can be much more sophisticated; e.g., a significance factor – such as a percentage from 0–100 (or 0.00 to 1.00). Some risks may be assessed low enough to eventually be ignored.

Another common phase in this step is to rate the likelihood that the risk will come to fruition and not be prevented. Again, a simple approach is high, medium, or low probability, or it could be more granular as 0.00 to 1.00 or a percentage.

1.1.1.3 – Rank

These two aspects of rating risk can be developed to a highly quantitative number and the results could then be plotted to assist in step three, to rank the risks. An illustration will show the potential efficacy of using this approach. First, suppose there were eight risks identified in the risk RECOGNIZE step (see column 1 of Exhibit 1.2). Management then proceeded to provide a rating for the significance factor and likelihood, both using a scale of 0.00 to 1.00, similar to a percentage (see columns 2 and 3 respectively in Exhibit 1.2). In order to obtain a "risk score", simply multiply the significance factor times the likelihood (see column 4 of Exhibit 1.2). The results can be ordered to provide the ranking objective of step three (see column 5).

EXHIBIT 1.2: Risk Score Matrix

RISK	SIGNIFICANCE	LIKELIHOOD	RISK SCORE	RANK
R1	0.60	0.25	0.15	7
R2	0.30	0.87	0.26	4
R3	0.74	0.61	0.45	3
R4	0.42	0.38	0.16	6
R5	0.72	0.79	0.57	1
R6	0.55	0.40	0.22	5
R7	0.69	0.76	0.52	2
R8	0.76	0.18	0.14	8

Another way to organize and rank risks, especially when the number of risks gets to be substantial, is to plot them in a scorecard manner. Using the same data as above, these risks could be plotted on a traditional scatter plot (see Exhibit 1.3).

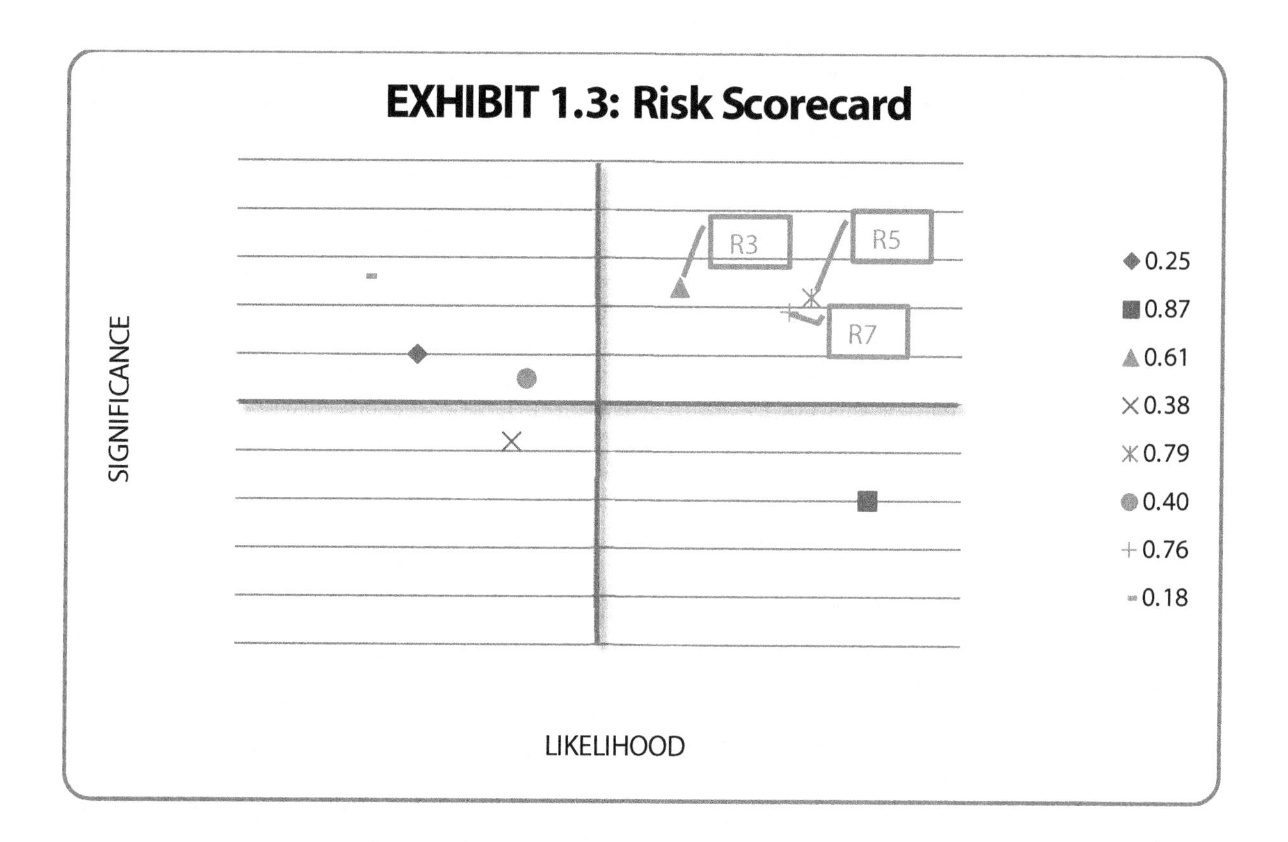

Then the scatter plot can be subdivided into four equal quadrants. The quadrant at the upper end of each axis (up and right) is generally considered the highest risk. The quadrant closest to the origin is the lowest risk quadrant. The other two quadrants are considered medium risk. This approach groups the risks into manageable units that could be more useful in risk management rather than a simple ranking. In the scorecard approach, risks R3, R5, and R7 end up in the "high risk" scorecard quadrant, R4 as low, and the others all in the medium quadrants. Note in the scorecard that R1 and R8 are actually ranked lower than R4 in the risk score matrix.

Thus the latter view is generally considered easier to assimilate because it is more visual, and provides a more efficient and effective application of risk assessment by ranking risks into groups of similar ratings (i.e., the quadrants). It also draws attention to the risks that need to be addressed by some order or precedence (Quadrant 4 {high}, then quadrants 2 and 3 {medium}, and last quadrant 1 {low}) that is probably easier to apply than the risk score matrix ranking of all risks.

Regardless of the approach, or its sophistication, management needs to do a formal ranking of risks, and use a structured process to get to that ranking. Management also needs to document the process (e.g., rationale, approach, methodology used) and results.

1.1.1.4 – Respond

The next step is for management to develop appropriate responses to the higher risks. Management should formally develop mitigating controls, actions, or plans to sufficiently mitigate all of the risks to an acceptable level[3]. Those responses can take a variety of forms such as insurance, controls, expertise (e.g., outsource), and other measures.

---

[3] Some risks will already be at an acceptable level of risk and therefore will not need to be mitigated further.

But the response is directly linked to both the specific risk and the assessed level of that risk. That is, it takes a high-powered control (or set of controls) to mitigate a high risk versus the type of control needed to mitigate a risk assessed less than high. The linking of both response to specific risk and the power or ability of the response to the level of risk is applicable in financial audits. The audit plan is directly linked to the RMM and further audit procedures in a similar manner.

Some risks will end up as exposures: i.e., risks for which there are no mitigating actions. One reason for bypassing addressing a risk is because the risk, risk score, or risk scorecard quadrant are below the threshold of risk that management has established as the level for which it is willing to accept the risk. Secondly, some risks will be subject to mitigation actions that are cost prohibitive. That is, the benefits of mitigating the risks are less than the costs of the mitigating action. Thus management will not mitigate all risks.

1.1.1.5 – Report

Now that management has identified, assessed, ranked, and provided mitigating actions, that information needs to be documented. Some report or document should be created by management in order to provide a formal and structured conclusion to the risk assessment process to this point.

This document is a key one for the CITP. In a financial audit, the CITP will want to ask for management's risk assessment report or documentation in order to gather evidence about risks associated with the audit. For instance, if management cannot provide a risk assessment report, that fact indicates a formal risk assessment has not been completed yet. The absence of a formal report means some relevant risk may not yet be identified at all. It also means management has not performed a risk aversion activity in this area. Generally, this situation raises the overall risk of the audit by some degree. If management also has no coherent thoughts or risk assessment activities to date, that increase of audit risk goes up by some degree again.

On the other hand, if management provides a well-written risk assessment report, the CITP has something that can assist him/her in gathering evidence and in assessing inherent risk and control risk (i.e., RMM). If the CITP discovers evidence that the report is reasonably thorough, uses common or sound methodologies, and the controls are in place and working effectively, it is possible those facts reduce IR and CR; that is, reduce the RMM. Or such evidence may otherwise provide assurance related to reliance on tests of controls.

Often the presence or absence of an effective risk assessment report is associated with "tone at the top", where management regularly uses due diligence in addressing risks and similar issues. The COSO element of control environment and risk assessment are related to the presence of a risk assessment report. That is, when a healthy tone at the top is present, management will likely know about COSO and exert due diligence to satisfy the five components, including risk assessment.

1.1.1.6 – Review

The IT world is characterized by rapid change. Thus any risk assessment, especially as it relates to IT, would certainly need regular review. Monitoring the risks, individually and in groups, and monitoring the risk mitigation effectiveness is certainly critical in keeping risk at an acceptable level. New risks can clearly emerge. Old risks can increase or decrease in assessed level (i.e., rating). Controls and other mitigations can lose effectiveness. Alternative mitigations can become more efficient or effective than the ones in existence. Thus a regular review is important to an effectual risk assessment and risk management. Therefore one thing the CITP would hope to see is not only all of the above regarding risk assessment, but also some formal and structured approach to monitoring risks and responding accordingly.

This step naturally leads management to return to step 4, respond. It also may lead through steps 1 (recognize), 2 (rate), and/or 3 (rank) before getting to step 4. Thus this approach is a life cycle approach to risk assessment.

1.1.2 – Enterprise Risk Assessment

The risk assessment related to IT that the CITP focuses upon should not be in isolation or independent of other risk assessments. The latest Committee of Sponsoring Organizations (COSO) model for internal controls, Enterprise Risk Management (ERM), has gotten a lot of attention and application (see Exhibit 1.4). COSO's ERM filled a void for the need of a generally accepted definition to risk assessment and management, and a need for a flexible, thorough structure that could not only describe risks but provide guidance on how the process should function.[4] ERM begins by defining ERM as:

> *"... a process, effected by an entity's board of directors, management and other personnel, applied in a strategy setting and across the enterprise, designed to identify potential events that may affect the entity, and manage risk to be within its risk appetite to provide reasonable assurance regarding the achievement of entity objectives."*

EXHIBIT 1.4: COSO ERM Model[5]

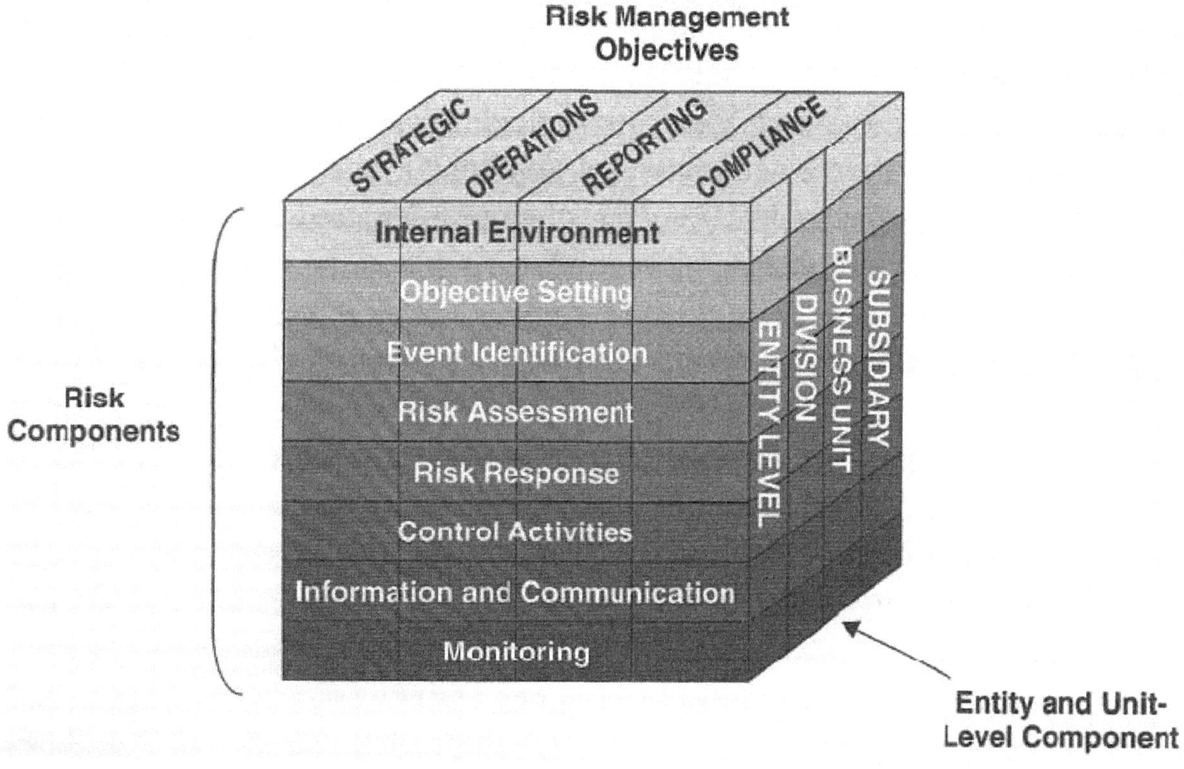

Risk Management Objectives
STRATEGIC
OPERATIONS
REPORTING
COMPLIANCE
Risk Components
Internal Environment
Objective Setting
Event Identification
Risk Assessment
Risk Response
Control Activities
Information and Communication
Monitoring
ENTITY LEVEL
DIVISION
BUSINESS UNIT
SUBSIDIARY
Entity and Unit-Level Component

COSO ERM has three dimensions (see Exhibit 1.4): risk components (8), risk management objectives (4), and the entity/unit components (proprietary to the entity). All of these should be of interest to CITPs in business and industry. For CITPs, the ERM model is a useful tool, partly because it can be applied to all

---

[4] Robert R. Moeller, "COSO Enterprise Risk Management: Understanding the New Integrated ERM Framework", 2007, John Wiley & Sons: Hoboken, NJ, page 52.

[5] Robert R. Moeller, "COSO Enterprise Risk Management: Understanding the New Integrated ERM Framework", 2007, John Wiley & Sons: Hoboken, NJ, page 53.

types of businesses and entities, and covers a broad scope of risks. It is also valuable because CITPs have a need to know, understand, interpret, and analyze risk and risk management issues in various aspects of their duties. For instance, areas of the entity are often selected because of "risk considerations". The CITP will need to be able to ask the right questions, determine the validity of areas chosen or not chosen, and to properly evaluate the risk management process of the entity.

The CITP may also find ERM valuable in the review of internal controls and in providing management comments at the end of the audit. In fact, it could be that the external CITP (IT auditor) finds ERM useful in reviewing and evaluating a client's risk management system and results, if the client has one, for purposes of the engagement's objectives.

1.1.3 – Financial Statement Risk Assessment

Risks associated with the financial reporting process are generally identified in the risk assessment phase of the financial audit (see Exhibit 1.5).[6]

During the risk assessment phase of a financial audit, the CITP will need to gather evidence about IT-related inherent risk in order to make a reasonable assessment of the RMM for that client in that fiscal year. The CITP will also be gathering information and evidence about controls, especially those embedded in IT, to assist in making an appropriate assessed level of relevant CR. This information will also allow the CITP to identify key controls that are missing, weak, or strong (that is, can be relied upon). Then the CITP will be able to provide input into the audit planning phase (phase two of the financial audit) to assess the RMM, and any IT-related procedures that might be beneficial for the further audit procedures phase (3rd phase) of the audit.

In fact, the RBA standards require further audit procedures (FAP) to be developed from a financial statement risk assessment, where the FAP are linked to specific risks. Not only are they linked to specific risks, but the level of the substantive procedure (or other FAP) should be appropriate for the level of risk. That is, for high risk RMM, the FAP needs to be one of the more powerful ones; e.g., re-performance.

In light of these requirements, and the specialized knowledge the CITP brings to the financial audit, the audit planning phase could benefit by the contributions of the CITP in developing these FAPs. For instance, the CITP might be able to identify an IT-related procedure that is either more efficient or more effective, or both, than an alternative manual substantive procedure. The CITP may also find opportunities for the use of Computer-Assisted Audit Tools (CAATs) for the same reasons. And finally,

[6] For business and industry, those risks are most likely the charge of the entity's internal audit function.

the CITP may very well have discovered some value add management comments related to the results of the risk assessment phase (IR, CR, and IT-related issues) that would be beneficial to communicate.

There are two key contributions by the CITP in the financial audit planning. First, the CITP is better able to recognize areas where the objective of an IT-related control overlaps with the objective of a substantive procedure. This situation is ideal for uncovering opportunities to use IT-related procedures versus labor-intensive substantive procedures. If the objectives overlap, then either a test of control (ToC) or a substantive procedure could theoretically serve the purposes of the need for a FAP. It is possible a ToC or IT-related procedure is more efficient and/or effective than alternative manual substantive procedures.

Secondly, it is possible, under the right set of circumstances, for the test of control to involve a test of one instance. Both Public Company Accounting Oversight Board (PCAOB) standards[7] and AICPA standards[8] have stated that fact. That is, the ToC may not be expensive to develop. One example of possible circumstances is if the outcome of the control is a dichotomous result. Another would be if the application control does not include a complex calculation.

The risk assessment phase typically should occur in the last quarter of the fiscal year under audit, and possibly in some other quarter during the fiscal year. For controls to be considered effective in audits of publicly-traded companies, those controls must be operationally effective throughout the fiscal year. Thus there is a need to review, observe, and/or test them more than once during the fiscal year. If controls are basically unchanged during the year, that makes it easier for the CITP to get assurance regarding that effectiveness.

Financial statement risk assessment can be viewed by two primary perspectives. The first is the financial reporting process that leads to the financial reports. The second is the financial statements themselves.

In order to effectively assess IR and CR during the risk assessment phase, some type of flowcharting of the financial statement data flow from initial capture to and through business processes and control procedures all the way to the financial statements themselves usually is beneficial. It could be that no appropriate flowchart exists, or that the one in place is not current. In those cases, the CITP may need to create one for the purposes of the financial statement risk assessment of the audit.

From the flowchart, the CITP should be able to identify all of the relevant systems, data sources, and the relevant processes, controls, and workflows that impact the financial reports or the financial reporting process. Use of flowcharts also may be beneficial in identifying IT-related IR. Identifying these objects becomes critical in properly identifying IT-related risks associated with financial statements. Of course it is possible, that the nature and complexity of the systems being audited do not provide an opportunity for flowcharts to be beneficial.

1.1.4 – IT Risk Assessment

Often, tracking the entire process using the aforementioned flowchart becomes critical for the CITP to be able to identify potential IT-related risks associated with the data that will end up in the financial statements, and risks associated with automated business processes and IT-embedded controls.

1.1.4.1 – Process: Applications

The documentation of key systems and applications allows the CITP to identify the possible IT-related risks associated with those applications. Specifically, customized software developed by the entity is

[7] Originally in AS2.

[8] Originally in SAS No. 94.

generally seen as more risky than customized software from a software vendor or commercial off-the-shelf software (COTS). The external CITP, in financial audits, will need to focus on those significant financial systems identified in the process above. In other words, focus only on those systems and ITGCs that are material to the financial audit to properly scope the financial audit (see also 1.1.1.1).

Of the three, the one with the highest IR is customized software developed by the entity. That is, there is a relatively high IR for applications developed in-house. There are controls that can mitigate that IR, and the CITP will want to examine, observe, review, and otherwise gather assurance that the IR of customized applications has been adequately mitigated.[9] The reason for the high level of IR is the nature of programming. It is very difficult to develop an application, even when tested, and put it into operations without any bugs or glitches. The probability of something not being quite right once an application is developed and implemented is almost 100%. This phenomenon could be referred to as "Murphy's IT law".

Sometimes vendors customize software applications for their customers. This situation is less risky, but carries the risk of bugs or fraud like any other application development project.

Generally speaking, the application situation with the least risk is when it is a COTS package AND the vendor is reliable. The assumption is that a vendor with a large set of customers where the application has been in existence for some years is relatively reliable; more reliable than customized applications.

Suppose that in the risks identified in Exhibit 1.2 and 1.3 above that R5 is a risk associated with a new application the entity has purchased from a software vendor where the version is 1.0, the vendor is new to software manufacturing, and the project manager for the entity is a sales person from the vendor. The reasons this risk may be high, even though it is a COTS package, are as follows:

(1) The vendor's reliability is unknown and being new to software manufacturing presents the same kind of risk as customized software.
(2) Version 1.0 is particularly risky (see discussion below).
(3) IT projects are relatively risky regardless of how well they are handled. Being managed by the vendor presents more risk than a project manager from the entity.

Version numbers provide information related to risk assessment. They use a format of MM.nn where MM represents a major change in the application, beginning with version number 1. Thus a version of 8.01 would mean an application that had been through 7 major changes since its inception, and likely to have been used for years by its customers. If the vendor were reliable (e.g., Microsoft, Sage, IBM, or some other well-known vendor with a substantial customer base), then 8.01 would generally be seen as fairly reliable, and there would be assurance that the application and its controls could be relied upon to some extent; or at least the risk of the application in the financial statement system is generally fairly low.

The number to the right of the decimal (nn) represents minor fixes, changes, or modifications within a major version. Thus 8.01 would mean 1 minor change had been made since version 8 (i.e., 8.00) had been released. Likewise 8.11 would mean 11 minor changes had been made.

One general risk avoidance situation is to avoid 1.00 at all costs, and wait for M.01 before implementing M.00 because a major change in the application follows Murphy's IT law. Put another way, the R5 scenario represents an IT-related risk where the magnitude (level) is at the peak of IR.

[9] See Dimension 3, internal controls and ITGC for more on the controls that could mitigate IR associated with applications.

Another general risk is whether the entity is relatively current with the version of the application it is using compared to the most recent version. That is, if the current version is 8.12 and the entity is using 6.9, there is likely some risk associated with the fact the entity is so far behind the current version. One actual risk is the fact software vendors generally do not support older versions of their software, at some point.

The above ignores one factor that is rather common, especially in medium to large-sized entities. Sometimes applications used in the financial reporting "trail" include some COTS and some customized, even if it is just one or two middleware[10] applications. These applications need to be evaluated independently, and the CITP will need to respond to whatever risks emerge.

1.1.4.2 – Process: Data Storage (Integrity, Security, and Reliability)

One of the IT-related risks that are fairly common is databases. The nature of the modern database is to be enterprise wide in scope; that is, a single database holds an enormous portion of the data the enterprise has captured. Thus, if an unauthorized party gains access to the entity's database, that person has access to a large portion of its data. Because of this fact, data storage has a relatively high IR. The CITP will want to examine the degree of that risk and, of course, what controls are in place to mitigate the risk.

For example, the above is why a database administrator (DBA) has such a high inherent risk. IR associated with a DBA is why there should be strict and broad mitigating controls, such as proper segregation of duties (SoD) for the DBA; e.g., no access to keying data, running applications, implementing applications, or developing systems.

One reason for the need for extra care and controls with the DBA is the fact the DBA may be able to circumvent strong network and application controls. For instance, an entity may have strong network controls regarding login credentials, strong SoD, and strong restricted access. Further, the entity may also have implemented separate and strong application controls to restrict access to applications and data. Together, these controls represent rather strong access controls to protect data. However, it is possible the DBA can use his/her access to bypass the network and application controls and directly access data files, whereupon he/she may change data, falsify data, or steal data, all despite the strong network and application controls.

One way to view the importance of data is to think through the idea of IT risks and what they include related to an object like financial reporting. In fact, it could be argued that financial statement data is the hub of all IT risks associated with financial statement audits. It can be argued, from the external CITP perspective, which it is all about the data.

In reality, the data is generally under the control of applications. That is, data is accessed, changed, and reported from applications (see Exhibit 1.6).[11] Put another way, generally access to data is obtained via the application that houses the data (known as the "front door"). Access to applications allows a user access to the data it houses. This fact is why it is so important to identify the key, relevant systems for accounting applications and financial statement reporting systems in order to assess this type of IT risk.

[10] Middleware is software written to coordinate communications of some kind between two systems. In this document, middleware is software used to transfer data between two systems, platforms, or databases. It is customized for the two different systems by a vendor, consultant, or in-house IT. It usually is a relatively small-sized program, and usually only one program; i.e., limited in scope somewhat compared to payables, payroll, etc.

[11] It is possible for unauthorized IT experts to gain access to raw data or files and make changes, steal data, corrupt data, or otherwise carry out malicious activities. While this scenario is possible, generally access to data is restricted to the application within which it is housed.

EXHIBIT 1.6: Data Focused Risk Assessment

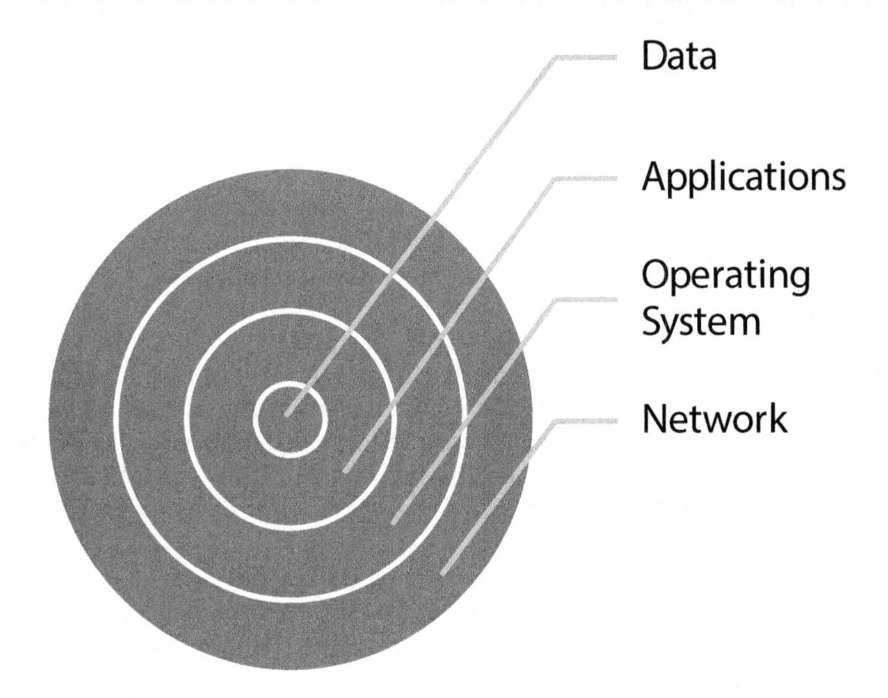

But the application and data are housed in an operating system (see Exhibit 1.6). That operating system (O/S), for the most part, controls who can obtain access to the applications – assuming the entity uses whatever access control is made available by the operating system. Unfortunately, the data can be accessed directly by the operating system as well (known as the "back door"). Administrators of the O/S have to be able to keep it working properly, and similar to a DBA, present a high IR. In fact, administrators with unrestricted access to the O/S are said to have "the keys to the kingdom" because they can access any data anywhere. Unauthorized access to the O/S also presents a high IR of access to data. Thus tight controls are needed over the O/S to mitigate these kinds of risky access to the database.

And operating systems are housed in networks. Generally speaking, it is the network level of an entity where users gain access, and the front door for unauthorized users who try to break into the system. Passwords and other logical access controls generally originate at the network level to control access to operating systems and applications.

By illustration, if the controls at the application level are strong, then there is less concern about unauthorized access at the network level. If an intruder did get in at the network level, they would likely be stymied by the strong access controls at the application level, or even the operating system level above it, if properly secured.

Thus the data is at the hub of almost all IT risks in a financial audit. The CITP can use this fact in reaching conclusions about the IT risk assessment and tracing IT-related risks (RMM).

1.1.4.3 – Process: Communications

Sometimes relevant data is communicated across networked lines or systems. This situation usually carries a relatively high IR because of the nature of communications; or more specifically, the susceptibility of intrusions or unauthorized interception. Most of these cases require a subject-matter expert (SME) to properly assess risks.

1.1.4.4 – Process: Data Transfers

A special type of communications is data transfers. Any time data is transferred from one system to another, that process is generally considered to be a relatively high IR. The transfer can be made in several ways. Generally, these can be classified as manual, semi-automated, and automated.

The manual process involves converting data in the originating system to a hardcopy printout and one or more keypunch personnel enter the data into the receiving (downstream) system (e.g., an electronic spreadsheet). This type of transfer would generally be considered the highest transfer risk. Much of that risk is associated with the high-risk manual rekeying of all that data. Part of the risk would also be associated with the fact that the receiving system is an electronic spreadsheet, as opposed to a computerized system or application. The situation where an employee is using a tool that is customizable, the employee makes raw data entries, the employee builds calculations or processes, or some combination of all of these, is referred to as end-user computing.

End-user computing (EUC) is generally considered to be relatively high in IR because of these employee-dependent circumstances. Usually, EUC involves employees who have an insufficient knowledge, ability, and expertise related to IT and controls, and who lack proper SoD (i.e., the user develops their own processing tool {such as formulas in Excel}, runs the tool, and has virtually sole custody of the tool).

The transfer could also be semi-automated where data is exported into some kind of file (e.g., text/ASCII {American Standard Coded Information Interchange}, Excel/csv {comma separated value}) and then manually imported into Excel or a similar tool. This type of transfer has a little less IR regarding the transfer because it does not have the manual rekeying of data. But it still has a receiving system that has a relatively high IR because it is an electronic spreadsheet. It also represents a significant IR related to fraud, as it is fairly easy for the end user to manipulate the data in the spreadsheet offline from the primary accounting information system (AIS).

These risks can usually be sufficiently mitigated, including the Excel and EUC risks. But the IR of these issues can be, and usually are, relatively high.

It could also be that either the entity or a third-party has written middleware[12] to transfer data from one computerized system to another – an automated transfer process. While this type of transfer is generally considered relatively high IR as a process, it is the lowest of the three because the data is transferred without human intervention and because the receiving system is an automated one – not a tool like an Excel spreadsheet or Access database.

1.1.5 – Security Risk Assessment (Audits)

Security audits are a special case of risk assessment. Some of a security audit is relevant to a financial audit, some of it is not, and some depends on the circumstances. As mentioned in 1.1.4, logical access plays a key role in assessing IT risk. Naturally, logical access is also a key in a security risk assessment. Thus these two overlap.

For a financial audit, some of the risks in a security audit would be irrelevant in a financial audit. The example above where an intruder gained access at the network level only to be frustrated by strong access controls at the application layer illustrate how the perimeter could be seen as irrelevant by the external

[12] Middleware is a term for a software application that exists as an interface between two systems, where the middleware gathers data from one system and transfers it automatically to the properly formatted data into the receiving system.

CITP in a financial audit in particular. However, perimeter weaknesses are of critical importance in a regular security risk assessment.

1.2 – UNDERSTANDING THE BUSINESS ENVIRONMENT & BUSINESS PROCESSES

There are many aspects of the business environment that relate directly to the role and responsibilities of the CITP in business and industry and public accounting. For instance, computer operations, IT general controls, and IT policies and procedures are all elements of the business environment, and all examples of areas the CITP has the expertise to make contributions, or is an area the CITP would examine in exercising his/her duties in performing risk assessment activities. The same is true for business processes. For example, automated controls are embedded in business processes that were automated. In order for a CITP to properly evaluate IT controls, it is imperative that he/she have an understanding of the entity's business processes.

This section will focus on risks associated with executive management functions, complexity of business entities, and business processes.

1.2.1 – Executive Management Functions

As plans relate to IT, executive management has to handle issues such as constant changes (including improvements) in hardware and software, how to integrate the IT function across all business units and other entity functions, how to make IT a strategic advantage, and how to efficiently and effectively manage all aspects of the IT function. All of these issues, and others, have the potential to introduce substantive risks to the business entity.

One way to frame these types of issues is to consider them in the framework of the primary functions of management: plan, organize, direct, and control. In these functions, one can identify areas of risks and opportunities for controls. Thus the CITP could benefit from familiarity with the IT risk implications and considerations of these functions.

1.2.1.1 – Plan

Executive management's role of planning includes the IT function. Whether it is several documents or a single composite strategic plan, the outcome should be a document or set of documents that define the IT function.

The first key plan related to IT is the strategic plan.[13] In the strategic plan, executive management should provide general guidance for the primary roles and responsibilities of IT in the organization. For example, management should provide a vision or purpose statement regarding the overall role of IT for the entity. Secondly, the strategic plan should provide general direction for future developments and changes in IT. Thirdly, the plan should include a formal mechanism for making sure IT meets strategic objectives, and is valued by some objective measure (e.g., return on investment {ROI} of some kind). Other long-term issues should also be provided for in this plan.

To illustrate, consider Southwest airlines. A primary goal of Southwest is to have a high number of turns at the airport gates in order to spread out the fixed cost of gate rentals across more flights than its

[13] The IT strategy could be embedded in the business's strategic plan or be a separate document. The latter tends to happen in larger sized companies.

competition. Therefore, part of its IT strategy is to develop systems that can facilitate faster turnarounds at the gate.[14]

A second key plan would be a risk assessment including plans to mitigate the identified risks. Executive management should do an IT risk assessment in order to effectively mitigate risks that can potentially adversely affect the business, its operations, its ability to compete effectively, its ability to reach its strategic goals and objectives, or even to just accomplish the business model.

Another key part of the strategic plan is for executive management to establish plans for an operational budget and capital budget for the IT function. The IT function will naturally need financial (budget) resources annually. In the case of the capital budget, the IT function will need funding for major IT projects to keep the IT portfolio efficient and effective, and for IT projects to satisfy strategic direction.

A parallel consideration is the need for executive management to plan how it will assess the value of IT as a portfolio, on individual projects, and as a strategic resource. The capital budget and strategic plan should be aligned with valuation (ROI) to mitigate the risk of IT inefficiencies.

While other aspects of plans may exist, one common planning document is the entity's policies and procedures (P&P). In this document, executive management establishes a methodology and control mechanism to ensure the employees function consistently within areas, across employees, and over time (including turnover of employees). Generally speaking, management is particularly interested in making sure business processes are standardized, function as prescribed, and are adjusted formally as needed.

This body of documents associated with planning provides the CITP with a source for assessing IT-related risk. That is, the CITP will want to obtain a copy of the strategic plan, business model, and associated plans. Using these plans (along with the IT policies and procedures), the CITP can review them for areas of IT-related risk.[15] Using a review of the strategic plans, especially the IT risk assessment, the CITP should be able to identify risks, measure risks, and even design follow-up procedures where necessary.

1.2.1.2 – Organize

A major responsibility of executive management related to IT is to ensure the entity acquires the resources necessary to accomplish the goals and objectives of the entity, especially those outlined in the strategic plan. Resources include: infrastructure, hardware, software, qualified IT personnel (hiring; professional development, qualifications, adjusting to changes in IT; terminating), finances, and facilities. Management should maintain a dynamic portfolio of its IT in order to manage it and to be effective in reaching its strategic direction and goals.

Management will also have to decide the best structure for the IT function – centralized (all IT resources available for a central unit) versus decentralized (some IT resources in each major business unit). Another aspect of organizational structure planning is the organization chart. This chart and structure is vital to risk because management could fail to properly segregate incompatible IT functions and thereby increase risk in all associated IT, systems, business processes, and automated controls. Likewise the appropriate SoD will decrease risks in those areas. Thus the CITP will want to review the organization chart, possibly job descriptions, and interview key personnel in order to determine if incompatible IT functions are properly segregated.

[14] This strategy explains why Southwest does not transfer luggage to other carriers.

[15] Actually, the review of the strategic plans could assist in identifying areas related to many other objectives the CITP might have.

One reason why this segregation is important is to minimize the opportunity for someone to add malicious code to a software application. If application development is segregated from application maintenance, the "second set of eyes" is a deterrent to malicious code as the independent second person has a chance of detecting it. There is also an operational benefit. Given that a different person is going to maintain the application, there is a good likelihood that adequate documentation of the original application exists. This specific SoD is also valuable in identifying coding errors that might go unnoticed by the original programmer and end users. The maintenance programmer has some probability of spotting erroneous code while maintaining it.

Another key separation is program development from operations. Because the programmer knows so much about the program, he/she is in the position of possibly knowing, or creating, ways around controls. Put another way, if a programmer were also a user, he/she is in a position to deliberately create errors or fraud with the level of knowledge he/she has of the program.

As mentioned in planning, executive management needs to provide an operational budget. That budget should be sufficient to take care of annual resources needed by the IT function. It would include the resources necessary for the operations of IT across the entity. However, executive management should also provide for capital IT projects as well, as mentioned in planning.

Actually, executive management has at least two options for major capital outlays for IT. One is to have a formal structure and process for developing a capital budget, and for awarding funding to competitive IT projects; that is, those that have a reasonable probability of satisfying the direction, goals, and objectives of the strategic plan. The alternative approach is for the CIO or equivalent to present business cases to the board of directors {BoD} or Chief Executive Officer {CEO} (or both) in an ad hoc fashion, and have the project receive approval, be postponed, or be declined. This latter process tends to seek funding for each IT project as a standalone project without necessarily fulfilling due diligence in examining the population of choices, without aligning projects with strategic plans, and without sufficient consideration of the value of IT.

The CITP will want to determine which of the methods is in place. The reason the choice matters is that the former reduces risk, and the latter increases risk. Those risks are that IT projects will fail to be delivered on time, on budget, and be fully functional, that they will fail to meet the strategies of the entity, that the IT function will not develop the most effective technologies and systems because of the results of adhocracy, and that the entity will spend more money than necessary (either on an individual project or one that is less effective than some alternative not considered).

The external CITP is interested in this information as it relates to ITGC (IT governance, project management, etc.) Any risk here is indirect to the financial statements, but could directly affect the ability to rely on tests of controls (if ITGC is not reliable, the financial auditors cannot rely on ToC). It also could lead to the RMM through a chain of events that the external CITP might have identified (e.g., the severe weakness in ITGC/IT governance and project management means program development of critical applications may have a high probability of error or fraud, and that error or fraud might be material and go undetected because of the absence of mitigating controls). The internal CITP would usually be interested regardless for operational reasons.

1.2.1.3 – Direct

The main purpose of management's direction function is to ensure compliance with objectives, policies, procedures, and business processes. Much direction revolves around management's ability to sufficiently motivate its employees to function coherently and consistently within those bounds.

In regards to the interaction of management's direct function and IT, communication of management is probably the most significant element. That communication would naturally include its policies and procedures; how IT personnel can receive more training, expertise, or knowledge; expectations (e.g., job descriptions); and the entity's formal processes related to the IT function.

1.2.1.4 – Control

The controlling function's purpose is to determine whether the actual procedures, processes, and practices of the IT function comply with management's planned activities. Controlling is probably the most relevant of the functions to CITPs as it naturally includes all types of controls, including any intended to mitigate risks, and, of course, any absent mitigating controls. Controls that have been implemented should also have been documented explicitly and formally.

Controls, in part, should be a natural outcome of extending the P&P into everyday performance. That is, a substantive portion of the internal control structure is essentially derived from P&P.

In addition, the CITP's IT risk assessment needs to consider whether controls are in place to appropriately mitigate IT-related risks. Some issues that need controlling in order to reduce IT-related risks follow.

The budgets have already been mentioned, but cost and spending needs to be controlled. That includes operations and IT capital projects. If the entity has a formal operational budget but ad hoc capital project process, that speaks to the level of IT risk associated with capital projects.

IT governance is one formal structure and formal process that can serve as a control for the IT organization, especially for major IT projects. IT governance is a mirror of corporate governance but instead of financial reporting, the object is IT. Thus the BoD should have an expert in IT, who is independent, and who will serve on a committee of the BoD to interact with the IT function by providing information and serving as a controlling function for the IT function. The IT capital budget would be assigned to that person's responsibility. That expert would also make sure IT projects aligned with the entity's strategic goals, objectives, and plans, and that IT projects are managed effectively (at a minimum, on time, on budget, fully functional).

It would also be incumbent on that person to make sure all IT investments added value to the entity (e.g., some kind of ROI approach). This particular objective has been difficult over the years, but best practices in IT governance, which have been developed over the last few years, provide methods of measurement of that value.

A surrogate for BoD involvement is a cross-functional IT steering committee (ITSC). The steering committee should represent all major IT user groups, all major business units, and IT itself. The chair should be independent of the IT function; that is, the Chief Information Officer (CIO) or other IT manager should not be the chair. The BoD should delegate its authority to the ITSC to award funding for IT capital projects. The ITSC should also be instructed to align IT projects with executive management's strategic plans, goals, objectives, and business model. Funding should be set aside at the beginning of the fiscal year by the BoD, and delegated to the ITSC for distribution. The ITSC should also provide some oversight of the IT capital projects to ensure they are delivered on time, on budget, and fully functional.

One key point is that best practices associated with IT governance, whether a formal structured IT governance or some effective surrogate, IS A CONTROL for certain risks (see 1.5.3 for more on best practices and controls). Likewise the absence of a formal IT governance structure increases the risk of IT in the ways already stipulated.

Another aspect of control is the computer operations as a whole. Risks here include: failure to timely resolve IT problems (e.g., help desk efficiencies and effectiveness), failure to have systems available adequately (e.g., downtime less than some percentage, usually less than 1%), restore operations after a major system failure or disaster (business continuity and disaster recovery), failure to follow standard methods (e.g., IT best practices or IT P&P), failure to maintain quality standards (e.g., data, information, processes), failure to document properly (e.g., new systems development), failure to manage IT projects efficiently and effectively, failure of appropriate security measures, failure to adequately control users (e.g., malicious activities by employees, failure to properly use systems and technologies), and failure to have satisfactory audits and reviews of IT.

An important control component is a formal, structured, and expert-driven process for ensuring all automated business processes have the appropriate automated controls embedded in the applications. This component is critical if the entity writes some or all of its own programs and software. If the CITP discovers that the IT function adds controls to its applications on an ad hoc basis, such as a dependency on the request of the project sponsor to include controls with the system requirements, then the risk that controls are absent can be relatively high.

These four aspects of management and some of the major repercussions regarding IT are summarized in Exhibit 1.7.

	EXHIBIT 1.7: Key IT-Related Outcomes of Executive Management
PLAN	• Strategic Plan (role and responsibilities of IT function) • Risk Assessment (IT) • Budgeting Plans (IT) • How to Value IT • Polices & Procedures (IT)
ORGANIZE	• Acquire resources to support IT function • Dynamic IT portfolio • IT function structure (centralize vs. decentralized) • IT organization (IT SoD) • Operational budget (IT) • Capital budget (IT)
DIRECT	• Communicating to IT personnel P&P • Communicating to IT personnel expectations • Communicating to IT personnel advancement opportunities • Communicating to the remainder of the entity the role and responsibilities of the IT function • Managing the IT function efficiently and effectively, especially addressing risks
CONTROL	• IT projects and costs by IT Governance (or surrogate) • Computer operations • Quality of systems and technologies • Quality of training of users • Data integrity, security, and reliance • Systems and technologies security • Adequacy of automated controls in applications

1.2.2 – Complexity of Business Entities

Business entities have become more and more complex over the last few decades. No longer can business entities be defined in simplistic terms. Complexity usually equates with risk; that is, the more complex an entity (or business process, or economic transaction), the greater the IR.

Complexity of the entity can have an indirect bearing on the risk assessment as it relates to IT. For example, if the organization is complex in its structure, scope of services/products, business model, or financing, these factors can have an effect of IT risk assessment as a whole.

The more important issue is complexity that has a direct bearing on IT risk assessment. That situation would involve issues such as complexity of business processes, transactions, or IT itself. The more complex business processes are, the more risk in performing those processes, the more complex transactions are, the more risk those transactions will be recorded, valued, and processed properly. But the more complex the entity's IT (at the individual, component, system, or entity level), the more risk there is in EVERYTHING it touches at that level.

1.2.2.1 – Assess the Level of IT Sophistication (Nature & Complexity)

On June 1, 2001, SAS No. 94, "The Effect of IT on the Auditor's Consideration of Internal Control in a Financial Audit" became effective and amended SAS No. 55.

In SAS No. 94, the standard states that the level of IT sophistication is not so much a function of the entity's size as it is the nature and complexity of the entity's IT. Thus a smaller-sized firm might have a complex IT environment, heavy reliance on that IT for financial reporting data and/or processes, and the nature of the IT might be one of high IR (e.g., e-Commerce, cloud computing, virtualization, wireless, transmission of applicable data over communication lines). The conclusion regarding this entity would be a high level of IT sophistication for audit purposes despite the fact that the entity is small in size. Likewise a large firm with a simple IT, COTS, and IT that is simple in nature would have a low level of IT sophistication for audit purposes.

This process can be facilitated by using a framework that categorizes various characteristics of an entity's IT into a simple taxonomy. For instance, Exhibit 1.8 uses four tiers of IT sophistication as a basis for assessing the level of risk related to IT sophistication.

CR can no longer be assessed at the maximum by default but it can be the maximum. If it is, the entity is in Tier 0 where controls will not be relied upon at all. However, the CITP may still find ways to contribute to the audit in providing IT-related procedures or support.

Tier 1 is a low level of IT sophistication. It is characterized by standard, commercial, and simple IT (including networks, software, and hardware). The nature of the IT environment is also simple: a few workstations (less than 20 relevant ones), one or two locations, one or two servers, and other similar characteristics.

Tier 2 is a moderate level of IT sophistication. This situation introduces a few IT risks above the Tier 1 such as a few servers, a few emerging technologies, more than 20 but less than a 100-200 relevant workstations, only a few custom applications (and these are limited in number and scope; e.g., middleware), and still using standard, popular applications and infrastructure.

Tier 3 is the layer where mostly the nature of the IT tends to be highly risky, and the IT tends to be complex in nature. The entity will be using some customer software, lots of workstations, heavy reliance internal controls over financial reporting (ICFR) embedded in IT, non-standard software or infrastructure

IT, and multiple platforms. For instance, applications that are custom written or the use of an Enterprise Resource Planning (ERP) application package generally will put an entity in Tier 3 automatically, as will entities that use multiple O/Ss. The same is true for most non-standard software or hardware. Certain industries tend to be Tier 3, such as banks and financial institutions because of the complex nature of IT needed. Tier 3 audits will require one or more SMEs because of the highly complex IT, and highly risky nature of the IT.

EXHIBIT 1.8: IT Sophistication Framework

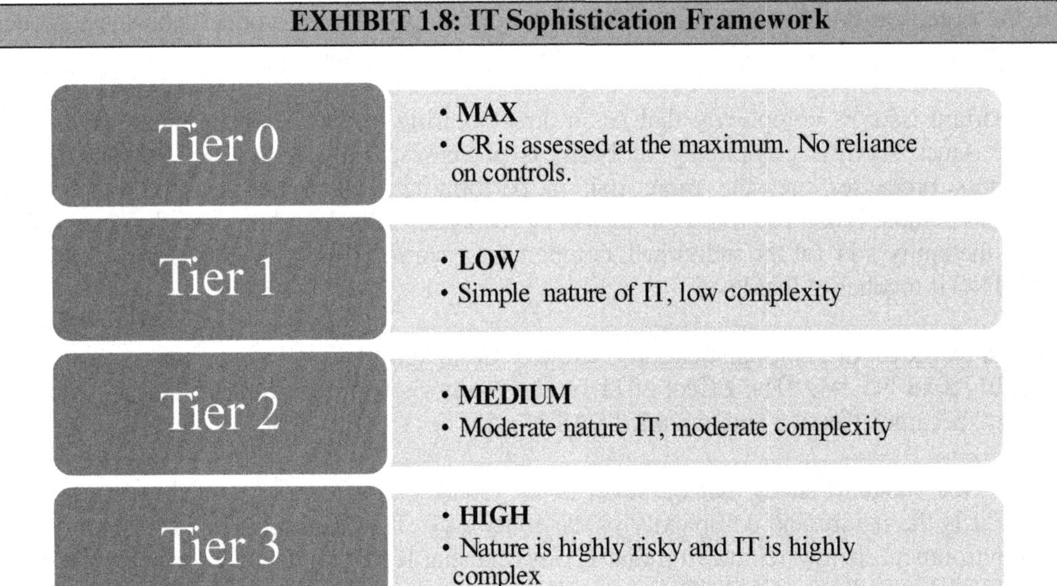

Once the level of IT sophistication has been determined, other decisions or procedures are easier than without this determination. For instance, in staffing and planning, the audit team will likely need a SME for tiers 2 and 3, and possibly multiple SMEs for Tier 3. Tiers 0 and 1, however, are simple enough that a trained financial auditor (e.g., CITP) should be able to fulfill his/her role and responsibilities adequately. Clearly, some CITPs will be SMEs beyond Tier 1.

1.2.2.2 – Determine the Degree of Reliance of Financial Reporting on IT

The more an entity relies on IT for financial reporting data or processes, the more the need for a CITP to analyze IT-related risks. The more an entity relies on IT, the greater the need for assurance IT is operating effectively, and the appropriate controls are implemented and operating effectively.

1.2.3 – Automated Business Processes

Business process (BP) as discussed herein focuses on automated ones. IT-related BPs are a key element of risk assessment, and a special case of controls – as alluded to in 1.2.1.4 above.

The best way to know for sure the extent of risk in BP is to gain a sufficient understanding of the flows and relationships of key data or transactions through all of the business processes, using some kind of flowchart of BP and/or systems.

This understanding is part of the responsibilities of the CITP in a financial audit regarding SAS No. 109, "*Understanding the Entity and Its Environment and Assessing the Risks of Material Misstatement*".

1.2.3.1 – BP Risks of Effectiveness

One risk of BP is whether or not business processes are being performed in an effective manner. IT-related business processes not only handle most of the activities associated with accounting transactions and events, but also it is generally where data is captured, processed, and reported. The IT risks in BP are associated with these factors.

Basically the question is whether BPs are compliant with management's directives not only in P&P but also in practice. The quality of the information from which management makes decisions is contingent on effectual business processes where the data is being captured and handled. It is the nature of organizations and humans that sometimes BPs drift from the moorings established by management without management realizing it. If this happens then there is some risk that BPs are ineffective and possibly inefficient and some risk that management's decisions are also ineffective.

1.2.3.2 – BP Risk and P&P

There are layers of controls that are needed in the business processes to assure management's P&P are being followed effectively. That compliance is often imposed on employees via IT. That is, in today's business world, most of the business processes of an entity are likely to be automated as a part of one or more applications, or a large accounting system (see 1.3.2.1 for discussion on automated vs. manual controls).

Thus the risk that, in practice, the entity is not compliant with P&P is actually an IT risk because it is the IT where the P&P are operating and being monitored for management.

1.2.3.3 – BP Risk and Controls

Thus business processes and key controls are usually inexorably combined in some automated process that is software-driven. This interaction is a key focus of risk. The primary IT risk is likely the process in place whereby controls are chosen, designed, embedded, and tested. In order to lower risk, that process needs to be deliberate, and use an expert for input, design, and evaluation of controls. It is also critically important to determine the operational effectiveness of automated controls.

1.3 – AUDIT RISK MODEL FOR FINANCIAL REPORTING

The AICPA has adopted the following audit risk model as an aid in determining the level of acceptable audit risk:

$$AR = IR \times CR \times DR$$

In the model, AR is the level of acceptable Audit Risk. That risk is a function of the three primary risks: Inherent Risk, Control Risk and Detection Risk. The following sections describe these risks and how they relate to the risks associated with the financial audit, and how they affect what IT auditors would do in a financial audit.

Audit risk is the level of risk that is acceptable to the audit firm. Inherent risk refers to a risk before controls are considered that could lead to a material misstatement in the financial reports (see 1.3.1 for assessing IR). Control risk refers to the ability of internal controls to prevent or detect a material misstatement in a timely manner (see 1.3.2 for assessing control risk). The risk-based standards define the combination of IR and CR as the Risk of Material Misstatement (RMM; see 1.3.3 for RMM). Detection risk is the risk that the audit procedures will fail to detect a material misstatement and basically reflects the level of substantive procedures and further audit procedures necessary to sufficiently minimize AR to an acceptable level based on the other three risks.

1.3.1 – Assessing Inherent Risk

Inherent risk means one evaluates the risk inherent to some object (person, place, or thing) without regard of possible mitigating activities and controls. Assessing IR involves identifying risks that are in some way inherent to the client and/or specific audit being conducted, even if the entity cannot affect it. They include, at a minimum, the entity's environment[16], and the entity's IT (including financial data, data processing, and usually financial reporting processes).

1.3.1.1 – The Entity's Environment

Entities have inherent characteristics that can potentially be risky to some degree. For instance, a large entity by its nature has lots of transactions which increase IR. It could be that executive management of the entity has a risky profile; always "pushing the envelope," resists compliance with society's behavioral rules and protocols, has a gambler's attitude regarding risk, and/or has a background of known relevant problems. Another risky situation is where management is lax, loose, or inattentive to risk, characterized by a lack of formal and structured management functions (see 1.2.1). Some combination of these kinds of factors could lead the CITP to believe the entity has some level or risk associated with its management. It is also possible that the entity's environment is affected by the current economy, its industry, or certain proprietary risks.

1.3.1.1.1 – Current Economy

The current economy can adversely affect risk assessment. For example, the economic downturn that began in 2008 was relatively widespread and affected a number of industries, not to mention a number of individual entities. In fact, many small businesses did not survive, especially those classified as discretionary or luxury items.

For instance, travel and entertainment are usually treated as discretionary spending for people. At the height of the economy, Las Vegas had unemployment of over 30%, and a large number of rooms were vacant regularly. Some casinos under construction were halted. In other areas of the country, condominium construction was halted, flower shops faltered, jewelry shops closed, and other similar effects occurred throughout the U.S. economy.

Thus the economy can certainly increase risk, if it significantly affects a particular business or industry.

1.3.1.1.2 – Industry Risks

Some industries were affected by the economic problems of 2008 and following months. But some industries are just inherently risky. Construction is generally considered to be risky as an industry quite often. When fuel prices soar, industries like automobile manufacturers and car lots suffer, as well as the airline industry and other industries that rely on fuel as a relatively large expense.

The CITP will need to make a determination as to whether his/her client or company has risk that is inherent to its industry, whether that risk is temporary or relatively permanent. That risk needs to be considered in the overall risk assessment process.

1.3.1.1.3 – Entity-Specific Risks

Large volumes of transactions naturally mean the probability of a misstatement being in that body is at some point directly proportional to its size. Entities that are located in certain geographic locations could have more IR (e.g., one located in a flood plain is more likely to be subject to a flood).

[16] See SAS No. 109 for more on the entity's environment.

Other proprietary circumstances that are likely to lead to entity-specific risks would be complex business processes, complex or sophisticated IT, use of ERP or enterprise-wide systems, a history of non-compliance, a history of not responding to auditors' reports on deficiencies, and heavy regulated entity.

1.3.1.2 – The Entity's IT

Inherent risks associated with the entity, in the context of the CITP BOK, includes aspects of the entity's systems, automated controls, computer operations (and other elements of ITGC), and technologies. Specifically, the question the CITP needs to answer is whether or not IT *itself* brings about risks to the entity or financial audit (RMM). For example, if the entity engages in e-Commerce, and has a sufficient volume of transactions that could lead to a material misstatement, then IT itself (the e-Commerce technologies) could possibly be the source of the RMM. The same is true for IT and IT-related issues such as:

- *Effectiveness of computer operations*
- *Emerging IT (e.g., cloud computing, virtualization)*
- *Programming code development (in-house)*
- *Third-party IT providers*
- *Significance of audit evidence in electronic form*
- *Logical access controls*
- *IT change management*
- *Backup and recovery*
- *Information security*
- *Data transfers/sharing*

The CITP will need to do a risk assessment of these types of areas of concern and IT risks in order to properly identify the RMM directly associated with IT and the risk it brings to the financial reporting process or financial statements.

For instance, if the entity transfers data from some COTS to a spreadsheet where adjusting entries, closing entries, and/or consolidations are made, then the fact that a spreadsheet technology was introduced to the financial reporting process is a risk *by itself* that can lead to the RMM on the financial statements as a whole. Everyone who has used a spreadsheet knows the inherent risks associated with handling data in one. Add to that risk the fact the financial reporting process is housed in a spreadsheet. While this IT-related risk can be mitigated, the point is for the CITP to identify it as a potential RMM in order to ascertain whether controls sufficiently mitigate it or not.

In other words, the CITP will need to assess inherent risks as they relate *specifically* to the entity's IT. Many of these risks exist in the ITGC area (see section 3.2 for more on ITGC and the following topics). One taxonomy for ITGCs is the IT control environment, change management, logical access controls, data backups and recovery, and third party IT suppliers. The IT control environment includes elements such as IT strategy, IT governance, project management, managing the IT function, and related topics. The goal is to minimize the risks associated with the IT function in general. Change management involves processes, structure, and P&P related to all changes in IT including all software and hardware changes, with the intent of controlling the risk associated with changes to IT. Logical access controls involve properly restricting access to applications and data in order to reduce risks associated with unauthorized or improper access. Backup and recovery involve risks associated with traumatic IT events from those that bring down systems temporarily (e.g., lockups) to pandemic events. Third party IT providers is the risks associated with outsourcing key or significant IT functionality to vendors, and the risks associated with their controls.

1.3.2 – Assessing Control Risk

Control risk indicates the likelihood that a material misstatement exists in some area of the transactions, events, disclosures, or account balances that will not be prevented or detected by the entity's system of internal controls in a timely manner.

In order to assess CR, the CITP will need to consider the nature of controls (automated vs. manual, key vs. non-key), and use some framework as to the adequacy and mitigation of controls (e.g., Preventive-Detective-Corrective/P-D-C model).

1.3.2.1 – Manual Versus Automated Controls

Manual controls rely on human intervention in order for them to operate. However, humans suffer from emotional, physical, and mental moments where their duties to perform a control might be adversely affected. That is, the human might either fail to perform a control, or do it ineffectively. For instance, if a manual control involves a human reviewing a book of authorized signatures as the control for verifying an authorization to pay an invoice signed by a business unit manager, that person may choose to skip that process for various reasons and the control fails to operate at all. Thus manual controls are subject to atrophy, complacency, and failures on each instance of operation.

However, automated controls do not fail to operate, and the IT performs the control on each and every instance in the same manner. Thus if the automated control can be tested for validity, it will operate over and over successfully until an environment change effects it. Generally speaking, therefore, an automated control is more reliable than an equally and effectively designed manual control.

It is for this reason that the PCAOB and AICPA suggested a test of one might be sufficient under the right circumstances.

It is possible that the control is partly manual and partly automated. These controls are sometimes referred to as IT-dependent or hybrid controls. They obviously have a mix of the two above conclusions about control effectiveness.

1.3.2.2 – The P-D-C Controls Model

One framework for evaluating risks associated with controls is the P-D-C model: prevent, detect, correct. The P-D-C model is used in systems development, information security and security audits, anti-fraud profession, and accounting controls.

1.3.2.2.1 – Preventive Controls

Preventive controls are designed to prevent the adverse event from occurring in the first place. For instance, preventive controls can be implemented to prevent certain data keypunch errors, fraud, or bugs in software development.

1.3.2.2.2 – Detective Controls

Likewise a detective control is designed to detect an adverse event should it occur. Thus if an error in data did occur a detective control is capable of identifying it. One example would be to use a CAAT to identify gaps or duplicates in check numbers for disbursements.

1.3.2.2.3 – Corrective (Mitigating) Controls

Sometimes an adverse event occurs and is detected, as mentioned above. At this point a corrective control would provide a means to correct the event and reestablish equilibrium, correct data, correct a workflow, etc.

One example is the use of error logs in applications. A program is written to read certain transactions and/or files searching for specified anomalies. If any are found, they are moved to some kind of cyber suspense file, and a notification (usually a report) is sent to the appropriate party. This part of the process involves a detective control. The appropriate person corrects the errors, resubmits the erroneous transactions, and they are reprocessed. This part of the process involves a corrective control.

The latter illustration brings up a point about the P-D-C framework. Usually, the ideal internal control system includes some of each. It is not possible to detect all errors, so some provision needs to be made to detect them and correct them. Likewise it is sometimes not cost-effective to prevent controls, and thus detective and corrective controls are even more important in that situation.

1.3.2.3 – Key versus Non-Key Controls

While auditors use the terms key control and non-key controls ubiquitously, neither PCAOB nor AICPA standards specifically describe key controls. That being said, it is an effective technique to identify key controls, especially as they related to SOX compliance in section 404, and the audits of management's evaluation. By definition, a key control is one that prevents or detects a material misstatement, and thus it relates to materiality and likelihood. Here is a list of possible key controls:

- A control or combination of controls that covers all of the risks, objectives, and assertions in a financial process related to the RMM
- The control at the pinnacle of a hierarchy of controls over the same process, risk, or assertion
- A control that is designed to mitigate the RMM arising from a process, and if it failed, the entity would fail to prevent or detect the material misstatement
- A control that covers a risk that no other control also covers is by default a key control

A non-key control would be a control that does not fit one of the criteria mentioned above. For instance, a control that is designed to prevent or detect only immaterial errors would be a non-key control.

1.3.2.4 –Control Gaps

One outcome of an effectual IT risk assessment is the identification of IT risks where no controls exist – that is, a control gap. Using the CITP BOK, the CITP should be able to identify the significant IT risks related to his/her current objective, and by examining controls, determine where none exist to mitigate one or more of those IT risks. If any IT risk has no mitigating control, this gap is an exposure, by definition, that the entity has, whether management is aware of it or not. Thus control gaps represent serious risk and significant flaws in the control environment. The CITP would want to identify any control gap, and make a recommendation to mitigate that gap/exposure, or use that information in evaluating audit evidence.

1.3.3 – Risk of Material Misstatement

The risk of material misstatement (RMM) is the result of performing a proper risk assessment related to IR and CR. Mathematically, it is the product of IR and CR. From a pragmatic standpoint, it is the risk that some event, process, or activity will lead to a material misstatement in the financial statements and not be prevented or detected timely. It includes not only account balances, classes of transactions, disclosures, management assertions, but also risks that arise strictly from the IT of the entity.

1.3.3.1 – Consider Applicable Account Balances, Classes of Transactions and Disclosures

An evaluation of the RMM would include the analysis of the financial statements, and knowledge of the entity's business processes and financial transactions in order to determine which account balances, classes of transactions, and disclosures could potentially be materially misstated. Thus if an account balance is below the materiality threshold, that account could not be materially misstated and is usually therefore eliminated from the need for FAPs.

If one of those objects is at or above the threshold for materiality the audit team will need to determine the effectiveness of controls in order to properly develop a body of FAPs necessary to detect any material misstatements that might exist. However, the audit team should include a CITP so it does not limit this analysis to numbers, amounts, and financial transactions. That is, the RMM can also result from adverse effects of the entity's IT. For instance, a bug in a software application at a local university inadvertently issued financial aid in excess of what the students should have received, and did so for years. By the time the application error was detected, the university was having serious financial difficulties, and was giving away millions of dollars erroneously. Those errors were not the result of an audit trail that was missing or not balanced but rather an IT error that went undiscovered.

This particular scenario could have been avoided with a CITP applying the BOK. For instance, a review of IT risks should have identified the custom application used in financial aid. Reviews of project documentation, interviews of key personnel, tests of the application could all have aided in early discovery. It would also have been discovered with the appropriate tests of details using a CAAT and financial aid data, compared to what it should have been.

1.3.3.2 – Combine Inherent Risk and Control Risk

Besides the mathematical combination of IR and CR to assess the RMM, there is the practical aspect of the combination. There is some inherent risk associated with processes, transactions, and events. But controls may exist to mitigate that IR to some degree. Once that degree of mitigation is determined, the IT auditor reduces the original IR level by some amount and reaches some "residual" risk. That residual risk, and its level of risk, becomes a primary factor in audit planning and developing FAPs.

1.3.3.3 – Apply Risk of Material Misstatement to Relevant Financial Statement Assertions

Lastly, this residual RMM is applied to the relevant assertions of account balances or the financials as a whole. This process of reaching a conclusion about residual RMM and developing FAP can be seen in exhibit 1.9. An illustration of the RMM framework is provided in Exhibit 1.10.

EXHIBIT 1.9: RMM Process Framework

STEP	DESCRIPTION
IR	*Identify the account balances, class of transactions, or disclosures that have a RMM*
Type of Risk	*Error or fraud*
Risk Level	*The relevant assertion regarding the IR or the financial statement as a whole*
Controls	*Identify the controls that could mitigate the IR's identified*
CR Assessed	*To what degree are these control effective in reducing the RMM*
RMM	*Combine the IR and CR to determine the level of risk for each specific RMM*

EXHIBIT 1.10: Illustration of RMM Process Framework	
#1. Risk Subject:	**Inventory Tracking and Reporting and COGS Calculation**
Background	The client uses a custom financial application for the purposes of inventory management including inventory valuation and reporting and cost-of-goods sold calculation. The client's technical and financial personnel make frequent changes to this application. Inventory represents approximately 60% or more of the client's asset valuation.
Inherent Risk	Inventory and Cost of Goods Sold (COGS) could be misstated due to errors made as part of authorized changes being made. There is potential for unauthorized changes being made that could affect inventory balances and COGS values. These account balances are very significant to the overall profitability of the entity.
Type of Risk	This risk is both from error and fraud. Program changes are inherently at risk of error. Financial personnel have the ability to make changes to the programs and this could enable them to change inventory balances and cost of goods sold fraudulently.
Risk Level	Assertion level for: • Inventory existence and valuation. • Cost of Goods Sold valuation.
Controls designed to mitigate this risk	**Change Control:** The client has developed and deployed policies and procedures associated with change control and SDLC (X-Ref W/P #). **Access Control:** The client has developed and deployed policies and procedures for access control over the application, database, and supporting network (X-Ref W/P #).
Control Risk Assessment	**Low:** The entity's controls effectively mitigate the inherent risks. **Change Control:** The auditor has determined that the entity has suitably designed standard operating procedures (SOP) for change management and that the SOP is placed in operation. **Access Control:** The auditor has determined that the entity has a suitably defined SOP for granting and managing logical access rights to the network and applications used for financial functions and that the SOPs are placed in operation, including appropriate logical access SoD.
Risk of Material Misstatement	**Moderate-to-High:** While the control risk is low, the inherent risk for this situation is very high.

1.4 – DEVELOP A WALKTHROUGH PLAN

A walkthrough is the act of tracing a transaction through organizational records, procedures, and business processes. The auditor's primary objective when performing a walkthrough is to develop an understanding of transaction flow – that is, how transactions are initiated, authorized, recorded, processed, and reported. It amounts to a nontechnical approach to learning how a particular process or transaction works. It also helps the CITP to determine what controls are being used and how effective they might be operating.

In AS5, the PCAOB states it is a procedure of choice when attempting to understand key processes and controls. At the points at which important processing procedures occur, the auditor questions the employee about their understanding of what is required by the entity's prescribed procedures and controls.

A walkthrough by itself is generally considered a preliminary step in the overall testing process [Federal Financial Institutions Examination Council {FFIEC}]. However, walkthrough procedures could include a combination of inquiry, observation, inspection of relevant documentation, and re-performance of controls. Together, they allow the auditor to gain a sufficient understanding of the process and to be able to identify important points at which a necessary control is missing, operating ineffectively, or not designed properly [PCAOB, AS5].

> *"Walkthroughs usually consist of a combination of inquiry of appropriate personnel, observation of the company's operations, inspection of relevant documentation, and re-performance of the control and might provide sufficient evidence of operating effectiveness, depending on the risk associated with the control being tested, the specific procedures performed as part of the walkthrough and the results of those procedures."*

In fact, walkthroughs are required when certifying financial reporting controls under SOX §404. Identifying transaction types that call for walkthroughs are largely a matter of auditor judgment.

1.4.1 – Determine Relevant Business Processes and Controls to Review

Based on the concept of key controls, the IT auditor will choose the BPs and controls that are relevant. They become relevant if (1) they are associated with financial statement data or the financial reporting processes, (2) they are IT-related or IT-dependent, and (3) they are related to the RMM.

1.4.1.1 – Primary or Key Controls

Section 1.2.2.3 discussed the difference between a key control and non-key control. Using that knowledge, and the filters described above, the IT auditor identifies the key controls associated with relevant systems, applications, and specifically business processes. That determination is usually assisted by the aid of an appropriate flowchart of the business processes, financial systems, and data flows. Key controls are sometimes called primary controls.

1.4.1.2 – Automated Controls

Section 1.3.2.1 discussed the difference between an automated control and a manual control including the advantages of automated controls. That section also described controls that are blended between the two hybrid controls.

The IT auditor has a dual focus on automated controls. One focus is the fact that automated controls are a key objective in an IT audit. Also, effective automated controls can be leveraged to reduce substantive testing in the FAP phase of a financial audit.

1.4.1.2.1 – Identify Relevant Controls Embedded in Automated Business Processes

Having identified the key controls via various methods, such as walkthroughs, flowcharts, interviews, observation, review of key documents, and others, the IT auditor then chooses those that are embedded in automated BPs, versus those that are totally manual.

1.4.1.2.2 – Benchmark Relevant Automated Controls

Then the IT auditor will need to measure and evaluate the "strength" (i.e., reliance) of that control. In order to make a valid measure of the relevant automated control in place the IT auditor needs a "ruler" or a benchmark. Usually, the benchmark is the designed purpose of the control. Another option is a best practice if an applicable one exists.

For instance, there could be an automated control associated with authorization of sales which checks for whether the customer is on an authorized customer list, and whether the customer has sufficient credit to acquire the goods or services. The test of that control would be to follow a transaction through the system where the customer is not an authorized customer, where the transaction puts the customer over its credit limit, or a customer who is already over its credit limit. If the result is some rejection of the transaction, the automated control would be operating effectively for that kind of transaction at that point in time. The process of testing these scenarios is called benchmarking, where the IT auditor established the effectiveness of a control against desired results (the "ruler").

1.5 – DRAFT RISK ASSESSMENT REPORT

Once the IT risk assessment is completed, the CITP will need to generate a report documenting the inputs, process and results with evidence for the conclusions. See Exhibit 1.11 for an illustrated example of a risk assessment report.

1.5.1 – Based on Evidence from Walkthroughs

Section 1.4 discussed walkthroughs, their purpose, and how they are conducted. For the purpose of IT risk assessment, it is critical that the IT auditor follow AS5 recommendations about combining observation, inquiry, and review of relevant documents as part of the walkthrough. Based on the information and evidence gathered from walkthroughs, the IT auditor should be able to assess risks associated with business processes and controls as they relate to IT.

1.5.2 – Based on Other Applied Procedures

The IT auditor will likely find a need to test controls or gather non-IT evidence in order to complete a sufficient and competent body of evidence to support the risk assessment. Those other applied procedures might include interviews, other inquiries, industry standards or metrics applied to the entity's performance, and other similar procedures.

1.5.3 – Usefulness of Best Practices

Risk assessment (and controls evaluation) requires the CITP to measure IT risks, IT effectiveness, controls effectiveness, etc. Thus the CITP needs a basis from which to make those measures and evaluations.

Best practices regarding certain IT processes (and technologies themselves) can serve as that basis. In fact, the presence of best practices being employed usually serves as a valuable control, in and of itself, to mitigate risk.

Exhibit 1.12 lists some of the best practices sets and how they generally apply to the IT risk assessment process.

Of course judgment from experience is invaluable as well.

EXHIBIT 1.11: Illustration of Contents of IT Risk Assessment Report	
IT CONTROL ENVIRONMENT	• Changes in last year? • Does an IT Strategic plan exist? Was it adequate? • IT mission/purpose statement? • IT P&P? • Evidence of effective management of the IT function including help desk.
RISK ASSESSMENT	• Is there a written IT risk assessment? Is it adequate? Is it recent? • What formal structured process exists to continuously monitor risks and controls?
IT GOVERNANCE	• Does some form of IT governance exist? IT steering committee? Review minutes of meetings. Evaluate its effectiveness. • How are major IT projects funded? How are they aligned to strategic plans? • How are major IT projects managed? How does management ensure they are delivered on time, on budget, fully functional? • Pull sample of IT projects. Report results of review.
BUDGET	• Does management have an operational budget? Review results of budget and actual result. Indicates quality of process. • Does management have a formal structured process for funding IT capital projects? Was that budget determined before the fiscal year began? What was the formal structured process whereby IT projects were funded?
BEST PRACTICES	• Were the best practices and principles of project management used on all major IT projects? If so, pull evidence and evaluate results. • Does the entity employ best practices and principles of IT governance? If so, pull evidence and evaluate results. In particular, review BoD minutes and interview at least one key board member to determine effectiveness of process and results. • If the entity writes some or all of its own programs/software, did the IT staff employ best practices and principles of SDLC? If so, pull samples, evaluate, and document results.
CHANGE MANAGEMENT	• Does management employ best practices of change management? • How does management provide for an appropriate method of selecting the changes to be made and vendors/products? • How does management ensure successful changes in its IT?
DRP / BUSINESS CONTINUITY	• How much downtime did the entity experience last year? What is the industry standard downtime (or other metric)? • Is data stored offsite at a reasonable distance from its facilities? • Is there a DR Plan? Has it been tested in the last 12 months?
INFOSEC	• Describe any security breaches of the last year. Pull documents, if one or more occurred, analyze, and document. • What are the controls for preventing malicious activities by employees? From outsiders? What controls exist at the perimeter? Operating effectively? • What is the logical access system? Does it provide for authorization and authentication controls? Are passwords changed routinely? • Evidence of effectual logical access segregation of duties. • Review administrative rights of O/S, networks, and systems. Same for DBAs.

EXHIBIT 1.12: List of IT Best Practices Sets	
SDLC	• Change management. • Systems development (SysDev). • Application development (AppDev). • Testing of IT projects.
PROJECT MANAGEMENT	• As integral part of IT Governance. • Managing major IT projects. • Ensuring successful IT projects.
IT GOVERNANCE	• Any entity with significant IT or significant reliance on IT. • Absolute if entity develops some of its own IT: software, hardware, etc. • Budgets, especially IT capital budget. • When the value of IT matters. • When an alignment of IT with strategy matters.
COMPUTER OPERATIONS	• SoD: new systems development from maintenance, systems development from operations, DBA from everything possible. • Computer operations. • Standards of quality on help desk and service (ITIL). • When downtime is problematic there is a heavy reliance on IT.
SERVICE ORGANIZATION CONTROLS	• When IT is outsourced. • Combined with vendor management to ensure reliable supplier. • SSAE No. 16 report or equivalent (e.g., SOC report).
VENDOR MANAGEMENT	• For all IT vendors to ensure reliable vendors and products/services.
CHANGE MANAGEMENT	• For all changes to infrastructure. • For all changes to applications, software, and software systems. • For all changes to hardware: PCs, laptops, hand-held devices, etc. • To reduce risks of implementing new IT.

Advanced Reading Recommendations:

AICPA. "AICPA Audit Guide: Assessing and Responding to Audit Risk in a Financial Statement Audit". Available from: http://www.cpa2biz.com/index.jsp.

AICPA/ITEC. "Information Technology Considerations in Risk-Based Auditing" (discussion paper). 2007. AICPA: online.

AICPA. SAS No. 104-111.

COSO. "Internal Control over Financial Reporting – Guidance for Smaller Public Companies", Volume I, II and III. 2006.

Moeller, Robert R. "IT Audit, Control, and Security". 2010. Wiley: Hoboken, NJ.

Raval, Vasant; Fichadia, Ashok. "Risks, Controls, and Security". 2007. Wiley: Hoboken, NJ.

Weber, Ron. "Information Systems Control and Audit". 1999. Prentice Hall: Upper Saddle River, NJ.

GLOSSARY:

Application Controls

Application Controls are internal controls, whether automated or manual, which operate at the transaction-level with the objectives of ensuring that:

- Proper authorization is obtained to initiate and enter transactions;
- Applications are protected from unauthorized access;
- Users are only allowed access to those data and functions in an application that they should have access to;
- Errors in the operation of an application will be prevented or detected and corrected in a timely manner;
- Application output is protected from unauthorized access or disclosure;
- Reconciliation activities are implemented when appropriate to ensure that information is complete and accurate; and
- High-risk transactions are appropriately controlled.

Assertion Level Risks

Assertion level risks are risks that are limited to one or more specific assertions in an account or in several accounts, for example, the valuation of inventory or the occurrence of sales. Assertion level risks are addressed by the nature, timing, and extent of further audit procedures, which may include substantive procedures or a combination of tests of controls and substantive procedures.

The risk of material misstatement at the assertion level has two components:

- Inherent Risk (IR), which is the susceptibility of an assertion to a material misstatement, assuming that there are no related controls. Inherent risk is greater for some assertions and related account balances, classes of transactions, and disclosures than for others.
- Control Risk (CR), which is the risk that a material misstatement that could occur in an assertion will not be prevented or detected by the entity's internal control on a timely basis. Control risk is a function of the effectiveness of the design and operation of the entity's internal control.

Automated Control

Controls automation involves leveraging technology to build and enforce internal controls with the least manual intervention possible. It can take many forms, including better use of available system configuration options of the kind common in enterprise resource planning (ERP) systems, to using workflow and imaging technologies to automate and drive processes from start to completion.

Control Risk

Control Risk (CR) is the risk that a material misstatement will not be detected or prevented by the entity's internal control on a timely basis. The auditor must consider the risk of misstatement individually and in aggregate with other misstatements.

Detection Risk

Detection Risk (DR) is the risk that the auditor will not detect a material misstatement in the financial statements of the entity being audited.

End-User Computing

In the context of this paper, end-user computing (EUC) is a function developed using common desktop tools, like spreadsheets, that are used in financial processes for purposes of determining amounts used for accounting and financial reporting purposes.

Electronic Commerce
Electronic business applications or processes that facilitate commercial transactions. Electronic commerce (eCommerce) can involve electronic funds transfer, supply chain management, e-marketing, online marketing, online transaction processing, electronic data interchange (EDI), automated inventory management systems, and automated data collection systems.

Source: Wikipedia; http://en.wikipedia.org/wiki/Electronic_commerce

Emerging Technologies
Changes or advances in technologies such as information technology, nanotechnology, biotechnology, cognitive science, robotics, and artificial intelligence.

Financial Statement Level Risks
Financial statement level risks are risks that may affect many different accounts and several assertions. Financial statement level risks typically require an overall response, such as providing more supervision to the engagement team or incorporating additional elements of unpredictability in the selection of your audit procedures.

Further Audit Procedures
SAS 110 defines further audit procedures (FAP) that include tests of the operating effectiveness of controls; whether relevant or necessary; and substantive procedures whose nature, timing, and extent are responsive to the assessed risks of material misstatement at the relevant assertion level.

Inherent Risk
Inherent Risk (IR) is the susceptibility that a relevant assertion could be misstated assuming that there are no other related controls. The auditor should consider the risk of misstatement individually as well as in aggregate with other misstatements, assuming there are no related controls.

Internal Control
Internal control is a process, affected by an entity's board of directors, management and other personnel, designed to provide reasonable assurance regarding the achievement of objectives in the following categories:

- Effectiveness and efficiency of operations
- Reliability of financial reporting
- Compliance with applicable laws and regulations

Key Concepts:

- Internal control is a process. It is a means to an end, not an end in itself.
- Internal control is affected by people. It's not merely policy manuals and forms, but people at every level of an organization.
- Internal control can be expected to provide only reasonable assurance, not absolute assurance, to an entity's management and board.
- Internal control is geared to the achievement of objectives in one or more separate but overlapping categories.

Source: COSO; http://www.coso.org/IC.htm

For additional resources on internal control over financial reporting visit www.cpa2biz.com for:

- *Internal Control—Integrated Framework* (product no. 990012kk), a paperbound version of the COSO report that established a common definition of internal control different parties can use to assess and improve their control systems. [http://www.cpa2biz.com/AST/Main/CPA2BIZ_Primary/InternalControls/COSO/PRDOVR~PC-990009/PC-990009.jsp]

- *Financial Reporting Fraud: A Practical Guide to Detection and Internal Control* (product no. 029879kk), a paperbound publication for CPAs in both public practice and industry. [http://www.cpa2biz.com/AST/Main/CPA2BIZ_Primary/FinancialManagement/Finance/FinancialReporting/PRDOVR~PC-029879/PC-029879.jsp]
- In July 2006, COSO released its guidance, "Internal Control over Financial Reporting—Guidance for Smaller Public Companies," which may assist companies and auditors in understanding the applicability of the COSO Framework to smaller entities. This publication can be ordered from the www.cpa2biz.com or through any of the sponsoring organizations. [http://www.cpa2biz.com/AST/Main/CPA2BIZ_Primary/InternalControls/COSO/PRDOVR~PC-990017/PC-990017.jsp]

Internal Control, Five Components of (COSO)

The Committee of Sponsoring Organizations of the Treadway Commission (COSO) outlines internal control in their *Internal Control-Integrated Framework*, as consisting of five related components that must be present for an entity to achieve effective internal controls. These five components are:

- The control environment
- Risk assessment
- Control activities
- Information and communication
- Monitoring

IT Auditor

An IT Auditor is a professional possessing the necessary knowledge and skills to understand and audit an entity's IT environment, systems, or applications, in support of a financial statement audit, internal audit, or other form of attestation engagement. The IT Auditor often has deep domain-specific knowledge or specialized skills (e.g., in use of computerized tools) that makes them particularly competent to understand the IT environment (and its associated risks) or perform IT-specific audit procedures.

IT Control Risk

IT Control Risk is a type of Control Risk where the source of risk is related to the use of IT in the processing of transactions or security of underlying data.

IT General Controls

IT general controls (ITGC) are internal controls, generally implemented and administered by an organization's IT department. The objectives of ITGC are to:

- Ensure the proper operation of the applications and availability of systems;
- Protect both data and programs from unauthorized changes;
- Protect both data and programs from unauthorized access and disclosure;
- Provide assurance that applications are developed and subsequently maintained, such that they provide the functionality required to process transactions and provide automated controls; and
- Ensure an organization's ability to recover from system and operational failures related to IT.

Logical Access Controls

Logical access controls are policies, procedures, and automated controls that exist for the purpose of restricting access to information assets to only authorized users.

Material Weakness

A material weakness is a significant deficiency, or combination of significant deficiencies, that results in more than a remote likelihood that a material misstatement of the financial statements will not be prevented or detected.

Source: AICPA; http://www.aicpa.org/Research/Standards/AuditAttest/DownloadableDocuments/AU-00325.pdf

Materiality

Materiality is "the magnitude of an omission or misstatement of accounting information that, in the light of surrounding circumstances, makes it probable that the judgment of a reasonable person relying on the information would have been changed by the omission or misstatement." Materiality is influenced by the needs of financial statement users who rely on the financial statements to make judgments about the client's financial position and results of operation and the auditor must consider audit risk and must determine a materiality level for the financial statements.

Source: AICPA; http://www.aicpa.org/Research/Standards/AuditAttest/DownloadableDocuments/AU-00312.pdf

Operating Effectiveness

Operating effectiveness is concerned with determining if "controls operate with sufficient effectiveness to achieve the related control objectives during a specified period." This is a function of how control is applied, the consistency with which it is applied and by whom it is applied.

Source:AICPA;http://www.aicpa.org/InterestAreas/InformationTechnology/Resources/InternalControl/DownloadableDocuments/ITEC_RBA_DiscPaper.pdf

Relevant Assertions

SAS No. 106 defines relevant assertions as those assertions that have a meaningful bearing on whether the account is stated fairly.

Risk Assessment Procedures

Risk Assessment Procedures are audit procedures performed to obtain an understanding of the entity and its environment, including its internal control, to assess the risk of material misstatement at the financial statement and relevant assertion levels.

Risk Assessment Procedures include:

- Inquiries of management and others within the entity
- Analytical procedures
- Observation and inspection.

Risk-Based Approach

Risk-Based Approach (RBA) is the methodology which provides assurance that significant risks associated with audit objectives have been identified, and that audit procedures address them to adequately gain assurance about the objectives of the audit, and the mitigation of those risks or nature of residual risk that exists.

Risk of Material Misstatement

The risk of material misstatement (RMM) is defined as the risk that an account balance, class of transactions or disclosures, and relevant assertions are materially misstated. Misstatements can result from errors or fraud.

The RMM consists of two components which are Inherent Risk and Control Risk.

Using the audit risk model to illustrate this concept: Inherent Risk x Control Risk = RMM

Auditors describe RMM as the combined assessment of inherent risk and control risk. However, auditors may make a separate assessment of inherent risk and control risk.

Significant Deficiency

A significant deficiency (SD) is a control deficiency, or combination of control deficiencies, that adversely affects the entity's ability to initiate, authorize, record, process, or report financial data reliably in accordance with generally accepted accounting principles such that there is more than a remote likelihood that a misstatement of the entity's financial statements that is more than inconsequential will not be prevented or detected.

Source: AICPA, http://www.aicpa.org/download/members/div/auditstd/AU-00325.PDF

Substantive Procedures

According to SAS 110, substantive procedures, "...are performed to detect material misstatements at the relevant assertion level, and include tests of details of classes of transactions, account balances, and disclosures and substantive analytical procedures. The auditor should plan and perform substantive procedures to be responsive to the related assessment of the risk of material misstatement."

Test of Controls

When the audit strategy involves relying on the operating effectiveness of the controls for some assertions in the design of substantive procedures or when substantive procedures alone do not provide sufficient appropriate audit evidence at the assertion level, the auditor should design and perform tests of the operating effectiveness of controls (ToC). Additionally, they will perform procedures to evaluate the design of internal controls and determine whether they are implemented.

CASE & STUDY QUESTIONS:

ABC Company has recently completed a self-risk assessment related to its IT and the following issues were identified:

(A) The anti-virus system being used is AVG. ABC is using the corporate license and AVG "pushes" updates to all desktops, laptops, etc. However, there are some configuration inconsistencies and there is an 88% chance that one or more such PCs could get infected with a new virus. The significance factor was based on the prediction that such an infection would take a full day for recovery of that PC, and that about 1/3 of the PCs had improper, inadequate, or missing configurations. The significant risk was rated at 12%.

(B) ABC uses Oracle's DBMS for its database, and the conventional ERP approach to implementing Oracle as its ERP. There is some change management issues related to infrastructure and the database such that there is a 66% probability of a temporary loss of the Oracle database due to a major infrastructure failure. Such a loss would lead to a temporary loss of access to all data in Oracle. Based on that fact, the significance factor was rated at 79%.

(C) ABC's financial reporting process includes the extraction of data from the Oracle Financials system which is exported to an electronic spreadsheet. This extraction and transfer is done using middleware which the IT department at ABC developed and implemented. These facts led the CITP to believe the probability risk of the data transfer leading to an error or fraud was 55%. The significance factor was rated at 30% due to the fact that these risks are associated with erroneous data in the financial adjustments and close processes as a result of a faulty data transfer.

(D) The CITP considered the risks associated with the electronic spreadsheet as another source of risk. Once the data is transferred to the spreadsheet, the controller's office makes final adjusting entries in order to obtain a trial balance from which to make closing entries, including any recommended by the financial auditors. Due to the relative ease with which errors can occur in using a spreadsheet, the probability risk was rated at 88%. The significance factor was rated at 24% due to these risks associated with the processing of transferred data and adjusting entry data in a spreadsheet.

1. Based on the information provided in the ABC case, which of the four risk scenarios has the highest risk score; that is, ranked #1?
   (A) The anti-virus risk associated with configurations
   (B) The infrastructure/database risk and temporary loss of Database Management System (DBMS)
   (C) The financial reporting data transfer/middleware
   (D) The financial reporting process embedded in a electronic spreadsheet

Key: B
Section Name: Rate (1.1.1.2), Rank (1.1.1.3), Process: Data Transfers (1.1.4.4)
Bloom's Taxonomy category: 2. Comprehension, 3. Application, and 4. Analysis
Reference: Moeller, Robert R. "IT Audit, Control, and Security" ICFR—Guidance for Smaller Public Companies. COSO, p. 49.
Solution:
The Risk Score formula is Probability X Significance. See Risk Score Matrix, Exhibit 2, and page 92 of Moeller book.

Stem (B): The Risk Score is .66 X .79 = 0.52; the highest score and thus ranked #1.
Option: (A): This Risk Score is .88 X .12 = 0.11
Option (C): The Risk Score is .55 X .30 = 0.165
Option (D): The Risk Score is .88 X .24 = 0.21

2. For your choice in question #1, which of the following would be the **BEST** response to the assessed level of risk and objective of an IT audit procedure to address that risk?
   (A) Make inquiries of relevant management
   (B) Make inquiries of relevant IT staff
   (C) Observe the actual IT processes involved
   (D) Re-perform the relevant processes

Key: D
Section Name: Respond (1.1.1.4)
Bloom's Taxonomy category: 2. Comprehension, 3. Application, and 4. Analysis
Reference: SAS No. 110
Solution:
SAS No. 110 requires auditors to "link" further audit procedures to identified risks by providing the type of procedure that can provide the level of assurance required for the level of risk. That is, a high risk requires a high-powered FAP. The types, from the least to the most assurance are: Inquiry, Observation, Inspection, and Re-performance.
Stem (D): Re-perform provides the highest level of assurance of these types of procedures. Since the risk is assessed as high, a high-powered procedure is used per RBA standards.
Option (A): Inquiries alone are insufficient as evidence, and provide the least assurance of types of procedures: Inquire, Observe, Inspect, Re-perform/Confirm.
Option (B): Inquiries alone are insufficient as evidence, and provide the least assurance of types of procedures: Inquire, Observe, Inspect, Re-perform/Confirm.
Option (C): Observe provides more assurance than inquiry, but provides less assurance than re-perform.

3. <Refer to Exhibit 10 for the following questions> Which of the following would describe an IT risk in the case?
   (A) COGS could be misstated due to errors made as part of authorized changes to the application
   (B) The client has developed and deployed policies and procedures regarding change controls
   (C) The client has developed and deployed policies and procedures regarding logical access controls
   (D) CR is assessed at low

Key: A
Section Name: IT Risk Assessment (1.1.4) and Risk Material Misstatement (1.3.3)
Bloom's Taxonomy category: 1. Knowledge, 2. Comprehension, 6. Evaluate
Reference: AICPA RBA Discussion Paper, ITEC, pages 13-14.
Solution:
Stem: (A): The risk of COGS being misstated is due to errors in an application. The source of this risk is IT.
Option (B): Change controls being deployed is a control, not an IT risk.
Option (C): Logical access controls being deployed is a control, not an IT risk.
Option (D): CR being assessed is not an IT risk but the result of assessing IT risks and their controls.

4. One useful tool for the CITP is a systems, data, or BP flowchart. Which of the following is true about the usefulness of an appropriate flowchart?
   (a) Using a flowchart is essential to any walkthrough of risk assessment activities
   (b) Using a flowchart may provide insights to the role of IT in financial processes
   (c) Using a flowchart may be useful in identifying IT-related inherent risks

i. All of the above
ii. (A) and (B)
iii. (B) and (C)
iv. (A) and (C)

Key: iii
Section Name: Financial Statement Risk Assessment (1.1.3), IT Risk Assessment (1.1.4), Risks Associated with BP (1.2.3), Primary or Key Controls (1.4.1.1), Identify Relevant Ones Embedded in BP (1.4.1.2.1)
Bloom's Taxonomy category: 1. Knowledge, 2. Comprehension, 6. Evaluate
Reference: AICPA RBA Discussion Paper, ITEC, pages 12.
Solution:
Stem: (iii): The use of flowcharts may be beneficial in providing insights to the role of IT in financial processes AND in identifying IT-related IR
Option (i): Flowcharts (A) are not essential to walkthroughs
Option (ii): Flowcharts (A) are not essential to walkthroughs
Option (iv): Flowcharts (A) are not essential to walkthroughs

5. Higher risks are associated with certain IT functions, changes, and activities. Which of the following is generally regarded as representative of relatively high risk (RMM)?
   (A) Backup and recovery of data and systems (e.g., disaster recovery)
   (B) Implementing new systems or significant changes to existing systems
   (C) Data communications within the enterprise's infrastructure
   (D) Network administrator

Key: B
Section Name: IT Risk Assessment (1.1.4, 1.1.4.1-1.1.4.4)
Bloom's Taxonomy category: 3. Comprehension, 3. Application, and 4. Analysis
Reference: "ICFR – Guidance for Smaller Public Companies", COSO, pp. 49-50.
Solution:
Stem (B): COSO explicitly states that the implementation of new systems or significant changes made to systems are considered relatively high risk for all instances.
Option (A): Back and recovery may or may not be high risk. The IR is low to moderate for most entities.
Option (C): Data communications may or may not be high risk. The IR is low to moderate for most entities.
Option (D): Network administrators can be risky, might not be risky, but never as risky as DBAs or new systems.

A precious metals mining company maintains significant quantities of gold in its warehouse. The company has three levels of controls to prevent unauthorized access to the gold inventory. First, all gold added to or removed from the vault is weighed and logged, with the log under the control of the mine manager. Second, the vault is secured in a separate room used only to pour and store the gold, with access to the room restricted to the mine manager, production manager, mill manager, and mine security. Third, the gold is stored in a vault with dual locks and only the mill manager and production manager each having one of the combinations.

6. Using the P-D-C model, which of these controls would **BEST** be described as a preventive control? (a) weighing/logging, (b) separate room for pouring/storing, (c) combination system

   i. All of the above
   ii. (a) and (b)
   iii. (b) and (c)
   iv. (a) and (c)

Key: iii
Section Name: P-D-C Model for Controls (1.3.2.2)
Bloom's Taxonomy category: 1. Knowledge, 4. Analysis, 6. Evaluate
Reference: "ICFR – Guidance for Smaller Public Companies", COSO, pp. 58-59. "IS Control & Audit", Ron Weber, pp. 35-36.
Solution:
Stem: (iii). *The last two controls are preventive in nature. The first one is detective in nature.*
Option (i): The first one (a) is detective vs. preventive in nature, detecting gold loss
Option (ii): The first one (a) is detective vs. preventive in nature, detecting gold loss
Option (iv): The first one (a) is detective vs. preventive in nature, detecting gold loss

FRAUD CONSIDERATIONS

Dimension 2

Consider the risks associated with IT and data related to fraud, forensics, litigation, and associated regulations. For financial audits, the focus would be material misstatement due to fraud. It also includes tools and techniques to react to, or procedures for, fraud suspicions, forensic investigations, and other similar activities. This part of the CITP BOK addresses knowledge requirements to issues such as computer forensics, digital evidence, data mining and analysis, security breaches, and relevant regulations (e.g., e-Discovery).

LEARNING OBJECTIVES

1. To understand the basics of fraud and forensics; e.g., fraud triangle, fraud tree (schemes and categories of schemes), scope of fraud (i.e., professional skepticism), and profile of fraudsters.
2. To have a good understanding of regulations and technical literature; especially SAS No. 99 (AU316) and how to apply it.
3. Generally, to be able to consider the risks of material misstatement due to fraud and determine specific techniques to detect fraud.
4. To understand how to use IT in fraud investigations.
5. To understand how to choose and employ the most appropriate digital acquisition tools and procedures in a fraud investigation.
6. To identify applicable sources of digital evidence in a fraud investigation.
7. To understand the basics of legal rules and procedures regarding digital evidence.
8. To understand the importance of state and federal laws regarding digital evidence.

2.0 – INTRODUCTION

Fraud has been a constant threat to the integrity of financial statements for 300 years, since the South Sea Bubble financial statement fraud of the early 18th century in England. Over those three centuries, financial frauds have been regularly perpetrated on the public and around the world. The financial auditor has responsibilities to detect these frauds, when they lead to material misstatements of the financial statements. The technical literature says:

> *"The auditor has a responsibility to plan and perform the audit to obtain reasonable assurance about whether the financial statements are free of material misstatement, whether caused by error or fraud."* [AU316.01]

AU316 is the codification of SAS No. 99, "*Consideration of Fraud in a Financial Statement Audit.*" This SAS is the most recent and most important standard related to fraud considerations in a financial statement audit. Fraud considerations, however, obviously also extend into business and industry (B&I). Those CPAs in key positions in B&I have a role and responsibility related to fraud considerations as well.

Because the context of all of these responsibilities and roles is a financial statement audit, an understanding of how fraudulent financial reporting may be perpetrated is useful (see AU316.06):

- *Manipulation, falsification, or alteration of accounting records or supporting documents from which financial statements are prepared*
- *Misrepresentation in or intentional omission from the financial statements of events, transactions, or other significant information*
- *Intentional misapplication of accounting principles relating to amounts, classification, manner of presentation, or disclosure*

This dimension of the CITP content focuses on the role and responsibilities of the CITP in fulfilling this responsibility related to fraud considerations as they pertain to the risk of material misstatement (RMM). Those roles and responsibilities will be presented as (1) prevention and deterrence, (2) digital evidence, and (3) detection and investigation.

The key standard regarding fraud consideration is SAS No. 99, which is now AU316, "*Consideration of Fraud in a Financial Statement Audit.*" The content of this dimension will be presented from AU316 to a large degree and cross referenced to the appropriate paragraph, page, or section.

2.1 – DESCRIPTION & CHARACTERISITICS OF FRAUD

In order to consider the risks associated with fraud, it is important for the CITP to be knowledgeable about the basics of fraud including a definition of fraud, the fraud tree (categories of frauds), the fraud triangle, the scope of fraud, and the profile of a fraudster (see AU316.05-.12).

2.1.1 – Definition of Fraud

There are numerous definitions of fraud that are used, but this dimension uses the one contained in SAS No. 99 because of the context of the knowledge; that is, assessing the RMM in a financial statement audit related to fraudulent financial reporting. According to AU316.05:

> *"Fraud is an intentional act that results in a material misstatement in financial statements that are the subject of an audit."*

Because any fraud could end up in court, a legal definition of what the courts deem as fraud is helpful. According to the U.S. Supreme decision in 1887, fraud is defined legally as:

- The defendant has made a representation in regard to a material fact
- Such representation is false
- Such representation was not actually believed by the defendant, on reasonable grounds, to be true
- It was made with the intent that it should be acted upon
- In so doing, the complainant was ignorant of its falsity, and reasonably believed it to be true
- That it was acted upon by complainant to his/her damage

2.1.2 – Fraud Tree

A framework for categorizing frauds is very important for CITPs in fulfilling their roles in both public accounting and B&I. There are several taxonomies of frauds but SAS No. 99 chose to use part of the Association of Certified Fraud Examiners (ACFE) fraud tree, so that is the framework used herein (AU316.06).[1] The ACFE "Fraud Tree" (see Exhibit 2.1) classifies frauds as (a) corruption schemes, (b) asset misappropriation schemes, and (c) fraudulent statement schemes (see AU316.06 that discusses the latter two).[2]

EXHIBIT 2.1: ACFE Fraud Tree

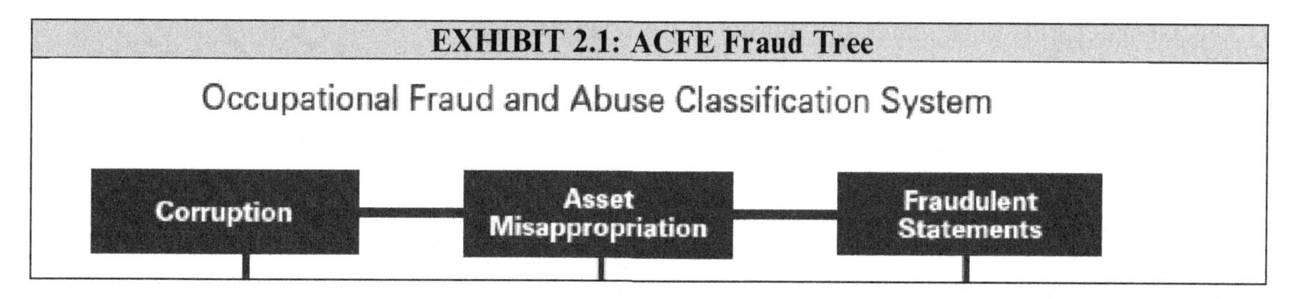

For CITPs involved in financial audits and financial reporting, obviously the latter is the primary focus. This dimension of the CITP body of knowledge focuses on the risks of material

[1] It should be noted that Joe Well, founder of the ACFE, was on the task force that drafted SAS No. 99.
[2] AU316 (SAS No. 99) omits corruption as a scheme and focuses on asset misappropriation and financial statement frauds.

misstatement. For B&I, it is likely the former two will be of more importance. The reason for that declaration is because of the correlation of materiality with the three schemes, and the role of independence with the three schemes, and the role of external auditors (including CITPs) versus internal auditors (including CITPs).

Fraudulent statement schemes are more likely to be material than the other two categories of frauds. For instance, the 2010 ACFE "Report to the Nation" (RTTN) is a survey of reported frauds from which the ACFE drew statistics to assist those whose role included some aspect of antifraud. One of those statistics is the average amount of loss per category of fraud (see Exhibit 2.2).

The average loss of corruption ($250,000 over about 18 months[3], or about $160K per fiscal year) and asset misappropriation ($135,000 over about 18 months, or about $90K per fiscal year) are likely to be immaterial, for the majority of frauds in those categories. However, the $4M average for fraudulent statements is much more likely to be material.

EXHIBIT 2.2: ACFE RTTN – Losses By Category of Fraud	
Corruption	$250,000
Asset Misappropriation	$135,000
Fraudulent Statements	$4,000,000

Thus the financial auditors and CITPs in public accounting would likely be more concerned about fraud in the financial statement category. Because external auditors are unlikely to address those first two categories due to the immateriality aspect, management in key positions of business and industry will need to focus on them, or else they will have little to no attention on them at all. Therefore, management and auditors working in B&I will need a slightly different set of knowledge, skills, and abilities, and even a slightly different perspective on fraud related to asset misappropriation and corruption schemes.

SAS No. 99 states that asset misappropriation, where usually the amount of loss is much smaller than fraudulent financial statements, can be large enough where the effect of the theft causes the financial statements to be materially misstated (see AU316.06).

For example, in 2009, an asset misappropriation scheme was detected at Koss Corporation, a public company subject to SEC reporting requirements. In December of 2009, American Express contacted the CEO of Koss to notify Koss of unusual charges to the corporate AMEX card: a charge to two jewelry stores of $382,400 and a charge at a clothing boutique store of $1.4M. The charges were made by Koss' principal accounting officer (VP Finance and Secretary), Sujata Sachdeva. Revenues in fiscal year 2009 were $38.2M, with a net income of $2M. The subsequent restatement was $8.5M in 2009, and the total fraud was estimated to be $31M over four years. Fiscal year 2008 was also restated. This case illustrates that it is possible for an asset misappropriation to occur where the effect is material to the financial statements. Therefore, the application of SAS No. 99, and the principles in this dimension, can be critical success factors in

[3] In the ACFE 2010 *Report to the Nation*, the average fraud had a median of 18 months before being detected.

appropriately assessing the RMM due to fraud when the misstatement is due to an asset misappropriation fraud.

Also, there is the independence aspect. Because financial statement frauds are almost always perpetrated by C-level executives, it is very difficult for internal discovery of those frauds. C-level managers can override controls, force subordinate accountants and others to comply with fraudulent transactions and activities, and work effectively to hide the fraud from prying eyes (see AU316.08). Thus it is difficult for the entity to discover fraudulent statements from within. However, the external auditor is independent of those factors, and by applying due diligence to comply with SAS No. 99, there is a good probability that the CPA and/or CITP will be able to find evidence of a financial statement fraud should one exist, because it is likely to be material, and financial audit procedures are designed to detect material misstatements. That caveat is possible as long as the CPA does not inadvertently lower his/her professional skepticism and get duped with phony explanations for anomalies and cover-up activities.

2.1.3 – Fraud Triangle

Another key framework in the RMM due to fraud is the fraud triangle. Fraud research shows that all frauds have three things in common regarding the fraudster: pressure/incentive, opportunity, and rationalization/attitude (see AU316.07).[4]

Pressure refers to something personal to the fraudster that motivates that person to commit a fraud.[5] For employees who commit asset misappropriation, it usually is financial pressure. But for executives committing financial statement fraud, it could be financial pressure but is more likely to be a motivation like greed, power, or ego. Again, this difference is a useful differential in evaluating the RMM as it relates to fraud. An executive with a huge ego (numerous CEOs who committed financial frauds could be described in this manner) or excessive greed for material wealth (e.g., valuable stock options based on financial performance) can be a fraud consideration when combined with other "fraud risk factors" in assessing the RMM due to fraud. Stock prices are often at the center of financial statement frauds, whether it is the object or the vehicle to the object (e.g., bonuses based on stock performance).

Another key factor for CITPs is the key role stock prices usually play in financial statement frauds. There are many potential ways to detect frauds during a financial audit, but one fairly common factor for financial statement frauds is the fact that the fraud is intended to drive up stock prices which, in turn, allows the C-level perpetrator to obtain his/her hidden goal (i.e., Enron, World.Com, HealthSouth, etc.). That goal could be low-cost stock options, increasing personal wealth related to stock being held, bonuses related to stock prices, or power. The very first financial fraud in history focused on driving up stock prices (South Sea Company "bubble" in 1720's) in order for the original stock holders to reap significant gains from the sale of their stock. Thus when the CITP sees C-level executives pay too much attention to stock prices, or have an inordinate focus on them, that is a factor that should raise professional skepticism regarding the RMM in financial statements.

---

[4] See Donald Cressey's book, *"Other People's Money"* for details on the research and findings.
[5] AU316 also refers to this aspect of a fraud as incentive.

Opportunity refers to the knowledge and opportunity to commit the fraud. It begins with the fact that a fraudster is in a position of trust. Thus a fraudster has gained the trust of some key people in order to be appointed to a position of trust, typically at the C-level for financial statement fraud. Second, it is related to the tenure of the employee. Usually, a fraudster has been with the entity a relatively long time. That length of service, especially in the position of trust, provides the fraudster with the knowledge to commit the crime and how to hide it from board members and external auditors. For CEOs and others, that knowledge is more of a factor of the knowledge the person has gained in his/her work experience. Also, opportunity is about internal controls. At this point, it is self-evident that CEOs, CFOs, and others have an ability to override controls that exist under them. In fact, the AICPA has written guidance entitled, "*Management Override of Internal Controls: The Achilles' Heel of Fraud Prevention*"[6] to assist CPAs to maintain professional skepticism and a proper perspective regarding executive management.

The 2010 ACFE RTTN reports statistics on internal controls that support this statement. The primary internal control weaknesses observed for frauds committed were, in order of frequency, lack of internal controls (37.8%), overriding of existing internal controls (19.2%), and lack of management review (17.9%). The second weakness listed is clearly about management override of controls.

The 2010 ACFE RTTN also reported statistics on internal controls that were modified or implemented in response to a resolved fraud. They were, in order of magnitude, increased segregation of duties (61.2%), management review (50.6%), and surprise audits (22.5%). This statistic indicates that the optimal response to a fraud is to increase SoD, something difficult to do with C suite executives and financial reporting.

Rationalization is about the mental process a fraudster goes through to justify why he/she is NOT committing a crime. That is, the fraudster juxtaposes the fraudulent activity with his/her personal code of ethics and comes up with a reason why it is permissible for them, in their circumstances, to commit the fraud. For instance, the fraudster may see an entitlement, and say to himself, "I deserve (need) a lavish life style as a CEO (etc.), so it is not wrong for me to take the money via financial fraud that increases my stock value (wealth)." Or the fraudster may find justification by using some of the ill-gotten gain for charity. There are many other reasons fraudsters may find to justify their financial statement fraud. AU316 also refers to this element of the fraud triangle as attitude. In the case of financial statement fraud, "attitude" may be a more appropriate term. For instance, a rogue CEO or CFO who becomes a fraudster is often referred to as a "wheeler-dealer," which describes an attitude.

The CITP should mentally question whether these three factors of the fraud triangle are present when performing audits. Observations such as a preoccupation with stock prices of the entity can be indicative of something currently unobservable that is happening; i.e., a fraud. Likewise the absence of pressure (motivation, incentive) could lead the auditor to believe fraud is less likely, and thus reduce the RMM related to fraud.

---

[6] CITPs should read the AICPA's guidance entitled, "Management Override of Internal Controls: The Achilles' Heel of Fraud Prevention". This guidance was developed for audit committees and oversight over financial reporting fraud, but contains useful information for external auditors and CITPs.

2.1.4 – Scope of Fraud

The basic conclusion from the scope of fraud is simple: a fraud CAN occur here! According to the 2010 ACFE RTTN, experts estimate that 5% of annual revenues are lost to fraud. The ACFE has conducted fraud surveys in 1996, 2002, 2004, 2006, 2008, and 2010. That percentage has been between 5% (2006, 2010) and 7% (2008) in all years (6% in 1996, 2002, and 2004). A review of newspapers and other news media (e.g., *Forensic & Valuation Reporter*) show a relatively constant flow of frauds being reported. Too often, when a fraud occurs, stakeholders never expected it to happen. The application is one of professional skepticism for the CITP in every engagement, or in every business.

2.1.5 – Profile of the Executive Perpetrator

The profile of a fraudster can be summarized by this statement: a fraudster (white-collar criminal) does NOT look like a crook. When a fraud occurs, it is often said by key stakeholders, "He/She was the last person I would have suspected!" Fraudsters are in a key position, have earned the trust of management or stakeholders, fairly educated, been an employee for a relatively lengthy tenure, often religious, and usually have a personal code of ethics. In fact, the fraudster looks more like employee of the year rather than a crook. These facts are true whether it is an executive C-level manager committing financial statement fraud or an employee committing an asset misappropriation fraud. The application of this fact, once again, is to maintain one's professional skepticism. By the nature of the job requirements, CEOs and CFOs who commit financial statement fraud usually are very articulate, can lie with a straight face, have a good image in the business community (or segment, such as stock analysts), and have a reasonably good personality.

2.2 – SAS No. 99 & ASSESSING RMM DUE TO FRAUD

SAS No. 99, "*Consideration of Fraud in a Financial Statement Audit*", describes the process whereby auditors assess the RMM related to fraud. It also describes certain factors that should be present throughout the audit. Thus applying this standard should be the best way to assess the RMM related to fraud in a financial statement audit.

The role of the CITP in fulfilling SAS No. 99, and is assessing the RMM due to fraud considerations is in understanding the implications of IT in perpetrating a fraud, and in a tool for detecting a fraud. IT can be a tool used by the perpetrator, and CITPs need to understand how a computer system or technology could be used by a perpetrator to conceal a fraud material to the financial reports. For instance, false transactions could be "coded" by the C-level person so he/she can keep distinguish the phony transactions from the legitimate ones.

Much of the following will focus on the C-suite executives because financial statement fraud is almost always perpetrated by a person in that position.

2.2.1 – The Importance of Exercising Professional Skepticism

One of the key factors in assessing the RMM due to a fraud is for CITPs and CPAs in financial audits to exercise professional skepticism. Professional skepticism is clearly an ongoing process for the CITP and CPA throughout the audit (see AU316.13).

Professional skepticism involves an attitude that includes a questioning mind, and critical assessment of audit evidence. Professional skepticism understands that a material misstatement due to fraud could occur in the current audit, despite past experience with the entity and regardless of the auditor's perception about management's integrity. The auditor would also not be satisfied with audit evidence that is less than suitable and the corroborating evidence is only an explanation from management; that is, seek independent verification.

It is natural for auditors to build a friendly social relationship with executive managers because of the natural and traditional interaction, and because that manager is a customer. However, CITPs need to remember that, should a financial fraud be perpetrated, it is almost always a C-level manager, and usually one with a good personality who is very charismatic. That makes the fraud situation difficult to discover apart from heightened professional skepticism.

The bottom line in the context of this dimension is that financial statement frauds are almost always perpetrated by C-level managers. Thus it seems some effort to ascertain the integrity of C-level managers needs to be put forth in financial statement audits, at least in the first year of the audits, and when executive management changes. For example, the audit firm could conduct a background check on executive management that includes financial and criminal information, or ask legitimate and legal questions of former employers, or question references.

Although it is simple, and intuitively obvious, CITPs should not forget that fraud is purposely clandestine, being deliberately concealed by the perpetrator (see AU316.09). The reality is that, if a financial fraud is being perpetrated, the C-level person is working feverishly to hide it. Financial statement fraudster such as Barry Minkow (ZZZZ Best financial fraud) and Sam Antar (Crazy Eddie's Electronics financial fraud) confess to the levels of social engineering and use of personal charm they used to fool auditors. Thus professional skepticism is a key antifraud technique for CITPs.

2.2.2 – Fraud Risk Factors

The key to an appropriate assessment of the RMM due to fraud is to understand, recognize, and respond to the fraud risk factors (FRF), such as those listed in SAS No. 99 (see AU.316.85, /Appendix A). Antifraud professionals often refer to FRF as "red flags" of fraud (e.g., Exhibit 2.3); that is, something that increases suspicion or skepticism that a fraud exists. As such, they should be treated similar to misstatements. Generally speaking, the larger a red flag is, the greater the risk of fraud. Also, red flags can be aggregated just as misstatements are treated in the aggregate – that is, the more red flags are identified, the higher the risk of fraud. For instance, a post office box and no physical address is a red flag for certain vendor schemes (e.g., shell vendor). But, that is a "small" red flag. However, if in applying CAATs to paycheck data, the CITP discovers two checks to the same person with the same amounts on the same date with the same check number, that red flag would likely be evaluated as a "large" red flag. Specifically, the former is possible in legitimate data but the latter should never happen and is an anomaly.

EXHIBIT 2.3: Behavioral Red Flags of Executives Committing Financial Statement Fraud	
Control issues, unwilling to share duties	33.3%
Wheeler-dealer attitude	26.7%
Financial difficulties	24.0%
Living beyond means	22.7%
Excessive pressure from within organization	21.3%

The basis of the FRF is a combination of the fraud tree (see 2.1.2), minus the corruption category, and the fraud triangle (see 2.1.3); or more aptly, it is a matrix on those characteristics containing six cells of FRFs by a combination of the fraud category and the aspect of the fraud triangle (see AU.316.85). Exhibit 2.4 summarizes the model used by SAS No. 99 for FRFs, and includes one example from Appendix A in AU.316.85 for each cell.

EXHIBIT 2.4: SAS No. 99 Model for Fraud Risk Factors	
Fraudulent Financial Reporting:	***Asset Misappropriation:***
Incentives/Pressures	**Incentives/Pressures**
Financial pressures such as: significant decline in customer demand and increasing business failures in either in the industry or overall economy	*Adverse relationships between the entity and employees with access to cash or other assets susceptible to theft may motivate those employees to misappropriate those assets*
Opportunities	**Opportunities**
Assets, liabilities, revenues, or expenses based on significant estimates that involve subjective judgments or uncertainties that are difficult to corroborate	*Inventory items that are small in size, of high value, or in high demand*
Attitudes/Rationalizations	**Attitudes/Rationalizations**
Excessive interest by management in maintaining or increasing the entity's stock price or earning trend	*Behavior indicating displeasure or dissatisfaction with the company or its treatment of the employee*

The FRF examples provided in SAS No. 99 are intended to illustrate the types of FRF rather than be an exhaustive list of FRF, especially a prioritized list. That is, the auditor needs to think about the six cells (the model) and what FRFs might be useful for in the audit being planned, including FRFs <u>NOT</u> in Appendix A.

A word of caution is pointed out in AU.316.85 regarding the use of the above model of FRFs. There is a problem with identifying the attitudes/rationalizations aspect of the fraud triangle and associated fraud risk factors.

> *"Risk factors reflective of attitudes/rationalizations by board members, management, or employees, that allow them to engage in and/or justify fraudulent financial reporting, <u>may not be susceptible to observation by the auditor</u>." (emphasis by author)* [AU.316.85.A2, page 300-8]

Thus extra professional skepticism may be necessary because rationalization and pressure are not easily observable.

2.2.3 – Behavioral Red Flags of Executive Fraudsters

There are some common behavioral red flags or characteristics that are associated with executives who commit fraud. The last attitude/rationalization listed for fraudulent financial reporting illustrates one of those behaviors:

> *"Domineering management behavior in dealing with the auditor, especially involving attempts to influence the scope of the auditor's work or the selection or continuance of personnel assigned to or consulted on the audit engagement."* (AU.316.85, page 300-9)

This behavior is present in many publicized cases such as Sam Antar, by his own confession, in the Crazy Eddie's fraud. It could also describe Enron executives, the Tyco CEO, and many others.

According the ACFE 2010 RTTN, these behavioral red flags (FRFs) begin with control issues (associated with the pressure leg of the fraud triangle and ego), wheeler-dealer attitude (likely the rationalization leg of the fraud triangle), and excessive pressure from within the organization (associated with pressure leg of the fraud triangle). Exhibit 2.3 is a list of the top five behaviors per the 2010 RTTN for executives and the frequency of the presence of that red flag in financial statement frauds resolved in the 2010 survey.[7] Opportunity is present with any C-level executive because he/she has the ability to override all of the entities controls.

Some of the discussion above concludes with an application of maintaining one's professional skepticism (see Exhibit 2.5). These factors give the CITP some specific reasons or ways to maintain, or sometimes increase, professional skepticism (see AU316.13).

EXHIBIT 2.5: Recap of Factors for Professional Skepticism	
Fraud Tree	Be aware of opportunity, incentives, and attitudes that lead to fraudulent financial statements
Executives/Perpetrators	Be reminded that fraudulent financial statements are perpetrated by C-level managers, who have reputation, appearance, verbal skills, and business knowledge that makes it hard to detect
- Clandestine	The perpetrator is working feverishly to hide the fraud, increasing the difficulty of detection
- Stock Prices	Because of the common purpose of financial statement frauds is to drive up stock prices, an inordinate attention to stock prices by executives deserves special attention and skepticism
- Behaviors	There are some behaviors common to executive fraudsters who perpetrate fraudulent financial reporting, for which auditors should be aware and increase skepticism accordingly
Scope of Fraud	In every audit, assume a material fraud could occur here
Behavioral Symptoms	Control issues (unwilling to share duties), wheeler-dealer attitude, financial difficulties, living beyond means, excessive pressure from within organization

[7] See page 72 of ACFE 2010 *Report to the Nation*.

2.2.4 – Management Override of Controls

AU316.86, "Management Antifraud Programs and Controls", describes in detail how management can build a thorough and effective antifraud program, and this information is also useful to auditors and B&I CPAs who are responsible for identifying and measuring the risk of fraud. Management clearly has the primary responsibility for assessing fraud risk, developing an antifraud program, implementing antifraud controls (e.g., preventive and detective), and monitoring for fraud. The fraud risk assessment should include the susceptibility of the entity to all types of fraud (financial statement fraud, corruption fraud, and asset misappropriation fraud), including the probability of any of those frauds leading to the RMM of the financial statements. It also includes fraud influences such as organizational antifraud effectiveness, industry fraud, and the economy's effect on fraud. Thus the auditor potentially can benefit from examining the auditee's fraud risk assessment, antifraud program, results of management's monitoring activities, and any evaluation of antifraud controls—if they exist. If management has done its due diligence, identifying and measuring fraud risk will be more efficient and effective.

2.2.5 – The SAS No. 99 Process – Assessing the RMM Due to Fraud

SAS No. 99 takes the same approach as the risk-based standards (SAS No. 104-111) and is called the risk-based approach (RBA). This approach is top-down, involves brainstorming/collaborating, and starts each audit with no predispositions about where fraud risks lie, but rather a conscientious risk assessment. The RBA gathers information, identifies the risks (i.e., inherent risk), assesses controls (i.e., control risk) and uses that information to evaluate the "residual risk" (i.e., how much risk is left after taking the controls and compensating controls into account; also known as RMM in a financial audit). Then the auditor takes the higher risks and addresses them by developing the appropriate audit procedures. That process is described in AU316.02 and summarized in Exhibit 2.6, along with potential contributions by a CITP.

It should be noted that it is management's responsibility to design and implement programs and controls to prevent, deter, and detect fraud (AU316.04).

EXHIBIT 2.6: SAS No. 99/AU316 Process		
SAS No. 99 Process	***Para.***	***CITP Contribution***
Discussion among engagement personnel regarding the RMM due to fraud	.14-.18	Understanding of IT and systems, and the implications to fraud as RMM
Obtaining information needed to identify RMM due to fraud	.19-.34	Data mining, data analysis of key data files. Analyze logical access for networks, applications, and operating systems.
Identifying risks that may result in a material misstatement due to fraud	.35-.42	Bringing specialized knowledge about logical access, automated processes, IT controls, and systems that lead to fraud risks
Assessing the identified risks after considering controls	.43-.45	<same as above, for risk assessment>
Respond to results of fraud assessment (i.e., NTE of audit procedures)	.46-.67	Ability to bring IT-related procedures that might be more effective and/or efficient than alternative substantive procedures
Evaluate audit evidence	.68-.78	Data analysis of data extracted
Communicating fraud, if discovered	.79-.82	Explaining IT implications of the fraud
Documenting auditor's consideration of fraud	.83	Documenting IT-related procedures and evidence of a fraud

2.2.5.1 – Brainstorm

Using techniques, skill, and knowledge, the auditors begin the process by brainstorming the possible fraud risks that could lead to a material misstatement. That would involve some of the fraud considerations and the fraud risk factors discussed above. The goal is to brainstorm how and where the auditors believe the financial statements might be susceptible to material misstatement due to fraud; how executives could perpetrate and successfully conceal a financial statement fraud, and how assets of the entity could be misappropriated and hidden from view. But the key factor in this analysis is that fraud risk *could* lead to a material misstatement.

The CITP can add value to brainstorming by gaining an understanding of the accounting systems and technologies and bringing that information to the session. The CITP is uniquely positioned to identify and explain the fraud risks related specifically to IT. That is, something about IT that creates the RMM due to a fraud.

For example, if the CFO has administrative rights to the operating system at root level, and there is no compensating control for "back door" activities, then the CFO could access data files, change data, the changes be material, and that change not be detected (assuming no compensating control exists). That scenario is specifically an IT risk, as opposed to fraud risks due to a business process risk or accounting control risk. Risks other than logical access exist in the IT space that need to be considered, such as fallibility of systems, technologies and software applications (including system development risk), other control environment risks, backup/recovery risks, third-party IT providers risks, change management risks, application control risks, etc.

2.2.5.2 – Obtain Information

Obtaining information necessary to appropriately assess the RMM due to fraud includes making inquiries of management (AU316.20-.27), unusual/unexpected relationships in analytical procedures (AU316.28-.30), identifying fraud risk factors that exist (AU316.31-.33), and other information (AU316.34).

It is also possible that the CITP could be used to do some preliminary analysis of data files in order to proceed to the next step with sufficient information. For example, an analysis of journal entries made on the weekend, large amounts made near the end of an accounting period, large round figures, and other anomalies could be extracted and analyzed in order to determine the exact risk associated with journal entries. This data analysis might be supplemented by a logical access evaluation of the nature of C-level managers' access via the "front door" (network and application access controls) and the "back door" (operating system access controls).

The CITP can add value by providing feedback on IT-related responses to discussions. For instance, the CITP can evaluate logical access to compare what is actually in operation versus the understanding management and key personnel may have. It is not uncommon for C-level managers to believe certain logical access controls are in place when something different is actually operational. Without the expertise of the CITP, that fact might get overlooked.

The CITP can also provide valuable insights into the identification of existing fraud risk factors, specifically the IT implications of those factors.

2.2.5.3 – Identify Risks

The information gathered in the above step should then be juxtaposed to the fraud triangle legs (incentive/pressure, opportunity, and rationalization/attitude) for the audit team to examine for potential fraud risks. The auditors should be aware that it is not always possible to observe all three legs, and, in fact, indirect evidence is probably needed to identify incentive/pressure and rationalization/attitude (AU316.35-.40). The identification of a RMM due to fraud includes the consideration of the attributes of the risk including (AU316.40):

- The *type* of risk that may exist (asset misappropriation or fraudulent financial reporting)
- The *significance* of the risk (material or immaterial)
- The *likelihood* of the risk
- The *pervasiveness* of the risk (financial statements as a whole, or particular assertion, account, or class of transactions)

SAS No. 99 asks auditors to presume that improper revenue recognition is a fraud risk (AU316.41) and to always consider the risk of management override of controls (AU316.42) when identifying fraud risks.

The CITP can bring specialized knowledge that often will be useful in identifying fraud risks. That knowledge includes logical access (see example in obtaining information), automated processes, accounting controls embedded in IT (e.g., controls), controls over IT operations, data structures, and how transactions flow through systems and database to the general ledger and financial statements. This knowledge can be beneficial in either identifying risks related to the IT aspects of the systems that can lead to a fraud-related RMM, or mitigating controls IT provides in reducing certain fraud risks.

2.2.5.4 – Assess Level of Risk in Fraud Risk

At this point, following the RBA methodology, the auditors review controls and programs that address the risks identified as potential fraud risks. This step is actually evaluating control risk, and the measure to which specific antifraud and accounting controls address the risks identified (i.e., mitigate the fraud risk), and the identification and evaluation of any "downstream" compensating controls that address the entity's ability to prevent and detect a material fraud. After considering the level to which those factors are able to reduce the RMM for the identified risks, the auditor team now has a level of risk associated with each fraud risk. Those that have been satisfactorily reduced to below the RMM can be considered out of scope. Of course any risk that still has a high risk, the RMM, must be addressed in the audit program. Either way, the audit team is required to document this process and the conclusions.

In this step, the CITP can provide the same kind of specialized knowledge that was described in "identifying risks" in the last step, which now would be used to help assess the control risk. The CITP can be especially helpful in evaluating relevant controls embedded in IT (e.g., applications), logical access controls that provide effective segregation of duties (SoD), and other control risk factors that are affected by IT or associated with IT.

2.2.5.5 – Respond to Assessed Fraud Risks

It is important to understand how C-level fraudsters could create false journal entries or transactions through their systems, how they could be concealed, and what response the audit team should make—assuming the assessment concluded that it could be material to the financials and there is no compensating control. That response would likely include some IT-related procedure that a CITP could perform to gather applicable evidence to determine if a material fraud exists.

The CITP can add value by providing feedback on IT-related responses to those fraud risks that represent the RMM. The CITP has knowledge on how to perform certain data mining or data analysis procedures that can be beneficial in detecting possible fraud. For example, the CITP should know how to analyze the data for journal entries using data mining/analysis tools to detect potential fraud (too close to end of period, too large, weekend dates of posting, etc.). This method may be more effective or efficient than alternative substantive procedures. The same could be said about any data relevant to those risks that were identified as being a RMM due to fraud. For instance, the CITP may be able to get credit card data to analyze for unauthorized charges (see Koss case above as an example of when this tactic may be useful).

2.2.5.6 – Evaluate Audit Evidence

Conditions may be identified during the field work that support, or change, a judgment about the risks that were assessed as a RMM due to fraud. Those conditions include (AU316.68):

- Discrepancies in accounting records such as:
    - Transactions that are not recorded in a complete or timely manner

- Transactions that are improperly recorded as to amount, accounting period, classification, or entity's policy
    - Unsupported or unauthorized balances or transactions
    - Last-minute adjustments that significantly affect financial results
    - Evidence of employees' (logical) access to systems and records inconsistent with what is necessary to perform their duties *
    - Tips or complaints to the auditor about allegations of fraud
- Conflicting or missing evidential matter including:
    - Missing documents
    - Documents that appear to be altered
    - Unavailability of documents
    - Documents available only as photocopied or electronically submitted documents, when original documents are expected to exist *
    - Significant unexplained items or reconciliations
    - Inconsistent, vague, or implausible responses from management or employees arising from inquiries or analytical procedures
    - Unusual discrepancies between entity's records and confirmation replies
    - Missing inventory or physical assets of significant magnitude
    - Unavailable or missing electronic evidence, inconsistent with the entity's record retention policy *
    - Inability to produce evidence of key systems development, program change testing, and implementation activities for current year's changes *
- Problematic or unusual relationships between the auditor and management including:
    - Denial of access to records, facilities, certain employees, customers, vendors, or others from whom audit evidence might be sought
    - Undue time pressures imposed by management to resolve complex or contentious issues
    - Complaints by management about the conduct of the audit or management intimidation of audit team members
    - Unusual delays by the entity in providing requested information
    - Unwillingness to facilitate auditor access to key electronic files for testing through the use of Computer-Assisted Audit Techniques (CAATs) *
    - Denial of access to key IT operations staff and facilities, including security, operations, and systems development personnel *
    - An unwillingness to add or revise disclosures in the financial statements to make them more complete and transparent

    ** The CITP should be a subject-matter expert (SME) on these factors and possibly others.*

Analytical procedures play a role in evaluating evidence. The auditor should evaluate whether analytical procedures that were performed as substantive tests or in the overall review stage indicate a previously unrecognized RMM due to fraud. If no analytical procedures relating to revenue were performed in the overall review stage, they should be performed through the end of the reporting period. Some examples are:

- The relationship of net income to cash flows from operations
- Changes in inventory, accounts payable, sales, or cost of sales from the prior period to current period might be inconsistent
- A comparison of the entity's profitability to industry trends may indicate differences for further consideration
- A comparison of bad debt write-offs to comparable industry data may provide unexplained relationships that could indicate a possible theft of cash
- An unexpected or unexplained relationship between sales volume as determined from the accounting records and production statistics maintained by operations personnel may indicate possible misstatement of sales

Note that should analytical procedures indicate the need for further procedures or review that could be facilitated by CAATs, the CITP needs to be prepared to conduct data mining and data analysis to gather more evidential matter.

In fact, the CITP needs to understand the systems, data, and business processes in order to be able to gather audit evidence out of electronic files should it be necessary. In other words, the CITP should be engaged and able to contribute to the audit program by suggesting ways IT-related procedures would be effective in gathering evidence related to the RMM due to fraud, or suspicion of fraud, because of results of substantive testing such as the analytical procedures mentioned above.

2.2.5.7 – Communicate

SAS No. 99 gives specific guidance on how to communicate misstatements related to fraud: (1) misstatements that may be indicative of fraud (AU316.75); (2) misstatements that are or may be the result of fraud, but the effect is not material to the financial statements (AU316.76); (3) misstatements that are or may be the result of fraud and either has determined that the effect could be material to the financial statements, or has been unable to evaluate materiality (AU316.77); and even circumstances where the auditor should consider withdrawal from the engagement (AU316.78). Guidance is also provided regarding the parties to which communications should be made; management, audit committee, and others (AU316.79–.82).

2.2.5.8 – Document

SAS No. 99 also provides guidance on what should be documented regarding the process of assessing the RMM due to fraud (AU316.83).

2.3 – PREVENTION & DETERRENCE

Effective fraud prevention and deterrence is based on the forensic basics presented in sections 2.1. For example, fraud prevention begins with an appropriate fraud risk assessment. An entity cannot defend itself against something which is unknown to the entity. Once fraud risks are properly identified, effective fraud prevention is then based on knowledge about fraud schemes: how they are perpetrated, what red flags are associated with them, who is likely to commit that fraud and why, and what countermeasures are considered best practices. Section 2.2.2 through 2.2.5 above presents that type of information.

The primary factor in prevention and deterrence is to increase the perception of detection. Perception of detection (PoD) is the environment that leads potential fraudsters to perceive/believe that if they commit a fraud, they will get caught, and they will go to jail. The potential results theoretically cause some potential fraudsters to forego frauds out of fear.

Examples of antifraud activities that potentially can increase the PoD include: surveillance, anonymous tips and complaints system, surprise audits, mandatory vacation/rotation of duties, prosecution of a fraudster who was caught, and background checks. While some of these are traditionally considered detective measures, if the entity does them effectively, they actually also increase the PoD because the potential fraudster fears he/she will get caught by that detective activity (e.g., surprise audit). That is, early detection controls might serve as a preventive control because it might increase the PoD.

The CITP can provide assistance in prevention and deterrence by making suggestions for IT-related antifraud preventive activities. It is possible that IT-related controls can be built into automated business processes whose purpose is to prevent a fraud. For example, the CITP could develop automated antifraud controls that prevent an unauthorized vendor from being added to the authorized vendor list to prevent a shell vendor scheme (e.g., using logical access to segregate duties). There are many ways the CITP can provide expertise in developing antifraud IT-related preventive controls.

2.4 – DETECTION & INVESTIGATION

Effective fraud detection and investigation is also based on the forensic basics presented in sections 2.1. Fraud detection and investigation begins with suspicion of fraud or discovery of one or more fraudulent events. Like fraud prevention, knowledge of fraud schemes is an important factor in effective detection and investigation.

Detection should be clarified to say *early* detection. Controls and anti-fraud activities should be focused on detecting frauds early rather than simply detecting fraud. For example, some antifraud controls have an ability to detect earlier than others.

Investigation also is included in this phase. Once a fraud is detected, the entity needs to decide whether a fraud investigation is necessary and how to conduct one if it is. Clearly investigation is distinct from detection itself.

2.4.1 – Use of IT Skills in Fraud Investigations

A fraud investigation should begin with an appropriate scoping process–something the antifraud profession calls the "fraud theory". In that process, the team attempts to identify the potential frauds that could be occurring. That scoping process necessarily takes into account an understanding of business processes, systems, and manual controls; IT controls; and logical access.

2.4.1.1 – Evaluating Relevant Systems and Software

One basic skill in a fraud investigation is simply to identify the relevant systems, applications, and operating systems for a specific fraud investigation. Controls, data, and relevant digital sources are mostly dependent on an understanding of data flows, systems processes, databases, and files from capture of information to the general ledger and financial reports. It also includes gaining an understanding of relevant software applications which is where the relevant data and controls exist. Obviously, one of the keys in fraud detection and investigation is to understand where data exists in operational and transactional systems relevant to the objectives of the investigation or fraud audit, and how that data could be subject to unauthorized access or manipulation.

The CITP is a SME who can map that data to the systems, platforms, and databases for possible data extraction, data mining, and data analyses. The proper identification or mapping of applicable databases to the fraud risk assessment (fraud theory) is key to effective and efficient data mining, data analysis, and gathering of digital evidence. But the CITP can also provide other beneficial services to the fraud investigation team.

2.4.1.2 – Evaluating IT Antifraud Controls

A critical factor in identifying the scope of a fraud is to understand the control environment, especially the IT controls, embedded in systems and software for business processes that are associated with potential fraud schemes. Thus the team needs to gain a thorough understanding of the control environment and how it affects the scope of the investigation.

When there is a suspicion of fraud, or when one or more fraudulent transactions come to the attention of a stakeholder, it is important to understand what frauds that person could have perpetrated. One of the reasons for this approach is the fact that of the fraudsters who get caught, they tend to escalate their crimes by taking more from a fraud, or by extending their activities into other types of frauds. In order to conduct an appropriate investigation, therefore, the investigation team needs to have some idea of the scope of the investigation, which is related to the IT antifraud controls, including their absence, presence, and operating effectiveness.

2.4.1.3 – Logical Access

When conducting a fraud investigation or fraud audit, it is helpful to see what kind of segregation of duties (SoD) is being used by logical access. The absence of strong logical access SoD is usually considered a serious weakness for fraud and thus affects the scope or direction of the investigation.

Therefore, in scoping a fraud, the CITP should examine logical access. That is, what access does a suspect have to data and systems (especially applications)? A logical access evaluation will enable the investigative team to understand the fraud risk associated with access via the "front door" (network and application access controls) and the "back door".

The back door is a slang term meaning access to data or applications via bypassing the normal access controls interfaced with networks and applications, and accessing them via operating system (OS) controls. Without proper OS access controls, an employee, especially a manager, could have the "keys to the kingdom"—missing or weak OS controls allowing that person to gain access to virtually all databases and/or applications.

2.4.1.4 – Observable Digital Data Sources

Some data can be easily observed in electronic form on electronic devices. It can be seen through operating systems, applications, and other interfaces. That type of data will be called observable data, not because it can be seen with the naked eye, but because it can be seen with common cyber lenses. Other data is more elusive, more difficult to observe with common means, and thus will be referred to as nonobservable, even though it can become observable with the right tool. This distinction is necessary in order to demonstrate the difficulty of detecting the nonobservable type, but also the possibility of gaining access to the nonobservable type.

As stated above, there should be an abundance of digital data in the operational systems of the victim entity.[8] The CITP is a SME that can help identify the relevant digital data sources including the entity's network system (routers, servers, etc.), email servers, computers, laptops, printers, application databases, and other sources, and then map those sources to the applicable fraud risks identified by the team.

Because of the special knowledge CITPs and other SMEs have about IT, it is possible for an investigation to overlook other potential sources of evidence. With the proliferation of IT in recent years, there are a number of digital sources that need to be considered in a fraud investigation including but not limited to:

- Home computer
- Server (email or data)
- Laptops
- Smart phones/PDAs/Cell phone/etc.
- Printer memory
- iPods
- Email
- CDs
- DVDs
- External drives
- Flash/Jump/USB drives
- Digital watch
- Flash cards (camera memory)
- Digital voice mail

Not only should the CITP be able to identify relevant digital sources, but he/she should also have sufficient skills to investigate these digital sources for potential evidence.

2.4.1.5 – Nonobservable Digital Data Sources

It is also possible that data exists in forms that are typically not observable, sometimes not even known to users, and not in the transactional data; referred to herein as nonobservable data.

One type of this data is metadata. Metadata is defined as data about data. Metadata can be the properties of Microsoft Office documents that are not viewable in the document, but can be viewed with the properties function of the Office application. This metadata records the author of

[8] The term extractable is used to refer to data that is normally visible and observable through the associated technologies and tools. For instance, using an operating system (e.g., Windows) viewer (Windows Explorer), a user can view a list of files stored in a folder. Non-extractable refers to data that is normally NOT visible and observable without an additional tool and special knowledge to even know it exists.

the document (something that can be valuable in fraud detection and investigation), modified/created/accessed dates (also valuable), revision number, total editing time, stats on the document contents, file location, and other facts entered by the author (title, subject, keywords, category, status, and comments). Metadata also exists in the following (Singleton & Singleton, 2010):

- Email headers
- Spreadsheet formulas and linked data
- Database structures and relationships
- Editing history (e.g., track changes in Microsoft Word)
- System logs of users' activities
- Windows NFTS/FAT files (directories)
- Certain HTML code
- Certain aspects of XML files

Another type of nonobservable data is latent data. Latent data is undiscovered, concealed, misplaced, missing, or hidden data on disk drives that under normal operating circumstances are not converted to observable information. The data is usually not accessible by applications. Latent data is very fragile and subject to loss by its nature. Examples of latent data include the following:

- Deleted files (which sometimes can be recovered)
- Slack space (download temporary files stored there)
- RAM data (if computer is powered up)
- Temporary files (from application processes)
- Windows swapped files
- Stored printer images

2.4.2 – Use of IT in Fraud Investigations

Many times, the use of IT in a fraud investigation is critical to a successful investigation. Often, this criticality revolves around data mining and analysis. As stated above, the SME/CITP should have been involved with the investigation team in identifying potential digital/data sources, especially for the purposes of data mining and data analysis. That process would not only consider operational and transactional data, but spreadsheets, end user documents, and other digital files of interest. It even may include credit card data, be it corporate or personal credit cards.

Data mining is extracting patterns from data, modeling and knowledge discovery, and/or matching transactions against specific criteria. The context for this discussion is patterns of fraud, modeling/discovery of fraud, or identifying transactions that are evidence a fraud has or has not been committed.

2.4.2.1 – Data Mining/Analysis

Data analysis is the process of inspecting data with some goal or benchmark in mind. For this discussion, the goal or benchmark is to determine whether or not it is evidence of fraudulent transactions.

Data mining and analysis are particularly beneficial in a fraud investigation when:

1. Events or transactions are voluminous within which potential evidence of fraudulent events or transaction exists
2. When paper documents are voluminous but the same information exists in data
3. When multiple and disparate systems are being used (often purposely designed to obfuscate a fraud)
4. When data mining and analysis are clearly more efficient than alternative substantive or manual detective/investigation procedures

When the suspicious events or transactions are buried in large volumes of transactions, then the ability to isolate or identify the fraudulent transactions become very difficult to do manually. But data mining and analysis are capable of examining the population of data, not a sample, with efficiency and effectiveness. If the above mapping and identification of data has been properly done, then the SME/CITP will know which files contain the data necessary to gather sufficient and competent evidence that a fraud did or did not occur. The SME/CITP would extract the relevant data and conduct the appropriate tests and procedures to mine or analyze the data. Those tests are primarily driven by an understanding of the nature of the schemes identified in the risk assessment, and are basically looking for the red flags (FRFs) also already identified.

When the paper documents abound but there are data or systems available, the only option available may be to meld the systems' data together for data mining and analysis. It might be cost prohibitive to examine millions of sheets of paper to gather evidence, but it may be possible to use IT tools to examine the data available.

Sometimes a fraudster will use disparate computers that are deliberately difficult to operate in order to hide the fraud; that is, either the systems are not integrated, or are integrated manually, and/or are difficult to operate. When this situation exists, data mining is probably critical to gathering effectual evidence.

It is the SME/CITP who can best make that assessment. Obviously, data mining is only as successful as the proper identification of the useful data stores and a successful data extraction.

2.4.2.2 – Proper Digital Data Acquisition Tools & Procedures

One way to describe the overall process of acquiring the relevant data and using the appropriate tool is as follows:

- Set the audit objectives
- Identify/map the relevant data and the associated systems, applications, and platforms
- Choose the appropriate data mining, data analysis, and computer-assisted audit tool (CAAT) tools (see Exhibit 2.7)
- Meet with the data owner and/or programmer
- Request the data (usually most difficult step)
- Extract the data into usable format

- Import data into the tool
- Verify the integrity of the data imported (vs. operational data)
- Gain a general understanding of the data (data mining at high level)
- Analyze the data for specific objectives, drill down, directed tests/procedures

The audit objectives have been discussed above, as well as the identification and mapping of relevant data to be used by the data mining tool. Next, the SME/CITP will choose the appropriate tool by matching the tool to the data and investigation. That means taking into consideration the nature of the digital evidence, the type of platform that contains the data files, the objective of the fraud detection and evidence gathering procedures, the export options available to extract the data, and the abilities of individual tools.

EXHIBIT 2.7: Data Mining Tools Model

Level	*Description*	*Example of Tools*
LOW	Simple functionality, smaller data files, simple procedures needed, delimited text file/Excel format export available	Excel
INTERMEDIATE	Moderate functionality, file size too large for Excel, moderate procedures needed, delimited text file/Excel format export available	Excel Plug-in (Active Data) Microsoft Access (or similar)
HIGH	Highly sophisticated functionality, largest files, complex or sophisticated procedures needed, text file/dbf/pdf/XML extract available	ACL IDEA Monarch Panaudit

Generally, the tools can be divided into the nature and complexity (strength) of the tool (see Exhibit 2.7). For example, suppose the procedures are relatively simple (i.e., able to be performed with sort, autofilter, and other standard Excel functions), the size of the data is relatively small (i.e., will operate efficiently in Excel), and the data can be exported as a delimited text file. Under these circumstances, the CITP/SME may well choose to extract the data in a format compatible with Excel, import the file into Excel, and use Excel's functionality to perform the appropriate procedures. But if the data is more complicated, or if the size is large, or if the procedures are more complex, then Excel will not be the best tool.

The Model is not an absolute but a guide based on four basic factors. That is, if a file size is too large for Excel to handle efficiently (too slow handling the data and/or commands), then that factor alone is sufficient reason to consider an intermediate or high tool. Obviously, if the data cannot be exported as a delimited text file, the low and intermediate tools may not be the best fit based on that factor alone.

Next, the SME/CITP needs to actually acquire the identified data by meeting with the appropriate IT person, requesting the data, and establishing the specific data to be extracted and its format. Once the data is obtained, the SME/CITP will import it into the tool. This step is the most difficult of the processes.

In getting the data, the SME/CITP starts with the goal of getting the data as "clean" as possible, and in the easiest format to be imported into the tool. The "ideal" format is one where the first row contains the names of the columns (i.e., data fields), and the rows below contain the data in tab or comma delimited format (see Exhibit 2.8). All rows need to be contiguous. However, it is not always possible to extract data in the ideal or easier formats and thus the SME/CITP is prepared to use techniques to "clean" the data, or alternative formats for importing more efficiently (e.g., pdf files, print to file, pull data directly using SQL/ODBC/etc.). Data formats by order of ease and efficiency of use are: dBASE, pdf (not a scanned image), Excel (.xls etc.), delimited text file, and XML. The rest of the options are fairly time consuming and difficult to use.

EXHIBIT 2.8: Ideal Data Extraction Format

ID	NAME	ADDRESS	CITY	ST	ZIP	PHONE	CRDT LMT	BALANCE
1	ABC Co.	101 Main St	Anywhere	FL	33333	123-4567	$50,000.00	$24,000.00
2	Cranky Repairs	211 Elm St	Anywhere	FL	33333	234-5678	$10,000.00	$1,200.00
3	Mild Soap Inc	314 Oak Ave	Anywhere	FL	33333	345-6789	$30,000.00	$5,000.00
4	Sunny Side Inc	411 Pine St	Anywhere	FL	33333	456-7890	$25,000.00	$26,000.00

Once the data is imported, the SME/CITP needs to gain assurance about reliability risk. That is, perform some procedure about the integrity of the data to ensure the data being mined and analyzed is exactly the same data in the operational data files.

After gaining assurance over the data integrity, the SME/CITP will take the necessary measures to ensure that the data being examined is read-only (RO). The "high" level tools usually treat the data as RO automatically. But clearly if the data is in Access, Excel, or similar tools, the data is subject to change and thus errors or data inadvertently changes. Precautions need to be taken to ensure that does not happen.

Data mining usually begins with gaining an understanding of the data set as a whole. For instance, the SME/CITP might run some descriptive statistics on the file to see if relevant data fields have a normal distribution, negative amounts where none should exist (and vice versa), identify outliers, and other informative statistics.

Based on the results of the general understanding, the SME/CITP may, based on professional judgment, decide that he/she needs to drill down on suspicious results. For example, if the stats reveal negative quantities in receiving reports, the SME/CITP would likely conclude that is an anomaly. The next step is likely to be a data mining procedure to isolate those entries containing the negative quantities, which then could be examined to identify possible reasons for the anomaly—which is either fraud or error.

The SME/CITP would then complete the procedures and tests necessary to meet the investigation objectives regarding digital evidence.

2.4.3 – Regulatory Standards

The primary technical literature is SAS No. 99 (AU.316) which has been discussed above. The Forensic Valuation Services (FVS) section of the AICPA issues guides and information to assist the CITP in fraud considerations. Regulatory standards for IT procedures and digital evidence do include federal and state laws regarding evidence (see section 2.5 below for more).

Federal regulations include the Foreign Corrupt Practices Act (1977), the Financial Fraud Detection and Disclosure Act (1986), the Sarbanes-Oxley Act (2002), and other laws.

The Foreign Corrupt Practices Act (FCPA) of 1977 was passed to address the fact that U.S. corporations were guilty of corruption fraud; that is, bribing foreign government officials to do business in those countries. FCPA was passed to prohibit bribery and make it illegal. It also required SEC registrants to establish and maintain financial records, accounts, and books. FCPA also required the establishment of internal accounting controls.

The Financial Fraud Detection and Disclosure Act (FFDDA) became law in 1986 and applies to issuers. FFDDA was passed because at the time, auditors had no obligation to report illegal acts of fraud to anyone other than management. FFDDA requires that auditors include specific and substantive procedures for detecting financial fraud as a part of the audit plan, and that they evaluate internal controls. Auditors are required to provide public disclosure of known or suspected fraudulent activities discovered during the financial audit, and gives auditors a responsibility for assuring such disclosure. FFDDA requires that auditors report known or suspected illegal activities to the appropriate government, regulatory, or enforcement authorities. It also provides complete legal protection for auditors who perform duties under the Act in good faith.

In response to large financial scandals, the U.S. Congress passed the Sarbanes-Oxley Act (SOX) on July 30, 2002. SOX has numerous provisions in it related to fraud, but the bill basically put requirements on management and not the auditors. It requires certain good corporate governance practices, such as independence and financial expertise for audit committees, and oversight of anonymous tips and complaints systems by the audit committee. However, auditors are required to opine on management's evaluation of internal controls, including antifraud controls (Section 404).

A summary of potential applicable laws for which the CITP needs to be aware are listed in Exhibit 2.9 (Pearson & Singleton, 2008).

EXHIBIT 2.9: Sample of Applicable Laws for Digital Investigation	
Copyright Laws, 1976 et al.	Intellectual property
Computer Fraud and Abuse Act (CFAA), 1984	Computer fraud, hacking
Health Information Portability Accountability Act (HIPAA), 1996	Privacy, medical
Gramm-Leach-Bliley Act (GLBA), 1999	Privacy, financial services
Sarbanes-Oxley Act (SOX), 2002	Financial reporting fraud
Fraud and Related Activity in Connection with Computers, Title 18 U.S.C. 1030	Computer fraud

2.5 – DIGITAL EVIDENCE

Digital evidence knowledge is critical because of the fact that if the evidence needs to be presented in a court of law, the digital evidence rules need to have been implemented from acquisition and throughout the process. That is, digital evidence can be tainted, made inadmissible, up front unintentionally, if the applicable rules and laws are not followed properly.

2.5.1 – Legal Rules & Procedures

Basically, one of the goals for an investigation is to ensure that digital evidence collected will be admissible in court if necessary. Courts use primary evidence as the best evidence, and primary is not only material, relevant, and competent, but in the same exact state as when initially captured "at the scene of the crime". That means digital evidence MUST be presented in court in the exact condition it was in when initially captured. Secondly, a chain of custody must be established to ensure that no one can tamper with the digital evidence. Lastly, the investigation team needs to make a working copy of the original in order to conduct tests and procedures to gather evidence.

It is essential, therefore, to capture the digital evidence (especially drives, computers, and other digital sources) without disturbing the digital data. For instance, if a personal computer is on, does one turn it off, pull the plug, or shut it down naturally? Turning on a computer can taint the digital data on the hard drive of that computer, so if it is off it should not be turned on. Main frames cannot have the plug pulled. If it is possible that digital evidence exists in RAM, that is another factor as well. But the SME/CITP must determine the course of action that preserves the digital evidence as is at the point of capture. All digital sources need to be "bagged and tagged", and maintained in its condition at the point of acquisition.

Secondly, the original evidence needs to have a chain of custody established at the point of capture by initiating a chain of custody log containing sufficient information to uniquely identify each digital source, and facts such as date, time, and location. The original evidence should be locked up in a closet or room with limited access. Every time that evidential matter is removed from the closet, the custody log needs to reflect exactly who had custody, what was done with it, and when it was returned.

Lastly, a working copy of the original needs to made without disturbing the original. Usually, that requires making a bit streaming backup of the original disk drive. Thus the SME/CITP should be aware of the tools and techniques available to perform that function properly (e.g., Encase software). Special tools could also include write blockers to prevent the original data from being changed. The same type of approach is used for email headers, tracers, audit logs, and other security-related sources. (Pearson & Singleton, 2008)

Therefore, even if it is uncertain, or even unlikely, that an investigation will end up in court, care should be taken at the point of digital acquisition just in case it does need to be presented as evidence in court. That is, the investigation should treat the acquisition as if it were going to end up in court because of the uncertainty about whether a fraud case will be litigated.

2.5.2 – E-discovery Rules & Procedures

Rule 34(a) provides that litigants in federal courts may request computerized data during legal discovery, recognizing that electronically stored information (ESI) is a type of discoverable information. Requesting parties have the ability to test or sample materials sought under the rule, specifically:

> *"...to produce and permit the party making the request, or someone acting on the requestor's behalf, to inspect, and copy, test or sample, any designated documents or ESI..."*

Rules are in place to ensure adequate notice from opposing counsel, and to limit the ESI data provided.

The issues for the CITP involve basic knowledge of e-discovery from the legal perspective, and to understand it from the IT practitioner's perspective.

In the case of the latter, the issues will include:

- Locating, mapping, where the ESI requested exists
- What resources will be necessary to extract the ESI requested (time, personnel, special software, etc.)
- Specifically, what efforts are necessary to satisfactorily extract the ESI
- How does the practitioner ensure the data provided is limited to that requested (it will usually be necessary to filter or cull databases after extraction but before delivery)
- Inadvertent release of privileged information
- A clear understanding of the format of ESI as a deliverable

From a B&I perspective, e-discovery means entities need to establish a policy for retention of email and other data. That is, establish an effective policy for routine destruction of electronic data. It also means the entity needs to establish software and data storage to facilitate an e-discovery request for ESI. That may mean specialized email software, for example.

It is important to not only have a reasonable policy and procedure for archiving email and electronic documents, but to strictly adhere to that policy. Should an entity be lax in adherence, that situation could allow the opposing counsel to expand the request for electronic documents despite the policy, because he/she knows the entity is archiving more than P&P states.

2.5.3 – Federal & State Laws

The use of digital evidence in court has increased in recent years. Courts allow: email, digital photographs, ATM transaction logs, word processing documents, spreadsheet documents, instant messaging (IM) histories, data files from accounting software, databases, Internet browser histories, contents of RAM, computer backups, computer printouts, Global Positioning System (GPS) tracks, logs from electronic door locks, and digital video or audio files.[9] But rules of evidence are somewhat different in state courts than federal courts.

2.5.3.1 – Federal Law

Federal law for digital evidence is taken from the "*Federal Rules of Evidence*". This document governs the admissibility of evidence in federal courts. The document is the codification of rules that existed in 1975, and has been modified by U.S. Congress. Topics covered include:

- General Provisions
- Judicial Notice
- Presumptions in Civil Actions and Proceedings
- Relevancy and its Limits
- Privileges
- Witnesses
- Opinions and Expert Testimony
- Hearsay
- Authentication and Identification
- Contents in Writings, Recordings, and Photographs
- Miscellaneous Rules

The more relevant sections, and their relationship to digital evidence, are as follows.

2.5.3.2 – Witnesses

There are two kinds of witnesses allowed in court. The first is a fact witness. A fact witness testifies as to facts personally observed (usually limited to the five senses), but does not include any second hand information (i.e., hearsay), or opinions.

The second is an expert witness, which is explained in the next section.

2.5.3.3 – Opinions and Expert Testimony

This part of the Rules allows the court to recognize an "expert" who has special technical knowledge that will assist the trier of fact (i.e., judge or jury) to understand technical evidence. In order to testify as an expert, that person must be qualified as an expert in the applicable field. An expert witness can express an opinion in court, but that opinion must be based on evidence (digital evidence in this context) already presented to the court.

2.5.3.4 – Authentication and Identification

In general, court rules about admissibility of digital evidence are the same as any evidence. Thus the evidence must be relevant, material, and competent evidence related to the case. The strength of evidence can be ordered in this manner: primary evidence, secondary evidence, and (acceptable) hearsay evidence.

[9] Taken from wikipedia.com, September 28, 2010.

Primary evidence is the original business documents, or in case of digital evidence, the original computer/hard drive containing the original digital business documents. This court rule is the reason digital sources must be captured and immediately maintained in the exact same condition as when captured.

Secondary evidence would include things like: a photocopy of a business document, testimony of witnesses, or transcripts of the evidential contents. However, the court will not accept secondary evidence unless an attorney satisfactorily explains why the original is not available.

Chain of custody is another authentication factor. Digital evidence needs to be uniquely identified immediately upon capture, and a log kept tracking any movement or use of the digital source/evidence.

2.5.3.5 – Hearsay

Hearsay evidence is not admissible with a few exceptions. One exception is "business entries made in the normal course of business", which would include digital entries.

2.5.3.6 – Treatment of Digital Evidence in Federal Courts

Generally speaking, courts will determine if digital evidence being presented meets the authentication criteria (relevant, material, and competent), then determine it is primary evidence and NOT hearsay evidence (with the possible exception stated above), before it will be admissible. That is, many courts apply the federal rules of evidence to digital evidence in a similar manner it applies them to paper documents.

However, some courts treat digital evidence different. The basis for differential treatment of digital evidence is in applying authentication, hearsay, and primary evidence based on: the voluminous nature of digital data, it is easily modified, it is easily duplicated, it is more readily available, it is more difficult to destroy, and it is potentially more expressive.[10] Thus digital evidence, in some federal courts, is more easily admissible than in others, who apply the general rules strictly in evaluating admissibility of digital evidence.

In 1996, new federal rules were implemented requiring the preservation and disclosure of electronically stored evidence (see *General Court Rules* above). Digital evidence is often questioned by opposing counsel with the claim that it is relatively easy for one to tamper with digital evidence, but most courts reject this argument without proof of actual tampering.

Another federal rule [Federal Rules of Evidence Rule 1001(3)] allows output, such as printouts and summaries, of primary evidence when the evidence itself is complicated or voluminous.

> *"If data are stored in a computer … any printout or other output readable by sight, shown to reflect the data accurately, is an 'original'."*

That output often can be charts or diagrams which are useful in summarizing digital information. The court considers such a printout from digital evidence as primary evidence (original evidence), although technically it is not.

---

[10] *Ibid*

It should also be noted that digital evidence must have been obtained with the proper authorization, such as a warrant, in order to not violate the fourth amendment (expectation of privacy principle).

2.5.3.7 – State Law

States laws vary from state to state, and sometimes take precedence of de facto federal laws and rules. One example is validating the qualifications of an expert witness.

The de facto rule allows a judge to challenge and validate the qualifications of an expert. This evaluation follows certain specified rules. But state laws sometimes allow opposing counsel to challenge the qualifications of an expert witness. This challenge is based on a case by the same name, the *Daubert* challenge. But a *Daubert* challenge varies from state to state. Other differences exist between states, and between state rules and federal rules.

The bottom line is the CITP needs to be aware of the *Federal Rules of Evidence*, as they apply to digital evidence, be up to date on specific rules that apply to digital evidence {e.g., rule 1001(3)}, and know any unique state rule that will apply–especially where the state rule will affect normal federal rules.

One good tool is the National Institute of Justice's "*Forensic Examination of Digital Evidence: A Guide for Law Enforcement*".

Advanced Reading Recommendations:

AICPA, (2009), *The Guide to Investigating Business Fraud*. AICPA: NY.

AICPA, (2006), *SAS No. 99*. AICPA: NY. {AU316}

Golden, Thomas W., Steven L. Skalak, & Mona M. Clayton, (2006), *A Guide to Forensic Accounting Investigation*. John Wiley & Sons. NJ: Hoboken.

Wells, Joseph T., (2008), *Principles of Fraud Examination*, 2e. John Wiley & Sons. NJ: Hoboken.

GLOSSARY:

Application Controls

Application Controls are internal controls, whether automated or manual, which operate at the transaction-level with the objectives of ensuring that:

- Proper authorization is obtained to initiate and enter transactions;
- Applications are protected from unauthorized access;
- Users are only allowed access to those data and functions in an application that they should have access to;
- Errors in the operation of an application will be prevented or detected and corrected in a timely manner;
- Application output is protected from unauthorized access or disclosure;
- Reconciliation activities are implemented when appropriate to ensure that information is complete and accurate; and
- Ensuring that high-risk transactions are appropriately controlled.

Asset Misappropriation Schemes

The use of one's occupation for personal gain through the deliberate misuse or theft of the employing organization's resources or assets.

Control Risk

Control Risk is the risk that a material misstatement will not be detected or prevented by the entity's internal control on a timely basis. The auditor must consider the risk of misstatement individually and in aggregate with other misstatements.

Corruption Schemes

A set of fraud schemes that involves someone inside the victim organization working with someone outside the entity to defraud the entity. Includes bribery, kickbacks, conflict of interests, bid rigging, economic extortion, and illegal gratuities.

Data Mining

Data mining is examining data by extracting patterns, modeling and knowledge discovery, and/or matching transactions against specific criteria.

e-Discovery

Discovery in civil litigation which deals with the exchange of information in electronic format, often referred to as electronically stored information (ESI).

Fraud

An intentional act that results in a material misstatement in financial statements that are the subject of an audit.

Fraud Investigation

The processes involved with conducting an investigation into possible fraud from the law enforcement and legal perspective. Fraud investigations include gathering accounting evidence, digital evidence, interviews, and other information that helps build a case to prove or disprove a fraud.

Fraud Risk Factors
Identifiers, indicators, situations, behaviors, and other evidence that a fraud has occurred, is occurring, or will occur. They are specifically related to a set of factors identified in SAS No. 99. See also red flags.

Fraud Triangle
Donald Cressey conducted research involving interviewing embezzlers who were incarcerated. From those interviews, Cressey identified three things that were present in all of the frauds: pressure, opportunity, and rationalization. These three facts have become known as the Cressey triangle or the fraud triangle.

Fraud Tree
The ACFE categorized occupational abuse and fraud schemes into a taxonomy that contains 50+ individual schemes. The nature of the taxonomy resembles a tree with branches. The trunk has three main branches: asset misappropriate, fraudulent financial reporting, and corruption.

Fraudulent Financial Reporting
The deliberate misrepresentation of the financial condition of an enterprise accomplished through the intentional misstatement or omission of amounts or disclosures in the financial statements in order to deceive financial statement users.

Inherent Risk
Inherent Risk is the susceptibility that a relevant assertion could be misstated assuming that there are no other related controls. The auditor should consider the risk of misstatement individually as well as in aggregate with other misstatements, assuming there are no related controls.

Internal Control
Internal Control is a process, effected by an entity's board of directors, management, and other personnel, designed to provide reasonable assurance regarding the achievement of objectives in the following categories:

- Effectiveness and efficiency of operations
- Reliability of financial reporting
- Compliance with applicable laws and regulations

Key Concepts:

- Internal control is a process. It is a means to an end, not an end in itself.
- Internal control is affected by people. It's not merely policy manuals and forms, but people at every level of an organization.
- Internal control can be expected to provide only reasonable assurance, not absolute assurance, to an entity's management and board.
- Internal control is geared to the achievement of objectives in one or more separate but overlapping categories.

Source: COSO; http://www.coso.org/IC.htm

For additional resources on internal control over financial reporting visit www.cpa2biz.com for:

- *Internal Control—Integrated Framework* (product no. 990012kk), a paperbound version of the COSO report that established a common definition of internal control different parties can use to assess and improve their control systems. [http://www.cpa2biz.com/AST/Main/CPA2BIZ_Primary/InternalControls/COSO/PRDOVR~PC-990009/PC-990009.jsp]
- *Financial Reporting Fraud: A Practical Guide to Detection and Internal Control* (product no. 029879kk), a paperbound publication for CPAs in both public practice and industry. [http://www.cpa2biz.com/AST/Main/CPA2BIZ_Primary/FinancialManagement/Finance/FinancialReporting/PRDOVR~PC-029879/PC-029879.jsp]
- In July 2006, COSO released its guidance, *Internal Control over Financial Reporting—Guidance for Smaller Public Companies*, which may assist companies and auditors understand the applicability of the COSO Framework to smaller entities. This publication can be ordered from the www.cpa2biz.com or through any of the sponsoring organizations. [http://www.cpa2biz.com/AST/Main/CPA2BIZ_Primary/InternalControls/COSO/PRDOVR~PC-990017/PC-990017.jsp]

IT Auditor

An IT Auditor is a professional possessing the necessary knowledge and skills to understand and audit an entity's IT environment, systems, or applications, in support of a financial statement audit, internal audit, or other form of attestation engagement. The IT Auditor often has deep domain-specific knowledge or specialized skills (e.g. in use of computerized tools) that makes them particularly competent to understand the IT environment (and its associated risks) or perform IT-specific audit procedures.

Logical Access Controls

Logical access controls are policies, procedures, and automated controls that exist for the purpose of restricting access to information assets to only authorized users.

Materiality

Materiality is "the magnitude of an omission or misstatement of accounting information that, in the light of surrounding circumstances, makes it probable that the judgment of a reasonable person relying on the information would have been changed by the omission or misstatement." Materiality is influenced by the needs of financial statement users who rely on the financial statements to make judgments about the client's financial position and results of operation, and the auditor must consider audit risk and must determine a materiality level for the financial statements.

Professional Skepticism

Having a questioning mind and critically assessing audit evidence (SAS No.99).

Red Flags
Signs that a fraud has occurred, is occurring, or will occur. They are similar to fingerprints in a traditional police investigation. The term can apply to fraud risk factors.

Risk of Material Misstatement (RMM)
The risk of material misstatement is defined as the risk that an account balance, class of transactions or disclosures, and relevant assertions are materially misstated. Misstatements can result from errors or fraud.

The RMM consists of two components:

- **Inherent Risk** is the susceptibility that a relevant assertion could be misstated assuming that there are no other related controls. The auditor should consider the risk of misstatement individually as well as in aggregate with other misstatements, assuming there are no related controls.
- **Control Risk** is the risk that a material misstatement will not be detected or prevented by the entity's internal control on a timely basis. The auditor must consider the risk of misstatement individually and in aggregate with other misstatements.

Using the audit risk model to illustrate this concept: Inherent Risk x Control Risk = RMM

Auditors describe RMM as the combined assessment of inherent risk and control risk. However, auditors may make a separate assessment of inherent risk and control risk.

Risk-Based Approach (RBA)
The methodology which provides assurance that significant risks associated with audit objectives have been identified, and that audit procedures address them to adequately gain assurance about the objectives of the audit, and the mitigation of those risks or nature of residual risk that exists.

SME
A subject-matter expert. One who has the knowledge, skills, and abilities to professionally address issues related to the topic.

STUDY QUESTIONS & CASE:

2.1 According to fraud principles and SAS No. 99 (AU316), there are three conditions that are generally present when a fraud occurs. Which of the following is one of them?
   (A) Auditors have a lack of professional skepticism
   (B) CEO has a "Wheeler-dealer" approach to business
   (C) Employee has an incentive or pressure
   (D) The assets are susceptible to fraud

Key: C
Section Name: Dimension 2.1.3, Fraud Triangle
Bloom's Taxonomy category: Knowledge
Reference: AU316.07; "Principles of Fraud Examination", 2nd Ed., Joseph T. Wells, Ch. 1, pp. 13–14.

Solution:
Stem: The three general conditions make up what is known as the fraud triangle (Cressey's triangle). They are: incentive or pressure, opportunity, and rationalization. Thus the correct response is C, incentive or pressure.
Option A: Professional skepticism is an attitude of the auditors that should be maintained throughout audits, according to SAS No. 99 (AU316), but is not a component of the fraud triangle.
Option B: CEO's who commit financial statement fraud often have a "wheeler-dealer" attitude. Employees who commit fraud usually do not. Wheeler-dealer attitude is not a component of the fraud triangle.
Option D: Assets susceptible to fraud are more likely to be stolen. But that fact does not relate well to financial statement fraud. And if the person is in a key position of trust, even assets not normally susceptible to fraud can be stolen. Susceptibility of assets to fraud is not a component of the fraud triangle.

2.2 "Delaying expenses" is a fraud scheme where there is a failure to accrue or record transactions for goods or services at period end. In which of the following categories of the fraud tree would this scheme be classified?
   (A) Fraudulent Statement
   (B) Asset Misappropriation
   (C) Corruption
   (D) Kickback

Key: A
Section Name: Dimension 2.1.2, Fraud Tree
Bloom's Taxonomy category: Comprehension
Reference: AU316.06; "The Guide to Investigating Business Fraud", AICPA/Ernst & Young, Ch. 3, pp. 37–38.

Solution:
Stem: Delaying expenses would cause the financial statements to be falsified and misstated. Therefore, the correct answer is A.
Option B: Asset misappropriation is the theft of the entity's assets by employees, not a scheme directly affecting the financial statements or financial reporting.

Option C: Corruption is a scheme whereby someone on the inside is working with someone on the outside to defraud the entity of its assets. It is not a scheme directly affecting the financial statements or financial reporting.
Option D: Kickback is a sub-scheme in the corruption category. It is not a scheme directly affecting the financial statements or financial reporting.

2.3 In developing an anti-fraud program, the board of directors and/or executive management should consider the role and responsibilities of internal and external audit functions. Suppose they are determining the best anti-fraud program element related to potential corruption schemes. Which of the following is the **BEST** scenario for these two functions; i.e., has the greatest potential benefit regarding corruption frauds?

(A) Ask external audit to include steps in the audit plan to detect corruption schemes
(B) Rely on the external audit to detect corruption schemes
(C) Ask internal audit to include steps in future audit plans to detect corruption schemes
(D) Ask internal audit to examine and evaluate effectiveness of internal controls

Key: D
Section Name: Dimension 2.1.2, Fraud Tree
Bloom's Taxonomy category: Application, Evaluation
Reference: "The Guide to Investigating Business Fraud", AICPA/Ernst & Young, Ch. 6, p. 117.

Solution:
Stem: Corruption would not become part of the external audit unless it reached a material level of risk, which generally does not happen. Anti-fraud programs should focus on both prevention and detection. Thus the **BEST** answer is for internal audit to examine and evaluate its internal control structure to ensure adequacy and effectiveness of internal controls to both prevent and detect fraud in a timely manner, regardless of materiality. Therefore, the correct answer is D.
Option A: Entities cannot ask external auditors to include steps in audit plans.
Option B: Financial audits are designed to detect material misstatements. A corruption scheme would only be discovered by a financial audit if it were material, or if the auditors discovered immaterial evidence during audit procedures. Even then, this approach ignores the prevention aspect of anti-fraud programs.
Option C: Asking internal audit to include audits for corruption schemes would not be constrained by materiality, but it would focus on detection and basically ignore fraud prevention.

2.4 During the risk assessment phase and audit planning meeting, the audit team concludes that a risk of material misstatement exists regarding the revenue account. Suppose you are a CITP on the audit team. Which of the following is the **BEST** recommendation to detect evidence of this type of fraud?

(A) Use vertical, horizontal and ratio analyses targeting the revenue account as part of the analytical procedures
(B) Change the nature, extent and/or timing of tests of controls to test controls used in recording revenues made by keypunch personnel
(C) Interview the IT personnel to determine how the revenue application processes entries and what controls it has
(D) Data mine journal entries made to the account, focusing on those at year end, made on weekends, and large amounts

Key: D
Section Name: Dimension 2.2.5.2, Obtain Information; 2.2.5.5, Respond to Assessed Fraud Risks
Bloom's Taxonomy category: Analysis, Synthesis
Reference: "Principles of Fraud Examination", 2nd Ed., Joseph T. Wells, Ch. 12, pp. 325, 327, 328, 331–332; AU316.31–34.

Solution:
Stem: If a revenue recognition fraud scheme is being perpetrated, it is most likely executive management who is responsible. If management is perpetrating this scheme, it would be through falsifying transactions, documents, or journal entries. Analytical procedures might detect a difference but only if the scheme falsified revenue without also adjusting other relevant accounts (e.g., COGS). Tests of controls would address the controls more than detect fraudulent revenues. Interviewing the IT personnel could also assist in understanding systems, automated processes, and automated controls, but not necessarily revenue fraud detection. However, revenue is often falsified by management through fraudulent journal entries. Those entries could be ones made on weekends (for secrecy), in large round amounts, or near year end (when the "target" revenue is more easily determined). Therefore, the correct answer is D.
Option A: Analytical procedures might detect a difference but only if the scheme falsified revenue without also adjusting other relevant accounts (e.g., COGS). Journal entries data mining is more likely to detect revenue fraud.
Option B: Tests of controls would address the controls more than detect fraudulent revenues.
Option C: Interviewing the IT personnel could also assist in understanding systems, automated processes, and automated controls, but not necessarily revenue fraud detection.

CASE:

As a part of the audit brainstorming, in fulfillment of the SAS No. 99 (AU316.14–18) requirements, the audit team determines that the risk of fraudulent disbursements is high, and could lead to a material misstatement in the disbursement class of transactions. Materiality was determined to be $5M for the balance sheet, and tolerable misstatement is $3M. During the substantive procedures, the IT auditor pulled all of the checks written, and checked the vendors against the data set containing all of the authorized vendors. Three checks were discovered to be written to an unauthorized vendor; that is, all three were written to the same unauthorized vendor. The amounts were all $100,000 and were documented as services delivered. The checks appear to have been approved by the accounts payable manager.

2.5 Which of the following is the **BEST** response to this situation?

(A) Report findings to the level of management responsible for disbursement transactions
(B) Report findings to senior management above the accounts payable manager
(C) Report findings to senior management above the accounts payable manager and the audit committee
(D) There is no obligation in SAS No. 99 for the auditors to report an inconsequential matter regarding fraud to anyone associated with the auditee nor any outside party

Key: B
Section Name: Dimension 2.2.5.7, Communicate (fraud evidence)
Bloom's Taxonomy category: Application, Analysis, Synthesis, Evaluation
Reference: "Principles of Fraud Examination", 2nd Ed., Joseph T. Wells, Ch. 12, pp. 329–330; AU316.79–82.

Solution:

Stem: SAS No. 99 (AU316.79–80) states that the auditor should report even inconsequential defalcations to the appropriate level of management. Because there is some concern the accounts payable manager is involved, and because the accounts payable manager is generally not considered senior management, the communication should be made to senior management above the A/P manager. Reporting to the audit committee is required if senior management or fraudulent financial statements is involved, but in the case above it is an asset misappropriation. Therefore, the correct answer is B.

Option A: The level of management responsible for disbursement transactions would be the A/P manager. However, that position is not generally considered senior management (which is what SAS No. 99 requires) and there is some suspicion the A/P manager is involved.

Option C: SAS No. 99 (AU316.79) requires the auditor to report to the audit committee if senior management is involved or if the fraud causes the financials to be deliberately misstated.

Option D: There is an obligation to report even inconsequential matters related to fraud evidence (AU316.79).

INTERNAL CONTROLS & INFORMATION TECHNOLOGY GENERAL CONTROLS ("ITGC")

Dimension 3

The concepts of internal control are critical to providing reasonable assurance regarding the reliability of financial reporting and the preparation of financial statements for external purposes and users of those reports, as well as business processes, IT operations, and financial reporting for internal purposes for those in business and industry. IT general controls have objectives that relate to the overall management of the IT function of the business enterprise. The level of effectiveness of ITGC affects the degree of IT-related risk the entity has, which could adversely affect its business operations and/or financial reporting, and directly impact the reliability of application controls. The concepts of information security are beneficial to an effective system of internal controls, including identifying, designing, implementing, and monitoring systems and processes used to enable the security of information and data.

LEARNING OBJECTIVES

1. To understand the internal controls frameworks and how to integrate them with financial reporting
2. To understand management considerations of internal controls
3. To understand issues in preparing an IT audit plan associated with internal controls
4. To understand the five basic areas of ITGC and how to assess the effectiveness of those controls: the control environment, change management, logical and physical access security, backup and recovery, and service providers
5. To understand how to assess the effectiveness of applicable controls related to information security: policies and procedures, hardware and physical controls, software and process controls, authorization and authentication, and encryption

3.0 – INTRODUCTION

Internal control usually plays a central role in almost all IT audits and reviews, whether it is in the context of a financial audit, other attest engagement, internal IT audit, management IT review, or a fraud audit. Thus a thorough understanding of internal control is a key element in the toolbox of a CITP. Over the last few years, ITGC has also become a focal point; in particular for auditing, regarding financial audits of issuers due to the Public Company Accounting Oversight Board (PCAOB) guidelines and standards, and even financial audits of non-issuers. Those CITPs in business and industry (B&I) need to fully understand the role of ITGC in reducing IT-related risks in financial reporting and business operations in general.

The CITP needs to be able to understand the specific body of internal controls in an entity, identify "key" controls, evaluate those controls, identify control deficiencies, and gather evidence about the operational effectiveness of controls. In particular, the CITP needs to know how to create or evaluate effective automated controls or identify relevant automated controls (especially in public accounting), know when they should be tested, and know how to test them for effectiveness.

This dimension of the CITP will provide an in-depth review of internal controls as they relate to professional standards, regulatory requirements, sound IT audit practices, and the role and responsibilities of the CITP related to them, whether in public accounting or B&I.

Generally speaking, controls are addressed in two broad categories: application controls and IT general controls (ITGC). Application controls are those embedded in software applications. ITGC are controls associated with all aspects of the IT environment; that is, where the controls are created, implemented, managed, and changed at all levels of the organization. The effectiveness of application controls is directly dependent on the sufficiency and effectiveness of ITGCs.

3.1 – INTERNAL CONTROLS

An appropriate understanding and application of internal controls involves an ability to gain an adequate understanding of a particular body of internal controls using some effectual framework. These frameworks are useful in evaluating the management of the internal control environment and developing an appropriate IT audit plan or IT review plan.

3.1.1 –Understanding of Internal Controls

In order to gain an appropriate understanding of internal controls, it is important to understand controls basics. Those basics include definitions, various types of controls (especially automated controls), the control development life cycle, implications of standards on controls, and frameworks available to develop, manage, and/or evaluate controls.

3.1.1.1 – Definitions

Part of understanding internal controls is to choose a definition. There are the definitions used in B&I, those used in public accounting, and those used in technical literature.

3.1.1.1.1 – General Definition

Because of the prevalence of the Committee of Sponsoring Organizations (COSO) definition, and the application of that definition for CITPs (i.e. both public accounting and B&I), that definition is the one used herein:

A process effected by an entity's board of directors, management, and other personnel, designed to provide reasonable assurance regarding the achievement of objectives in:

> *(a) the effectiveness and efficiency of operations,*
> *(b) the reliability of financial reporting, and*
> *(c) the compliance with applicable laws and regulations.*[1]

This process includes developing policies and procedures (P&P) designed to safeguard assets, ensure accuracy of data, ensure reliability of information, promote efficiencies in operations, promote effectiveness of accounting data and financial reporting, and measure compliance of the entity with these P&P.

3.1.1.1.2 – Technical Literature

While the technical literature for financial audit does not contemplate expressing an opinion on controls for private companies, there is a requirement for auditors when they detect control deficiencies. There is technical literature that does require expressing an opinion of controls for public companies (issuers).

The technical literature on control definitions evolved in response to the Sarbanes-Oxley Act of 2002 (SOX). Section 404 of SOX requires management of issuers to evaluate the entity's system of internal controls, and for the auditor to opine on that evaluation. In response to that, the PCAOB and the AICPA converged on definitions about control deficiencies.

That is, the technical literature focuses not on controls per se, but rather on control deficiencies of "key" controls. Control evaluation is not described as dichotomous (either "good" or "bad") but as types of deficiency. CITPs must be familiar with these terms, definitions, and the application thereof. Because of the convergence of technical standards, there is a common set of definitions for three types of control deficiency.

- **Control Deficiency (CD)**: The design or operation of the control does not allow management or employees, in the normal course of performing their assigned functions, to prevent, or detect and correct misstatements in a timely basis.
- **Material Weakness (MW)**: A material weakness is a deficiency, or combination of deficiencies, in internal control, such that there is a reasonable possibility that a material misstatement of the entity's financial statements will not be prevented, or detected and corrected in a timely basis.

---

[1] Per COSO. See www.coso.org or "Internal Control Over Financial Reporting – Guidance for Smaller Public Companies", Volume I, COSO, 2006.

- **Significant Deficiency (SD)**: A significant deficiency is a deficiency, or a combination of deficiencies, in internal control that is less severe than a material weakness, yet important enough to merit attention by those charged with governance.

These definitions are included in SAS No. 115, "Communicating Internal Controls Related Matters Identified in an Audit". The severity of such deficiency is further defined as a combination of magnitude (of misstatement caused by the CD) and probability (that such control will actually fail). There is also a list of MW indicators, and a list of CDs that would at least be SDs.

The PCAOB has identical definitions and information in AS5, "An Audit of Internal Control Over Financial Reporting that is Integrated with an Audit of Financial Statements."[2] Obviously, CITPs in B&I, where the entity is an issuer, will be concerned with the issues related to these terms. Because of the prevalence of this definition, all CITPs need to know and understand them.

3.1.1.1.3 – General Axioms about Controls

There are certain axioms about controls for which the CITP should have an understanding. These affect the management of controls for B&I, and affect the auditing of controls for public accounting. Six of the key axioms are:

(1) ***Controls are the responsibility of management.*** This affects CITPs in B&I in particular. That CITP is likely to be involved in internal controls, or at least should be considered an expert in internal controls, especially as they relate to IT-related controls, and application controls.

(2) ***Controls can only provide reasonable assurance***. There is no perfect system of internal controls. There are a number of reasons why controls may be missing yet acceptable. For instance, the benefits of implementing any internal control should outweigh its costs, but if not, then management may select not to implement that control. Some controls will be missing, but the exposure may be low in magnitude or probability or both. Obviously, there are also cases where controls are deficient or missing and need to be mitigated.

(3) ***There is always the possibility of error, even in automated controls.*** Just because an appropriately designed control has been implemented and is operating does not absolutely guarantee the elimination of error. This fact is particularly true of manual controls, ones requiring human intervention. Even automated controls can be affected by IT-related processes or human mistakes (e.g., coding) that could lead to an error.

(4) ***There is always the possibility of circumvention of controls***. For instance, two or more people in collusion could deliberately, and probably fraudulently, circumvent certain types of controls. Even a single person may be in a position to know enough to circumvent a control, especially a manual control.

(5) ***There is always the possibility of management override of controls***. Management at any level can generally override controls under its purview, scope of management. The higher up in management a manger resides, the greater the scope of the potential override. At the

[2] See Section 2.F for definitions of control deficiencies. AS5 also includes identical lists of SDs and MWs, and the same severity formula as SAS No. 115.

C-level, it is almost absolute override over ALL controls. All CITPs should keep this fact in mind.

(6) ***The control environment changes over time.*** The environment from within which the control operates changes over time, and sooner or later, one or more change will result in a decrease in operating effectiveness, or will even lead to a control becoming unnecessary. Thus controls need to be monitored to determine when changes in the controls are necessary.

(7) ***It is possible that downstream manual controls mitigate IT risk.*** Sometimes management will deploy strictly manual controls downstream from an accounting process to compensate for lack of segregation of duties (SoD) or other control weakness. Just because the downstream control is manual does not mean it is not effective. Therefore, care should be taken to develop or evaluate the body of controls and not exclude manual controls just because the weakness is an IT risk.

3.1.1.2 – Types of Controls

Controls have different tendencies based on the type of control it is. Generally, controls are of two types plus a blended type:

- Manual (human intervention)
- Automated (e.g., application control)
- Hybrid (partly manual, partly automated – referred to herein as "IT-dependent")

3.1.1.2.1 – Manual Controls

Manual controls are those that rely totally on human intervention in order to function. Because it depends on people, the tendency of manual controls is subject to atrophy. That is, the longer a manual control functions, the more likely slackness will be introduced into a full due diligence of performing that control. It is also subject to human frailties such as emotions, physical problems (e.g., lack of sleep, tired), psychological issues, political issues, and other human elements that could cause improper execution of a manual control.

Thus, generally speaking, a manual control is not as reliable as the same control activity that is automated (e.g., manually verifying credit limits vs. the application control mentioned below).

3.1.1.2.2 – Automated Controls

An automated control is a control that occurs automatically, usually through computer systems, based on predefined criteria, circumstances, times, dates, or events. Automated controls are designed to work within IT or applications and function automatically as the related business process or operational process occurs. For example, if management's policy of selling to qualified customers includes setting a credit limit for each customer, an automated control is likely to be employed. Specifically, the sales entry program application will automatically pull the customer's current balance, add the amount of a sale being processed, and see if the total is less than or equal to the credit limit. If so, the sale would be processed; if not, some kind of warning would be given to the person entering the data to alert the status of the customer's balance and credit limit, and prohibit processing the sale in accordance with management policy. Automated controls may also be tied to technologies, such as transferring data from one system to another (where some kind of automatic reconciliation may occur).

Automated controls tend to be more reliable that manual controls. Put another way, automated controls, once implemented, tend to operate in the same manner repeatedly (for the identical set of circumstances), for virtually an infinite number of occurrences. It is for this reason that AS5 and SAS No. 109 both say that it is possible, under the right set of circumstances, that a test of control *could* be a single instance.

3.1.1.2.3 – Hybrid Controls
Some controls are partly manual and partly automated. For example, some legacy systems, notably payroll, set automated flags in a series of programs that run to ensure the proper sequence of programs for that business process. At the end of each run, that program prints some kind of interim report, which is reconciled or reviewed offline by an employee. Once the reconciliation or review is completed, the next program in the series is initiated. If the automated flag from the previous program is set "on" (did run), that program will execute, usually leading to yet another printout and review. The final application will print some final report (e.g., payroll checks), and reset all of the automated "flags" to "off". Usually, there is a checklist to accompany the process to document each reconciliation/review and the series of process in general.

<u>3.1.1.3 – Control Development Life Cycle</u>
Understanding the control development life cycle (CDLC) is beneficial in understanding, evaluating, and managing controls. The cyclical phases are: design, implementation, operational effectiveness, and monitoring.

3.1.1.3.1 – Design
The design of controls begins with the presence of a formal, structured approach to control development by management. That is, how does management ensure that expert input and feedback is being consistently applied to the development of applications, systems, and technologies for automated controls, and the internal control system as a whole (manual and hybrid controls in particular)? That includes changes to any business process and controls necessary for their effective operation. How does the entity provide assurance that controls are being developed as needed, and designed effectively? Based on the identification of key business processes associated with material items related to financial reporting, or critical business processes, what controls <u>should</u> be in place to prevent or detect and correct material misstatements? What controls should be in place for the relevant assertions of material accounts? What controls should be in place to mitigate the higher risks identified in the risk assessment process (assuming one was performed)?

Once some expertise has been employed in a formal process to identify controls needed, the design of those controls should be subject to assessment of their design effectiveness (i.e. the control's ability to mitigate risk and/or prevent, detect, or correct material misstatements, errors, or failures related to P&P). Then management should document those controls, including the control objectives, how the control operates, and where in the entity's systems and business processes it is located.

The CITP will want to make sure whatever process is being used to identify and design controls is a formal and structured process rather than no process or even an ad hoc one. Having the business managers who request changes to IT also be responsible for requesting controls is a weak form of control design, and probably not very effective. It is also not a good example of a formal process. If, however, management involves a cross-functional team who reviews business cases for new applications, systems, and technologies, and a member of that team is an expert in controls (e.g., CITP) who provides input into controls needed and their design, then that process would be formal, structured, and suitable because of the expertise involved.

3.1.1.3.2 – Implementation

Once controls have been properly identified, and effectively designed, they *must* be implemented. In fact, SAS No. 109 asks auditors to examine controls to make sure they have been properly designed AND implemented. Clearly a control does no good unless it is put into operation. CITPs functioning as IT auditors in a financial audit need to use activities such as observation, inspection, and walkthroughs to make the determination as required by SAS No. 109. Management, and CITPs in B&I, needs some formal manner of making this determination as well.

3.1.1.3.3 – Effectiveness

It is not enough assurance for a control to be properly designed and implemented; it must also be operating effectively day after day (consistently) as it was designed to operate. Effectiveness is related to the control objective, which will likely be the mitigation of a business risk or financial reporting risk (i.e. risk of material misstatement). Effectiveness is also associated with consistent application of the control.

The ultimate assurance is a test of control (ToC). For external audit CITPs, however, ToCs should only be performed if the audit team plans to rely on the control. It cannot be relied upon if the ITGCs have a SD or MW. That is, the ITGCs need to be reliable as a whole before the external CITP can rely upon an automated control.

PCAOB standards and some IT attest engagements (e.g., SSAE No. 16, type II) require the assessment of controls to provide assurance that controls were operating effectively throughout the testing period. To accomplish this requirement, CITPs will probably be asked to test controls to be relied upon in such a way as to gain assurance to that end; that they were operating effectively across the testing period.

One way to gather evidence and gain assurance is to examine whether a key control was changed during the year. If not, often the IT auditor would likely test the control twice a year (e.g., 2nd quarter and end of 3rd quarter), possibly three times, the latter during the further audit procedures. The assumption is if the control did not change and operated effectively across 2–3 ToCs during the year, that control was most likely operating effectively the remainder of the year as well. If the control did change, the CITP would want to test the control before the change, close to the time of implementation of the change, and depending on the time of year implemented, maybe one additional time. In the end, the CITP will need to use professional judgment to determine the best way to gain assurance about the operating effectiveness of controls across the testing period, where applicable.

3.1.1.3.4 – Monitoring
Change is inevitable. And changes in the business environment will eventually affect the controls in the control environment. The question is whether management has a formal, structured process to know when one or more controls need to be added, deleted, changed, or replaced. What formal system does management use to perform this monitoring function?

An example might be the cross-functional team mentioned earlier, if it is charged with this responsibility, and if members do their due diligence. Another example is section 404 of SOX; management of issuers is basically forced to evaluate controls every year and thus is monitoring them (with some exceptions, public companies must evaluate controls each fiscal year).

The CITP auditor would need to determine if such a formal structured process is in place. This assurance should be attainable via inquiry of key managers, key employees, review of P&P or management/Board meeting minutes (where applicable), observation of the process, or other relevant procedures. The CITP auditor would want to ensure the process is formal and structured, and not informal or ad hoc.

3.1.1.4 – Understanding of Frameworks
The use of frameworks in understanding, managing, and evaluating controls is generally seen as beneficial. One of the benefits is the need to standardize an approach to controls across time, business units, or clients. Using the same framework helps to provide a consistency. Several frameworks are presented to provide a tool for the CITP and to illustrate some of the IT-related concerns, potentially beneficial activities, and effective evaluation methods. Each one takes a slightly different perspective of controls.

The COSO framework is a management perspective of controls, and more or less, a comprehensive view. The COBIT framework is IT process focused, and is known for its practical application in performing evaluation of internal controls. The systems model looks at controls from a data processing, or information systems, view. The P-D-C framework, more or less, looks at controls from the perspective of an undesirable event, in a chronological order.

Each framework makes its own contribution to the evaluation and proper operations of internal controls, and can work jointly with one or more of the others. In fact, it is fairly common to see COBIT used to evaluate controls (i.e., used to design and perform the IT audit procedures), and then the results mapped to COSO (e.g., for reporting purposes) – this joint use appears to be somewhat common for public companies and SOX section 404 compliance. The same kind of joint use and mapping could be done with the other frameworks as well.

3.1.1.4.1 – COSO
The Committee of Sponsoring Organizations (COSO) developed an integrated framework of internal controls between about 1985 and 1992. This model provides a way to view controls, specifically a management view of controls. COSO provides the following definition of internal control:

Internal control is broadly defined as a process*, effected by an entity's board of directors, management, and other personnel, designed to provide reasonable assurance regarding the achievement of objectives in the following categories:*

1. *Effectiveness and efficiency of operations*
2. *Reliability of financial reporting*
3. *Compliance with applicable laws and regulations*[3]

Internal control is divided into five elements, across the three-way definition above, and across the business units or activities of the entity (see Exhibit 3.1).

The ***Control Environment*** element is the set of control activities, policies, and procedures that sets the tone of the organization and provides the foundation for the other components. Control Environment includes factors such as communication, enforcement of integrity and ethical values (e.g., ethics and/or fraud policy), competency of employees, management philosophy and style, assigning authority and responsibility, organizational structure, professional development of employees, and the board of directors (BoD) involvement.

The control environment is associated with the element of ITGC by the same name. Thus the COSO details of this element potentially can be used to develop audit procedures or benchmarks for the CITP in evaluating controls at the entity level.

EXHIBIT 3.1 – COSO Model of Internal Controls

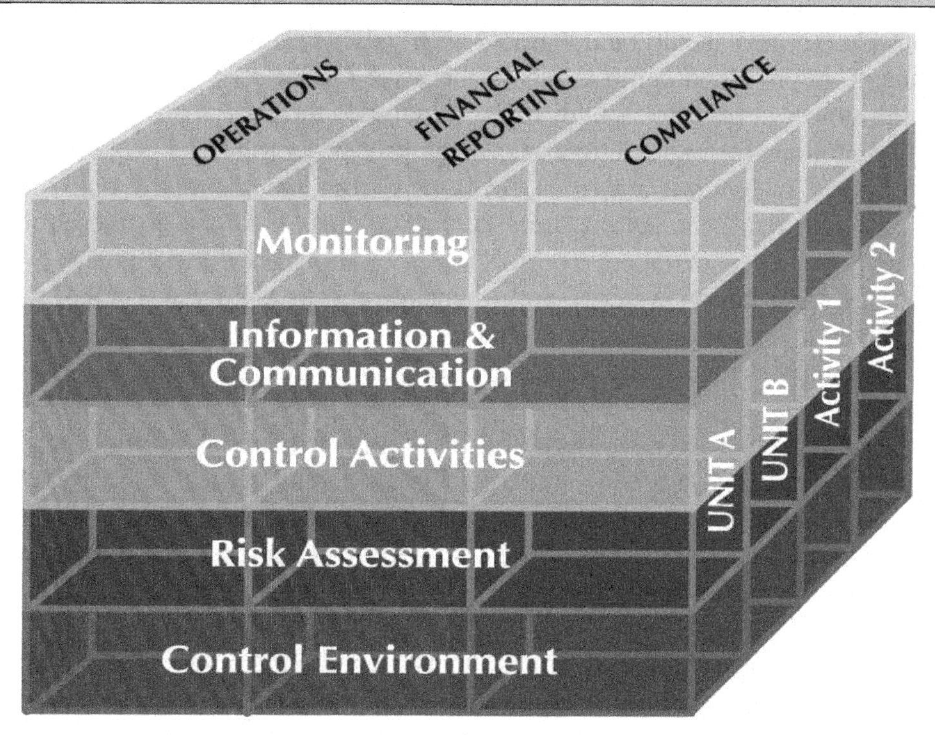

3 Reference: http://www.coso.org/IC-IntegratedFramework-summary.htm

The ***Risk Assessment*** element is the set of activities, policies, and procedures used to identify and assess the composite risks, both general business and accounting processes, that are significant enough to impair the entity's ability to achieve its business goals or control objectives. Every entity has its own external and internal risks that need to be identified, assessed, and managed (mitigated). Management's risk assessment activities should naturally lead to some kind of risk assessment document that the CITP would want to review in the context of an audit (public accounting), or in most risk-related reviews/audits (B&I). Because the internal and external environments are constantly changing, and thus risks are constantly changing, this document is dynamic (a living document) rather than static. Thus management would want to make regular updates to the entity's risk assessment document.

Two key roles of risk assessment are financial reporting risks and IT risks. If management has done this activity effectively, financial reporting risks will have been identified, as well as the IT risks. This information could be beneficial to the CITP in procedures, audits, and activities related to evaluating financial reporting, controls, and various types of IT reviews.

Risk Assessment is fundamental to effective control activities, monitoring elements, and the successful mitigation of risks, including IT-related risks. Thus it is a critical element of the system of internal controls.

The ***Control Activities*** element involves the internal controls operating on a day to day basis. A control is a task or action that has the intent to mitigate a particular risk for the respective control objective. Control activities should be integrated with risk assessment; that is, the risks identified in risk assessment are assigned controls where the level of control is linked to the level of the risk (e.g., a high-power control for a high risk). It includes the P&P that are designed to ensure management's guidelines for internal controls. If the process is followed properly (effective risk assessment, followed by control activities developed from the identified risks, with controls linked to the assessed risk), the actions necessary to address the risks to the entity's business model, goals, and objectives are taken. Control Activities should permeate the entity at *all* levels, business processes, information systems, and financial reporting processes. They would include important accounting activities such as authorizations, verifications, reconciliations, reviews, access rights, protection of assets, and segregation of duties.

Control activities are chosen and developed considering their potential ability to mitigate risks to achieving financial reporting objectives and key IT goals and strategies. In order to be deployed, controls are also subject to a cost-benefit analysis. That is, controls that cost more than the quantifiable amount of potential loss are simply not deployed, and an exposure exists, which will probably need to be covered by insurance or some other alternative means.

Control activities are generally seen to fall into two broad categories: physical and computer. Physical controls include controls whose objective addresses independent verification, transaction authorization, segregation of duties, supervision, accounting records and audit trail, and physical access controls. Computer controls are subdivided into general controls (see section 3.2 – IT General Controls for details) and application controls (see section 3.3 – Application Controls).

The ***Information and Communication*** element involves the timely identifying, recording, and communicating of relevant information necessary for employees and stakeholders to carry out their responsibilities. This element would include the financial reporting systems and their ability to properly capture data, report information, and assist management in decision making and managing the business. While this element obviously includes internal reporting, it also includes external reporting to the appropriate external parties (e.g., customers, vendors, regulators, banks, and shareholders). Information and Communication also includes information about internal controls as well as accounting and/or financial reporting information.

The ***Monitoring*** element involves control activities about controls themselves. Specifically monitoring involves regular reviews of controls to assess the ongoing quality of the control over time. This element would include some kind of formal, structured process of ongoing monitoring such as regular management review, supervisory activities, technology designed to monitor controls in an ongoing fashion, and other manual activities. The ongoing aspect could be literally 24/7, or it could be activities taken offline but done at regular intervals. The primary goal is to identify changes in the internal control system; that is, when a control needs to be changed or deleted, or when a new control is needed.[4]

Monitoring would identify internal control deficiencies and communicate them timely to the appropriate party. An example would be SOX section 404 compliance where key controls are evaluated every year for most public companies.

3.1.1.4.2 – ISACA Frameworks: COBIT & ITAF

Control Objectives for Information and related Technology (COBIT) is a framework provided by the IT Governance Institute (ITGI) of the Information Systems Audit and Control Association (ISACA), and is based on decades of its publications under similar names that documented best practices in IT audit. The current framework is provided in formats for management and auditors.

COBIT is from the IT process perspective, which includes four primary processes (called "domains") that are basically sequentially and circular: Planning and Organizing (PO), Acquire and Implement (AI), Deliver and Support (DS), and Monitor and Evaluate (M). Each primary process (domain) is broken down further into sub-processes, 34 in total (see Exhibit 3.2 for a summary of these two levels of COBIT). Each sub-process is then broken down into over 300 activities (life cycle) or tasks (discrete), which are essentially control objectives for that sub-process. The activities (life cycle) or tasks (discrete) can be used for designing audit procedures, evaluating IT controls, and even assessing IT risks.

COBIT has other beneficial aspects to it such as information criteria; the fact it includes business requirements, IT resources and IT processes; and questions for domains, processes, and activities/tasks. Exhibit 3.2 shows the main aspects of the framework.

---

[4] See the 4th phase of CDLC, monitoring, which is essentially the same thing as COSO's monitoring element – Section 3.1.1.3.4.

EXHIBIT 3.2 – COBIT FRAMEWORK	
Plan & Organize	***Deliver & Support***
PO1 – Define a strategic IT plan PO2 – Define the infrastructure architecture PO3 – Determine the technological direction PO4 – Define the IT organization and relationships PO5 – Manage the IT investment PO6 – Communicate management aims & directions PO7 – Manage human resources PO8 – Ensure compliance with external requirements PO9 – Assess risks PO10 – Manage projects PO11 – Manage quality	DS1 – Define service levels DS2 – Manage third-party services DS3 – Manage performance and capacity DS4 – Ensure continuous service DS5 – Ensure systems security DS6 – Identify and attribute costs DS7 – Educate and train users DS8 – Assist and advise IT customers DS9 – Manage the configuration DS10 – Manage problems and incidents DS11 – Manage data DS12 – Manage facilities DS13 – Manage operations
Acquire & Implement	***Monitor & Evaluate***
AI1 – Identify automated solutions AI2 – Acquire and maintain application software AI3 – Acquire and maintain technology infrastructure AI4 – Develop and maintain IT procedures AI5 – Install and accredit systems AI6 – Manage changes	M1 – Monitor the process M2 – Assess internal control adequacy M3 – Obtain independent assurance M4 – Provide for independent audit

COBIT is sometimes mapped to COSO or other frameworks for reporting results or summarizing evidence.

In addition to COBIT, ISACA also has the IT Assurance Framework (ITAF). This framework focuses on the design, conduct, and reporting of IT audit and assurance assignments rather than the IT processes of COBIT. Its stated purpose is to provide good practice-setting guidelines and procedures for formal IT audits and assessments of IT controls. Whereas COBIT is organized around a life cycle view of IT processes, ITAF is organized around the assurance or assessment activity, and focuses on internal controls (see table of contents summarized in Exhibit 3.3).

EXHIBIT 3.3: ITAF – Table of Contents

Section 1000 – Introducing the IT Assurance Framework
Section 2000 – IT Assurance Standards: Defining a Common Reference Point
Section 3000 – IT Assurance Guidelines: Putting the Standards Into Practice
Section 4000 – IT Assurance Tools and Techniques

3.1.1.4.3 – Systems Model

The systems model is a general model for any kind of system. All systems basically operate on the minimum of three processes: input, process, and output. For instance, the respiratory system of the human body takes in oxygen (input), exchanges it in the lungs with carbon dioxide (process), and exhales the CO_2 (output). A computerized system would add data storage to process as an interactive fourth element (data is processed, stored, retrieved, printed, etc.).

Input controls include those controls that are employed at the data entry stage and are used to filter bad data or missing data. That is, the controls are used to validate and verify data, as much as possible, as it is "input" into the system.

Process controls include those controls that are employed during the application processing of data to filter anomalies. These controls are used to ensure the validity and reliability of data being processed and stored. For example, when sales entries are made, and eventually the system posts the debits and credits to the general ledger, process controls make sure the data posted in the GL is the same data that was entered.

Output controls include those controls that are employed to safeguard information, especially printed objects, at the output stage of the business process. For instance, when payroll checks are printed, output controls would ensure that the figures on the checks are accurate. The same thing would be true for customer invoices, statements, and financial reports.

Often segregation of duties (SoD) is used to employ a person not associated with inputting or processing of data to take custody of printed materials and distribute them properly.

As can be surmised, application controls may be involved in all three phases of this model. There could be application controls used to validate certain data, process controls to maintain data integrity, and output controls to safeguard sensitive data (screen prints) or documents. For instance, the application could forward printouts to a certain individual for distribution, using appropriate logical SoD.

3.1.1.4.4 – P-D-C

The P-D-C model frames controls as preventive, detective, and corrective controls. The CITP in B&I will find this model helpful in developing a strong body of controls around risky events or transactions, and thus mitigating identified risks of operations and/or financial reporting. The external CITP auditor will find this model useful in evaluating controls in attest and audit engagements.

Preventive controls are those designed to prevent the risky event from occurring in the first place. Realistically, it is about mitigating the risk of some adverse event at the point it could occur. Controls can be designed to screen out aberrant events or transactions based on known aberrations and their characteristics.

Obviously, it is cost-effective to prevent an undesirable event from occurring rather than detecting and correcting it after it occurs and has created problems. For example, what control is in place to *prevent* a vendor's invoice from being paid twice?

One key way to prevent errors and anomalies from occurring is to have strong data entry controls on input screens. For instance, using lookup functions to find authorized customers or vendors, using a range control in the application to make sure the data is a reasonable entry, and forcing data entry clerks to enter something in data fields that should not be blank.

Detective controls are those designed to detect an undesirable event once it occurs, and do so early rather than later. Often these controls are based on comparing actual occurrences with pre-established standards of what those occurrences should be. When a departure from the standard is recognized, the transaction or event is "tagged" in some manner, and often an "alert" is sent to an appropriate party. For instance, transactions with missing data are flagged as incomplete, stored in a suspense file, not processed, and a report is either manually or automatically printed for the person responsible for correcting this type of error. If the violation is serious (e.g., fraud is recognized), the alert may be an email or similar response to a senior manager or internal audit manager (e.g., chief audit executive). The type of alert notification and timeliness of the alert are dependent on the level of risk associated with the anomaly.

To carry forward the example above, what control is in place to *detect* a double payment of a vendor's bill? If such a control exists, and if it detects a double payment, who gets notified and how?

Corrective controls are those designed to correct a deleterious event, as much as possible, once it is detected. Often these controls are a follow through for a detective control. For instance, an undesirable error is detected in a transaction, and the transaction was flagged as error and filed in a suspense file and not processed. A supervisor runs an error report at the end of each day which prints all of the transactions in the error file, along with an error code. That person then has to investigate each error, correct the data, and re-process the data. This series of steps would be a corrective control. Any control designed to reverse the adverse effects of some event or transaction would be a corrective control.

Using the example above, what control is in place to correct a double payment of a vendor's bill?

As can easily be seen, a strong set of internal controls would have some of each of these three types of controls so that all errors and anomalies can be prevented, where possible, or detected, when not prevented, and corrected properly when detected. Each of these types of controls could be automated, manual, or hybrid.

3.1.1.4.5 – Information Technology Infrastructure Library (ITIL)

The IT Infrastructure Library (ITIL) is a set of international best practices for IT generally divided into two main areas, Service Support and Service Delivery. These areas are divided into subareas known as ITIL disciplines. ITIL has been around for 20 years, and the current edition is version 3.

The objective of ITIL is to provide best practices as they relate to distributed computing for all aspects of the IT service life cycle. These holistic practices are designed to drive consistency, efficiency, and operational effectiveness for managing the IT function. ITIL is particularly useful in measuring the value IT provides to its customers. The life cycle is depicted in Exhibit 3.4.

EXHIBIT 3.4: ITIL LIFE CYCLE
SS: Service Strategy
SD: Service Design
ST: Service Transition
SO: Service Operation
CSI: Continual Service Improvement

The benefits of ITIL include: alignment with business needs, negotiated achievable service levels, predictable and consistent IT processes, efficiency in service delivery, and measurable and improvable services and processes.[5] ITIL has been mapped to COBIT, applicable International Standards Organization (ISO) standards (e.g., 27002), and many other frameworks.

3.1.2 – Management Considerations for Evaluating Internal Controls

A factor that has an important impact on any evaluation of controls is the history at that organization of any prior year reports and audits. This history speaks to two different concerns: first, the level of control deficiencies that exist and whether or not management is making improvements in controls; second, the degree of due diligence in managing the IT function. That is, does management correct CD in a reasonable time frame? If so, that fact presents evidence that management is effective in managing controls and IT risks (or vice versa).

3.1.2.1 – Management's Attention to Controls

As part of the evaluation of controls, the CITP will want to determine the level of attention management is placing on internal controls. If the pattern of management is to pay little attention to controls, have little to no formal structures for designing controls, then the control environment would likely be weak, and that would likely adversely affect control activities actually in operation.

3.1.2.2 – History & Prior Control Reports

Management may have a modicum of attention placed on controls, but fail to follow up appropriately on control deficiencies. Thus the CITP will want to evaluate how management addresses control deficiencies in the subsequent fiscal year. If, for some reason, management is consistently not addressing control deficiencies being reported, that in and of itself is a control deficiency, and a great concern to the CITP. The CITP would probably view this situation as at least a SD.

If, however, past reports or audits indicate effective design and operation of a control, and no changes have been made to the control or process in which the control resides, and ITGC is reliable, then walkthroughs to test operating effectiveness may provide sufficient evidence of operating effectiveness. The factors in determining if walkthrough evidence is satisfactory depends on the risk associated with control, the specific procedures performed as part of walkthrough, and the results of the walkthrough.[6]

3.2 – IT GENERAL CONTROLS

It is important to adequately identify and address the specific risks that IT introduces into financial reporting processes and data. Part of that risk emanates *indirectly* from IT General

[5] See "ITIL: The Basics, Compliance Process Partners, LLC, 1010 white paper. http://www.best-management-practice.com/gempdf/ITIL_The_Basics.pdf

[6] See AS5, paragraph 49.

Controls (ITGC). IT General Control is one of the two main types of IT controls (the other being application controls – see section 3.3). With regard to the role of the CITP, the purpose of ITGC is to provide assurance that the underlying automated controls and programmed accounting procedures are performing correctly and consistently throughout the period being examined (i.e. the things that *directly* impact RMM).

ITGCs are pervasive controls that operate within the IT environment. However, they generally do not directly lead to or cause the risk of material misstatements (RMM), but rather they affect some element of the financial reporting systems or process in such a way that the element affected leads to or causes the RMM. That is, there is a chain effect from ITGC to RMM.

For instance, the effectiveness of automated controls depends on the effectiveness of the ITGCs; that is, weak or unreliable ITGC necessarily implies the underlying automated controls are unreliable, which could cause or lead to the RMM.

Because there are a large number of IT general controls, an appropriate framework is useful in evaluating them. One such taxonomy is the one developed by the IT Executive Committee (ITEC) of the AICPA, and used by the AICPA's "IT Audit School". The framework consists of five basic areas: control environment, change management, logical access, backup/recovery, and 3rd party providers.

Another framework is ISACA's ITAF. As part of the ITAF mentioned above, section 3000 (*IT Assurance Guidelines*) provides guidance on enterprise topics, IT management processes, IT audit and assurance processes, and IT audit and assurance management. The IT audit and assurance processes section (3600) provides valuable information on internal controls, especially ITGC found in segment 3630 entitled "Auditing ITGCs". In that segment, there is a list of 16 ITGCs, with resources for auditors (such as mapping to COBIT) as well as guidance content (see Exhibit 3.5 for a list of topics in this segment).

3.2.1 – Control Environment

The control environment basically refers to management of the IT function. It would specifically include controls and activities at the organizational level as well as certain IT function activities. Some examples of control environment controls or activities would be: management of computer operations, IT governance, budgets (both capital and operating), managing major IT projects, employing best practices in programming (where applicable), managing IT human resources, IT strategy (especially strategic plans), IT investment, alignment of IT with the business model and entity goals and objectives, entity's IT risk assessment, and IT policies and procedures.

EXHIBIT 3.5: ITAF – 3630/IT GENERAL CONTROLS		
1. Introduction to ITGCs	2. Information Resource Planning	3. IT Service Delivery
4. Information Systems Operations	5. IT Human Resources	6. Outsourcing/3rd-Party IT
7. Information Security Mgmt	8. SDLC	9. BCP/DRP
10. Database Mgmt & Controls	11. Network Mgmt & Controls	12. Systems Software Support
13. Hardware Support	14. O/S Mgmt & Controls	15. Physical/Environment Control
16. Enterprise Portals	17. Identification & Authentication	

One of the primary goals of effective control environment is to ensure that the data processing that takes place in systems and technologies occurs in a controlled environment, supporting data integrity and security. This element of ITGC is basically equivalent to COSO's control environment and COBIT's Plan and Organize (PO) domain (see Exhibit 3.6).

3.2.1.1 – Strategic Planning

IT plays an important role achieving the business model, goals, objectives, and strategies of almost all entities. Part of controlling IT is to make sure it is not an ad hoc function, where changes are mostly by happenstance and the needs of the moment, but rather changes are planned with some due diligence of deliberation where IT is selected and managed with a strategic approach. That process would include certain management activities.

First, it should include an IT strategic plan. That plan could be a part of the entity's overall strategic plan or as a separate IT strategic plan. Either way, the objectives of such a plan is to make sure all of the IT function is aligned with the entity's strategies, goals, objectives, and leveraged to accomplish its business model. It would naturally include long-range plans and short-range plans.

Second, it should include a strategic approach to budgeting of IT. Budgeting for IT is divided into two parts: the operational budget (employees, operating expenses, etc.) and the capital budget (funding for major IT capital projects – systems, hardware, software, etc.). The latter should be an annual budget where funds are appropriated from the capital budget for IT projects to be awarded on a competitive basis, where decisions revolve around a proposal's ability to satisfy the IT strategic plan (i.e. its alignment with the entity's business model, goals, objectives, and strategies). It should also include some kind of ROI or investment analysis objective.[7]

EXHIBIT 3.6 – CONTROL ENVIRONMENT ASPECTS OF COBIT & COSO

COBIT – Plan & Organize:	**COSO – Control Environment:**
PO1 – Define IT strategic plan	Integrity & ethical values
PO2 – Define information architecture	Board of directors
PO3 – Determine technological direction	Management's philosophy & operating style
PO4 – Define IT organization/relationships	Organizational structure
PO5 – Manage IT investment	Financial reporting competencies
PO6 – Communicate management goals and direction	Authority & responsibility
PO7 – Manage human resources	Human resources (of IT function)
PO8 – Ensure compliance with external requirements	
PO9 – Assess risks	
PO10 – Manage projects	
PO11 – Manage quality	

[7] Note: It is customary for the IT infrastructure to be considered a "sunk cost" and thus a cost of doing business. Thus it often, maybe usually, does not get scrutinized for ROI or investment.

For instance, Wal-Mart has a high-tech strategic approach to the supply chain which they refer to as quick response. It involves bar coding, data mining, just-in-time (JIT) inventory, electronic data interchange (EDI), and other technologies. Wal-Mart also uses a strong control environment, the principles mentioned herein. Therefore when a business unit manager asks for new IT or updates to IT, the business case would need to show how the project will enhance Wal-Mart's ability to have an effective and especially efficient supply chain (which is its unique financial and strategic advantage in the market) in order to gain capital funds for the IT project.

Thirdly, some controls would need to be in place to make sure these objectives are being met. One control would be some group to report to the board of directors (BoD) about the IT function as it relates to strategic planning on a regular basis. That could be a subcommittee of the BoD, or a cross-functional IT steering committee, or even take other forms. This body would manage the capital budget funds, award IT projects, prioritize IT projects, oversee major IT projects, and in general, make sure that the IT function is satisfying the entity's needs related to strategic use of IT.

3.2.1.2 – Policies & Procedures

The control environment would not only include the strategic IT plan, but a body of policies and procedures (P&P) related to the IT function. Normally, the entity should have a separate P&P document for the IT function describing how the IT function will be managed for effectiveness, efficiency, and to meet management's expectations. The P&P should include the role, structure, and processes of IT governance and project management – when relevant – and standards for developing, deploying, and managing IT resources.

3.2.1.2.1 – IT P&P

The CITP will want to review the IT policies and procedures as part of examining the control environment. The IT P&P should be congruent with the entity's P&P. They should also include items that demonstrate the intent to align IT with enterprise goals, objectives, and strategies. P&P should cover professional development of staff (training, seminars, certification, etc.), support services for users, management of IT projects (especially development procedures, testing procedures, and deployment practices), budgets, change management, access controls (physical and logical), information security, business continuity planning/disaster recovery planning, vendor management (especially 3rd party providers of IT), data management, and other general IT function activities. Obviously not all of these issues will be relevant in all entities, but larger entities will likely have most if not all of these areas.

The other key to P&P is that it addresses the IT risks identified by management in its enterprise risk assessment (see 3.2.1.3 and Dimension 1).

3.2.1.2.2 – Role of IT Governance in Control Environment/ITGC

IT governance is a critical success factor for control environment, if it is relevant to the entity. That would be true if: the entity has major IT projects on a regular basis, writes its own software or modifies software, has risky IT projects (such as major changes to core, critical applications), has a high level of IT sophistication – and likely for medium level (nature and complexity of IT, see 1.2.2.1), and/or the business operations are highly reliant on IT. Even in the smallest of entities, or lowest levels of IT sophistication, some form of IT governance principles should be employed. For instance, there should be a formal basis for updating and replacing its commercial, standard IT. IT governance is simultaneously a process, a formal structure, and a monitoring system (see 3.2.2.2 for more on this topic).[8]

Assuming the entity qualifies for the need of it, IT governance plays a role in an effective control environment. The IT Governance Institute (ITGI) defines it as:

> *... a set of principles to assist enterprise leaders in their responsibility to ensure that IT is aligned with the business and delivers value, its performance is measured, its resources properly allocated, and its risks mitigated.*

The P&P should describe the specific nature of the structure for IT governance. It could be an IT expert on the BoD, and possibly a BoD subcommittee. It could be a cross-functional team that oversees critical aspects of the IT function and reports to the BoD at each meeting. It could take other forms as well. Evidence of the presence of the structure should be determinable from a review of the P&P and interview of the CIO or manager of the IT function.

An assessment of the level of effectiveness of that structure would involve gathering evidence of the processes involved and measuring results against the five objectives in the definition above (see 3.2.2.2 for the role of IT governance in change management). The substance of the IT governance process should be to meet the objectives indicated in the definition above. That generally involves capital budgets, regular reviews of the IT portfolio, the engagement of the BoD, and best practices for project management, change management, and IT governance in general.

3.2.1.2.3 – Role of Project Management in Control Environment/ITGC

The factors that determine whether IT governance is relevant are virtually identical for whether project management is relevant. Any entity that has large or risky IT projects should employ the principles of project management. The P&P of that entity should reflect the intent to follow project management principles, including the structure and processes of project management.

The Project Management Institute (PMI) defines project management in its Project Management Body of Knowledge (PMBOK) as:

> *... the application of knowledge, skills, tools, and techniques to project activities to meet project requirements.*

In other words, it involves planning, organizing, monitoring, and controlling the project activities in order to accomplish the project requirements. The three basic requirements are generally considered to be resources, time (deadline), and functionality – with quality and risks factors to

---

[8] Both IT governance (ITG) and project management (PM) have dual roles in the control environment and change management elements of ITGCs. For the sake of making the distinction, the control environment would focus on the structure (presence and form) of ITG and PM, and the stated objectives of those structures. Change management would focus on the processes of the two; what is done, compliance with the principles of ITG and PM, and how well they meet their control environment (P&P) objectives in their application.

be considered and managed as well. Thus the objectives of project management are associated with these five factors of IT projects. But effective project management clearly involves leading, planning, organizing, and controlling IT projects including personnel, resources, risks, and the environment; that is, effectively managing them.

Like IT governance, evidence of the presence of project management should become evident in a review of the P&P and interview of the CIO or manager of the IT function. However, an assessment of the effectiveness of project management takes more evidence, such as evaluating the processes associated with managing IT projects (see 3.2.2.3 for the role of project management in change management).

COBIT's planning and organizing process of "manage projects" (PO10) provides guidance related to this role, and project management in general as it relates to IT.

3.2.1.3 – Risk Management

Part of the control environment would be a risk assessment, specifically those risks related to IT. The outcome should be documentation of IT risk management (see Dimension 1 for more on IT risk assessment).

This aspect of control environment is basically identical with COSO's "risk assessment" (limited to IT here) and COBIT's planning and organizations process of "assess risk" (PO9). Thus those two resources provide information in developing an appropriate risk management structure, process, and objectives.

Specifically, management should have a formal due process of identifying IT-related risks – risks to the business operations, goals, objectives, and strategies. Naturally, that process should conclude in a written document. Then management should consider taking measures to mitigate the greater risks, or ones they can effectively and efficiently mitigate. Those decisions should be documented as well. Risk management of the control environment should involve a structure, process, and set of objectives related to IT risk management.

Some IT situations have a high inherent risk in almost all instances. For example: customized software (in house), transfers of data between two systems, communication of data from one system to another, and logical access controls (especially remote and Internet).

3.2.1.4 – IT Operations

Managing IT operations is likely to be a part of the control environment for all entities. This aspect includes the issues such as organization of the IT function, managing the IT portfolio, managing support and IT services, and using some kind of continuous improvement methodology (whether formal or informal).

3.2.1.4.1 – Consideration of portfolio of systems deployed and planned

The entity will want to not only manage changes to its IT (e.g., new hardware, upgrade or modify software, etc.), but will want to manage all of the IT as a portfolio. Obviously, that begins with knowing what is in the portfolio, or documenting the portfolio. Thus documents such as a network diagram and IT assets inventory are critical to proper IT operations. However, it does not stop with documenting the status quo of IT.

Management should evaluate the portfolio regularly to see what technologies should be replaced, retired, or changed. That process would include an assessment for adding new technologies as well, and should be integrated with IT governance and the IT strategic plan. Considering the portfolio when considering new technologies allows management to walk through the proposal to see if any unintended consequences can be identified, or if there is a conflict or obstacle to implementing the proposed IT. For instance, considering the portfolio allows IT managers to notice incompatible technologies or an infrastructure not ready for the new IT.

That regular review process would also include updating the documentation of the portfolio to make sure it is current; the portfolio is dynamic after all and not static.

3.2.1.4.2 – Documenting networks, systems, and the IT portfolio

As mentioned, documentation of the IT portfolio is essential to effective management of IT operations, and the documents should include more than a list of IT items. For example, a complete and accurate network diagram is critical to effective information security. Routers, PCs, servers, and especially firewalls need to be precisely identified on that diagram in order to assess the level of security the entity has in place and to effectively manage it in an ongoing basis.

The same is true for systems. For instance, the CITP begins the process of a financial audit by reviewing the financial reports, identifying material account balances, disclosures, and/or classes of transactions, and then identifying which systems "touch" those transactions or events. That is not a difficult process if there is a current and accurate systems diagram, but can be cumbersome and possibly time consuming if one does not exist. The fact management has an accurate and up-to-date systems diagram (or network diagram or IT portfolio documentation) speaks to the effectiveness of managing IT and management's efforts to minimize IT risks.

3.2.1.4.3 – Support services/Help desk

In order for data entry to be working effectively, as well as data processing, people along the systems path have to be performing their duties effectively. In order to do their job properly, employees need to be trained and supported. A measure of the latter is how the help desk or IT support service performs its function.

Generally, support service or help desk has a formal way of recording requests and responding to them – usually a ticket system (whether electronic or paper). Thus one way of assessing that performance is to examine the ticket system for timely and effective responses. Effective management will generally have done its own evaluation of the help desk or support services system to see if response time is adequate, to see if there are gaps in responding effectively, and even to spot repetitions of the same problem.

On a broader basis, there is a generally accepted set of best practices in Information Technology Infrastructure Library (ITIL).[9] ITIL is a set of concepts and practices for providing IT support

[9] The official website of ITIL is http://www.itil-officialsite.com/home/home.asp

services and includes topics such as service support, service delivery, infrastructure management, security management, application management, software asset management, planning to implement service management, and small-scale implementation. ITIL provides a benchmark of objectives from which the CITP could measure the effectiveness of the support services function in IT operations. (see section 3.1.1.4.5 for more on ITIL)

In addition, COBIT's domain of "deliver and support" has 13 processes of which most relate to this aspect of IT operations, and support services/help desk in particular.

3.2.1.4.4 – Continuous Improvement

There are several models in the IT profession that involve the concept of continuous improvement. For instance, the Capability Maturity Model (CMM) has been seen as a "good housekeeping seal" for software vendors around the world. In addition, as mentioned above, version 3 of ITIL has as a last step in its life cycle continual service improvement (CSI). Thus continuous improvement is usually seen as a part of effective IT operations.

3.2.1.5 – Human Resource Management of IT Personnel

Just as good corporate governance is built on sufficient competencies of key personnel (e.g., financial expert on audit committee, controller, CFO, and accounting clerks); the control environment and IT function as a whole is dependent on the overall competency of the IT personnel. That objective would involve the processes of identifying competencies, hiring, firing, performance evaluation, training, and professional development. The latter is of particular importance for the IT staff because of the rapid changes to the IT environment and individual technologies.

Sometimes the HR function does all of these processes, and sometimes the IT function shares part of them. For instance, sometimes the IT function takes charge of training and professional development and managing it, partly because of the special needs related to the rapid changes in IT or nature of the entity's IT.

This aspect of the control environment is associated with COBIT's process of "manage human resources" (PO7), which would provide valuable information on objectives and audit of this aspect.

3.2.1.5.1 – Proper IT skill set (competencies)

Somehow management needs to identify the proper set of skills needed by the personnel of the IT department. That is obviously dependent on the nature, complexity, and manufacturer of the IT being employed by the entity. Usually, that skill set will need to be identified by IT management, but the HR function will need it in order to recruit and hire the proper personnel. Inevitably, the IT function will collaborate and cooperate with HR function in making sure new hires and existing staff have the proper skill set for their job.

3.2.1.5.2 – Hiring and firing policies and procedures

HR management should document its objectives and the intended process in policies and procedures for hiring and firing IT personnel. Those objectives and processes would revolve around a sufficient body of competencies for the IT function.

Some key elements would be certification and education. The IT function would identify which credentials are needed for which jobs, and HR would ensure that employees hired hold those credentials – whether it is certification, education, or experience. The key is for the structure and process to be documented, to be objective driven, and to be effective in providing sufficient competencies in the body of IT personnel.

One key distinction in IT needs to be understood related to the hiring of managers of the IT function. Like other disciplines (e.g., engineering), there are strong technicians ("geeks") and there are strong managers of IT, and usually a person is one or the other. Executive management needs to understand that difference and be judicious in hiring IT managers. A good technician does not necessarily make a good manager. Quite often a good technician has a college degree from the arts and sciences segment of the college or university and thus probably has no business education. On the other hand, a person who has a MIS/IS/CIS degree for the business segment of the college or university has lots of business education and a modicum of education for the technical side of IT.

3.2.1.5.3 – Performance evaluation

Likewise, IT employees' performance evaluation, which would be performed by the IT managers, should be overseen by the HR function. Performance evaluation works in conjunction with the competencies (3.2.1.5.1) in making sure the state of competencies is always sufficient.

3.2.1.5.4 – Training and professional development

Management of the HR function will want to coordinate training and professional development for IT personnel for the same objective. The IT function may manage this process in some entities, but regardless, the objective is the same.

One reason why training and professional development is so important to the control environment for IT is because of the nature of IT to change substantially each year, such that in a relatively few number of years, IT employees could become relatively obsolete in competencies. Even if not, the IT of the organization will be constantly evolving and changing, and employees will need to be able to support these new technologies. Therefore, training and professional development is particularly important to IT.

For instance, if IT does not have a Project Management Professional (PMP) but the entity has major IT projects, then either the IT function could hire a PMP, or equivalent, or provide training for key IT personnel so its competencies related to project management would be sufficient for the needs.

Some questions and procedures the CITP might want to consider in order to properly assess and evaluate the control environment include:

- Were there any violations of ethics policy related to IT in the prior year?
- Does documentation exist on any recent IT ethical violations, including the resolution?
- What is the monitoring function that ensures compliance with the IT portion of the ethics policy?
- Review the organizational chart to gain an understanding of the IT function and SoDs

- Review relevant job descriptions of key IT personnel (e.g., manager of application development)
- Take a sample of major IT projects and review the documentation (e.g., look for best practices being employed)
- Perform interviews, walkthroughs, or other procedures to adequately determine whether best practices are being used in change management, project management, IT governance, and SDLC (where applicable)
- Perform interviews, walkthroughs, or other procedures to adequately determine the assurance related to initiation, authorization, development, testing, and implementation of IT, including user acceptance reports (testing), and BoD minutes (authorization)
- Review the written IT risk assessment (if one exists; if not, that says something about how this management is managing the IT function and especially IT risks)
- Review the professional development records for the year, and match it to relevant needs
- Examine the competencies of the IT staff corporately, and key IT personnel individually
- Examine the IT governance structure and process
- Examine the SDLC processes (if applicable)

3.2.2 – Change Management

For the CITP, the key aspect of change management is that program changes and systems acquisition, or development, are appropriately managed to ensure that the application software and automated controls adequately support financial reporting and/or business objectives. The CITP would consider whether the entity has identified the relevant risks that arise from change management and established mitigating controls effectively. Such controls would not only include properly designed and implemented application controls, but change management controls upon which application controls depend.

While change management focuses on application changes, it would also include related changes such as relevant hardware and systems, operating systems, and configurations – especially those that house financial applications.

The COBIT model lists change management as its own process (AI6), which is part of the phase acquire and implement. In AI6, COBIT describes the high-level control objective as managing changes to computer programs to ensure processing integrity; the formal management of IT changes via change control requests, authorization, risk and impact assessment, documentation, and proper scope of policies and procedures (see 3.2.2.1). The stated goal is to minimize the likelihood of disruption of IT processing, unauthorized alterations, and mitigation of programming errors.

<u>3.2.2.1 – Policies & Procedures</u>

The proper scope of policies and procedures would include subjects such as version control, release, distribution, implementation, testing, etc. The change process should be formalized and structured in the change management P&P, beginning with the initiation of a change request and authorization of all changes. The proper authority for approving changes would need to be identified, as well as the standardized process. P&P should include how to keep the project sponsor informed about the status of the request.

At a minimum, an appropriate set of policies and procedures needs to address the key aspects of change management mentioned above: changes to applications and relevant hardware, operating systems, and configurations. The P&P would address initiation, authorization, purchasing or developing, testing, deployment, and maintenance of the pertinent aspects of the IT portfolio.

3.2.2.1.1 – Configuration Management

The issue with configuration management is the fact that they can interact with applications. Generally, this type of configuration is related to commercial off-the-shelf (COTS) applications, and allows an administrator to customize or change certain factors in the software. For instance, configurations of COTS usually allow customization of the general ledger account numbers for standard accounting transactions (e.g., the debit and credit account numbers for a sale on account). Configurations often also provide authorization factors for initiating transactions – a key automated control.

In fact, according to one expert:

> *The importance of configuration management in ITIL cannot be overstated. Change management, problem management, incident management, security, and compliance all rely, to some extent, on the accuracy and scope of underlying configuration management data. (Configuration management data) will ultimately point to information about an asset, its importance, and role, and critical operational details such as the interdependencies among other assets and services. Ideally, configuration changes should be automatically captured when they are made, possibly using integrated tools.*[10]

As can be seen from the quote, the objective of configuration management is to control changes to configuration within a formalized structure, whether automated (as recommended above) or manual.

The more sophisticated the system, or the more key control factors (initiation, authorization, processing, recording, and reporting) are reliant upon the configuration, the higher the level of inherent risk, and more important configuration is to the CITP. Thus systems like enterprise resource planning (ERP) are generally high-risk configurations. Such configurations should be controlled and managed closely and are generally in scope for the IT/financial audit. It usually requires a subject-matter expert (SME) to audit/evaluate an ERP configuration. Things to consider are the same as the objectives for change management: authorized changes, limited access, documentation for changes/setup, a formal structured process for testing, and a formal structured process for approving and managing changes.

Specific guidance on auditing and evaluating the configuration is provided by ISACA's *IS Auditing Guideline* G37, "Configuration Management Process", and COBIT process DS9,

[10] See "Ten Simple Steps to ITIL Network Compliance", white paper, Netcordia, 2007. http://hosteddocs.ittoolbox.com/wp-itil-network-compliance-us.pdf

"Manage the Configuration" (see Exhibit 3.2). G37 includes COBIT information and therefore serves as a single source for configuration. DS9 includes objectives such as:

- Establishing a central repository of all configuration items
- Identifying configuration items and maintaining them effectively
- Reviewing the integrity of all configuration data periodically

Configuration measurements that can serve to facilitate the gathering of evidence related to these objectives includes the following examples:

- Number of business compliance issues caused by improper configuration of IT
- Number of deviations identified between configuration repository and actual IT assets
- Percent of licenses purchased but not accounted for in the repository
- Effective capture of configuration changes (e.g., authorization and access control changes)

Management of entities would want to consider these factors in developing a thorough policies and procedures related to configuration management. For example, handling certain malicious activities and certain errors are highly dependent on configuration changes.

3.2.2.1.2 – Software Management

Software management would include whatever applications the entity used in its accounting information system, whether it is COTS or custom software, or some hybrid.

For COTS, policies and procedures should be established to make sure that software is purchased from reliable vendors. Criteria should be developed that would make an effective determination of a reliable software vendor. The P&P should also include guidance on keeping the software up to date with version changes. It also should cover software maintenance, which usually includes version updates as well as help desk support.

For custom software, it should lay out procedures that would ensure risks of errors and fraud in development and deployment are mitigated. Special attention should be given to complete testing offline before deployment. It also is beneficial to stipulate compliance with best practices that can mitigate programming risks (e.g., SDLC).

The P&P should include pseudo software such as macros in end-user systems (e.g., electronic spreadsheets or databases), and formulas (electronic spreadsheets). The issues are basically the same as custom software: development, testing, and deployment practices that would mitigate the risks associated with end-user computing.

The COBIT process AI2, Acquire and maintain application, should be a beneficial source for objectives in this area for developing P&P.

3.2.2.1.3 – Operating System Management

The operating system (O/S) plays a key role in computer operations because applications run within an O/S environment, and the fact O/S need updating due to vulnerabilities from time to time. Also a user with administrative rights to the O/S has direct access to IT assets, which if present, represents a relatively high inherent risk. Thus P&P would include issues and objectives similar to software (version control, updates, development control, testing before deployment, etc.) but also includes logical access control. It would also address settings and parameters of the O/S and patches.

ISACA's ITAF, segment 3630.14, covers "Operating Systems Management and Controls", and should be a beneficial source for objectives and issues in this area for developing appropriate P&P.

3.2.2.1.4 – Network Management

The network is another critical piece of the infrastructure supporting financial applications and data. Developing network P&P would typically include internal and external networks, outsourcing, level of operating performance (e.g., availability), access controls (especially password policy), and security.

ISACA's ITAF, segment 3630.11, covers "Network Management and Controls", and should be a beneficial source for objectives and issues in this area for developing appropriate P&P.

<u>3.2.2.2 – IT Governance</u>

The IT Governance Institute (ITGI) defines IT governance as:

> *... to understand and manage the risks associated with implementing new technologies, and addressing enterprise challenges and concerns such as (a) aligning IT strategy with the business strategy, (b) cascading strategy and goals down the enterprise, (c) providing organizational structure that facilitates the implementation of strategy and goals, (d) insisting that an IT control framework be adopted and implemented, and (e) measuring IT's performance.*
>
> *IT governance is the responsibility of the Board of Directors and Executive Management. It is an integral part of enterprise governance and consists of the leadership and organizational structures and processes that ensure that the organization's IT sustains and extends the organization's strategy and objectives.*

IT governance actually takes three forms simultaneously, and they work together to result in effective change management: (1) a structure, (2) a set of processes, and (3) monitoring using appropriate measures/metrics. [11,12]

---

[11] De Haes, Steven and Wim Van Grembergen. "IT Governance Structures, Processes and Relational Mechanisms: Achieving IT/Business Alignment in a Major Belgian Financial Group". *Proceedings of the 38th Hawaii International Conference on System Sciences*, 2005.

Structure would include roles and responsibilities, IT organization structure, CIO, expert on BoD, IT strategy committee, and IT Steering committee. In general, structure involves the existence of responsibility functions such as IT executives and one or more IT committees.

Process includes activities such as strategic IT planning, Service Level Agreements (SLAs) with third party IT providers, application of COBIT/ITIL/other applicable frameworks and best practices, alignment of IT with enterprise goals and objectives, and governance maturity models. Basically, processes ensure strategic decision making and monitoring of IT effectiveness and efficiency.

Monitoring involves measuring IT performance using proprietary metrics. Traditional measures are cost-benefit and ROI, and a more modern one is balanced scorecard. It is advisable to consider intangible performance factors as well.

Two of the main purposes of IT governance are to effectively manage the IT function (plan, organize, and control IT activities) and effectively mitigate IT risks. Clearly these purposes provide assurance about the quality of IT overall, and specifically to provide assurance over aspects such as change management. When an entity has mature IT governance, there will be signs to indicate it. For example, in mature IT governance, IT priorities are driven by the business strategies, whereas in basic IT governance, IT priorities are driven by the IT community and/or IT department. This continuum from basic to mature IT Governance exists on a number of factors such as how IT adds value, BoD involvement, and portfolio management.

One reason IT governance is so important to reducing IT risks is because of its impact and scope across the entity. To illustrate, project management can be seen as a subset of IT governance, and project management principles are critical success factors in major IT projects (i.e., change management). But IT governance considers the enterprise, and the entire IT portfolio, in its processes, structure, and monitoring.

3.2.2.3 – Project Management

Project management (PM) would be applicable in direct proportion to the number or scope of major IT projects. All entities go through changes in its IT, but those that strictly use commercial, standard, and popular software, hardware, and infrastructure products have a low level of need for project management, or just some simple, basic application of PM principles. But, those entities that have a large scope IT projects, or write software, or modify commercial applications have a need to employ the full PM body of knowledge and principles to mitigate risks associated with changes in IT.

Project management best practices have a particularly positive impact on change management. The primary objectives of PM body of knowledge is directed at ensuring projects are on time, within budget, fully functional, at a high level of quality, and with proper consideration of

---

[12] Bowen, Paul L., May-Yin Decca Cheung, and Fiona H. Rohde. "Enhancing IT Governance Practices: A Model and Case Study on an Organization's Efforts". International Journal of Accounting Information Systems, Volume 8 (2007), pp. 191–221.

relevant risks. Empirical evidence suggests that while about 60–75% of IT projects fail on one or more of these factors[13], those that adhere to Project Management Institute's (PMI) Project Management Body of Knowledge (PMBOK) principles have far fewer failures and in fact generally succeed on all five aspects.

Project management fits within IT governance. The Software Engineering Institute (SEI) provides a model that demonstrates the role of project management and how it is incorporated into IT governance (see Exhibit 3.7). Certain projects roll up into "programs" – where projects work together or are integrated in operations. The Project Management Institute defines "project" in its PMBOK as:

> *A project is a temporary endeavor undertaken to create a unique product, service, or result, having a definitive beginning and end.*

Programs and individualized projects roll up into the IT portfolio. Programs and individualized major projects are managed by a Project Management Office (PMO) in a mature entity. The PMO would be staffed by those experienced in project management principles, such as those certified as Project Management Professionals (PMP). The IT portfolio is managed by the BoD or executive management, as a function of IT governance.

Project management is about leading, planning, organizing, and controlling the project stakeholders, resources, and environment such that the results are successful; that is, the project is on time, on budget, fully functional, and "right" quality.

EXHIBIT 3.7: PROJECT MANAGEMENT & IT GOVERNANCE		
GOVERN	IT Portfolio Management	Executive management & BoD Strategy and alignment: High level plans Exception reports Funding Direction
MANAGE	Program Management	Middle Management Project Management Office (PMO) & PMPs Broad management of all projects Funding, prioritizing, and monitoring major IT programs Tactical activities
EXECUTE	Project Management	IT staff (possibly others) Execute individual IT projects Detailed plans Changes communicated and incorporated

[13] Mango, Ammar W. "Project Management; Beyond the Formal Definition". *PM World Today*, Volume X, Issue IV (April 2008), pp. 1–4. [Note: Statistics come from 2006 data.]

One key aspect of IT governance is the structure of committees that have oversight of major IT projects (that is, changes to IT and thus change management functionality). One important part of IT governance process is the application of frameworks and best practices such as project management (particularly useful for change management). But basically the overall objective of IT governance naturally leads to the mitigation of risks associated with change management, and activities therein provide assurance of effective change management. Thus effectual project management reduces the risks in changes to IT.

3.2.2.4 – Systems Development Life Cycle (SDLC)

Like project management and IT governance, the need for SDLC to be included in an IT audit or review depends on the entity's particular systems development process. Some entities purchase all, or almost all, of its software applications. The more an entity writes code, or modifies commercial applications, the more SDLC becomes relevant[14].

One IT risk that usually has a high inherent risk is software coding. Thus the more an entity writes programming code, the more risk it has (assuming those applications are relevant). One way to mitigate the IT risks associated with AppDev is to effectively employ SDLC principles.

3.2.2.4.1 – Phases

Systems Development Life Cycle, like all life cycles, is made up of several continuous, cyclical phases. Different sources will offer different lists of these phases, but they all generally contain the same activities or functions. Exhibit 3.8 has one list that is an example of SDLC phases.

The first phase is generally considered to be ***IT strategic planning***, the same kind of activities and goals as discussed previously (see section 3.2.1.1), with the context of changing something in the software segment of the IT portfolio (e.g., new software application or system, major change to an existing application, etc.). Basically, this phase has the purpose of ensuring that the change being proposed has an effective business case that demonstrates how this project will facilitate achieving enterprise goals and objectives, and how this project adds value to the enterprise. This phase would benefit from a written IT strategy that is thorough, and a capital budget process including written objectives for that year's proposals.

The second phase is usually ***information requirements*** gathering. Here, systems analysts, project managers, or other IT professionals gather the requirements for the proposed system by talking to the project sponsor, end users in that functional area, and other relevant parties to determine the functionality the software application should include. This phase is also referred to as systems analysis. Key issues that should be included in mature organizations are the expert input on controls, any information security issues, and the scope of data to be collected (e.g., what is needed for effective business intelligence later on). As information requirements are gathered, they should be documented in some form standardized for that entity, and the process follow best practices of SDLC.

[14] Application development is known as AppDev, whereas systems development is known as SysDev. SysDev is broader and includes systems of technologies, and AppDev is about an application or core group of interrelated applications.

EXHIBIT 3.8: SDLC PHASES

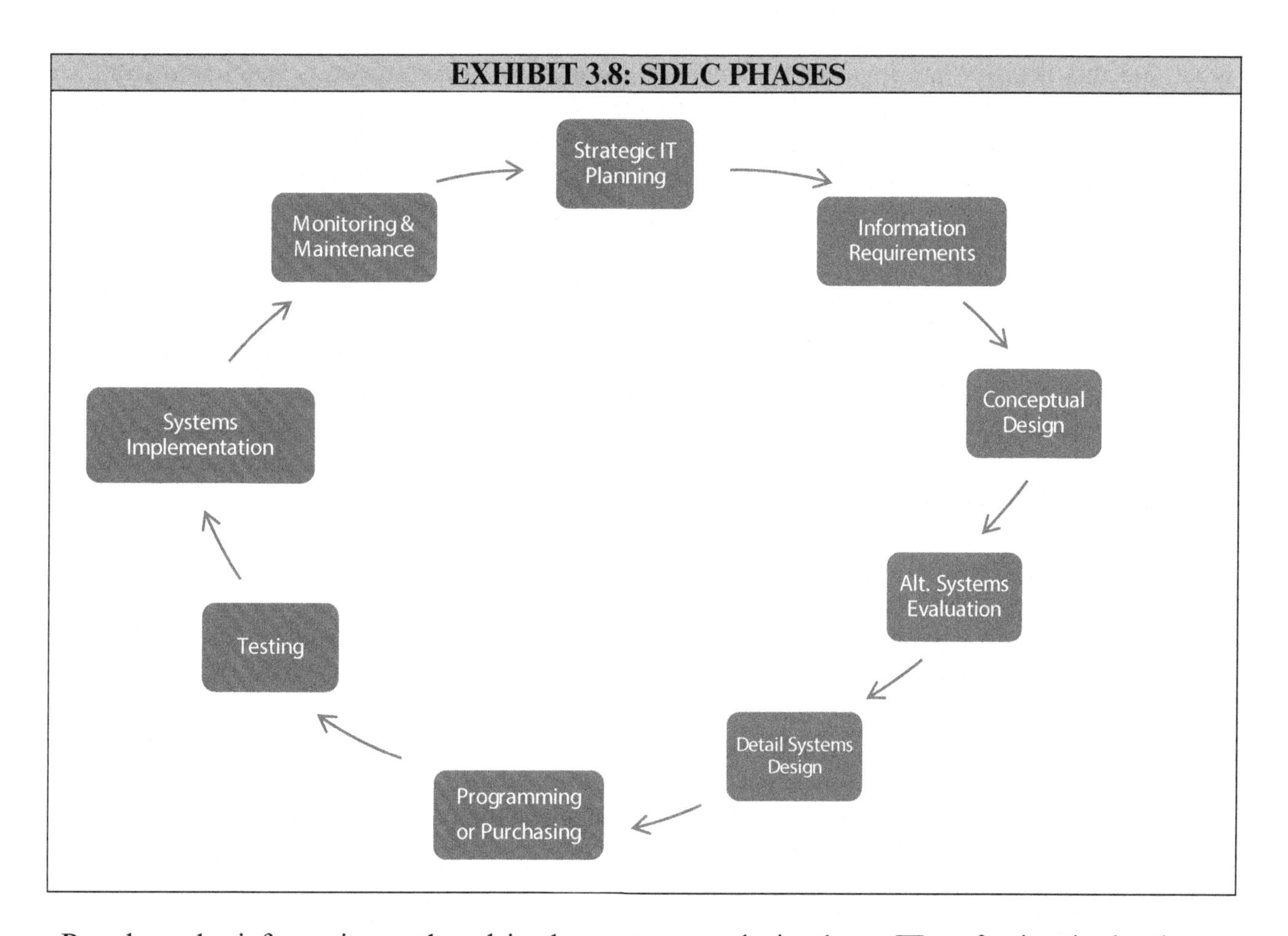

Based on the information gathered in the systems analysis phase, IT professionals develop a ***conceptual design*** of what the system looks like at a relatively high level; succinct and summarized in terms of details. This conceptual design should be a document that diagrams, or provides a schematic of, the proposed system in enough detail for software vendors to bid on the proposal, or for programmers and analysts to make reasonable estimates of time and resources to complete the project.

The next phase is the ***evaluation of alternative solutions***. Sometimes this process leads to a request for proposal (RFP) sent to a number of reliable vendors for bids. Sometimes the alternatives are to build or buy; that is, have the entity's own programmers write the code or outsource the programming to a reliable vendor.

The next element of SDLC is a ***detailed systems design***. Whether the choice was build or buy, there is a need for a detailed schematic of the proposed systems' functionality, including input documents (e.g., source documents, input documents), processing details, and output documents (e.g., screens, printouts, etc.).

At this point, the entity may have a choice of whether to buy a commercial product that can fulfill the information requirements and functionality needed, or build it by having internal programmers write the application, or outsource the coding to a vendor programming service organization. Because of the high inherent risk associated with customized programming, this issue and this decision are important. Generally speaking, if the software is purchased from a commercial vendor, there is probably a reduction in the risk associated with programming code. If it is outsourced to a group of professionals, a reliable vendor, then again that would usually be less risk than if the entity used its own employees. Even if the entity outsources the programming requirements, or uses a RFP to buy a standard commercial application, the other steps of SDLC described herein are beneficial in change management associated with the changes in software being implemented. If the entity writes its own application, it is even more important to reducing IT risks in change management.

Testing is a critical success factor in reducing IT risks associated with change management. Whether it is hardware or software, the IT being implemented should be adequately and appropriately tested offline before being deployed online. That process should be a formal, structured process that is planned, managed, and documented thoroughly.

For example, management may have developed a standardized testing plan (e.g., checklist) of standard, common testing procedures, and includes signatures of those performing the testing, and end users who verify the testing was successful according to their perspective and needs. Another best practice is to establish a "staging area" where systems similar to the enterprise system is housed and used strictly for testing (and maybe backup and recovery or other similar needs). This type of testing allows the isolated application or hardware to be plugged into the enterprise interfaced system of hardware and software where the best, broadest test can be performed. Testing is more critical if the entity writes its own code as the risk of errors in the code is generally greater there.

Testing should also include various perspectives or steps. Obviously the programmer(s) would need to test the application. But then the IT function should provide a quality assurance (QA) or quality control (QC) function to provide a second, independent test of the application. Then the application should be tested by interfacing it with all potential applications and modules – which is where the staging area becomes important. Lastly, the project sponsor, business unit manager, should provide users to test the application (fully integrated if possible), and upon successful completion of that testing, a user acceptance report, where the user signs off that the application is fully functional and the test was successful, is generally considered a best practice.

Only after a thorough and appropriate testing has been successfully performed would the entity ***implement*** the hardware or software. That is, the application or hardware is put into IT operations. This point of the process is a key one in terms of risk. Although a thorough testing has occurred, there is usually still some significant risk in the implementation of new IT. Generally, the IT department will have some higher level of alertness at the particular point in time the new IT goes into operations, keeping a close watch over its performance to be ready to handle any unexpected problems.

The final phase is ***monitoring and maintenance***. Two purposes related to IT risks and SDLC would be the effective operations and the determination of a need for a change. Effective operations clearly directly impact the automated business processes and automated controls associated with significant financial systems. The determination of further changes also reduces risk in a different manner in that it keeps the overall effectiveness of the enterprise systems and technologies at a high level.

3.2.2.4.2 – Best Practices

The principles of SDLC are best practices. As such, they can usually serve as benchmarks for evaluating and measuring the effectiveness of an entity's change management controls, especially for custom software.

One key benefit of using SDLC principles is that each phase has a document associated with that phase and its objective and activities. Some examples of the various types of documents that might be available are listed in Exhibit 3.9 below, organized by phase.

EXHIBIT 3.9: SDLC BEST PRACTICES – EXAMPLES OF DOCUMENTATION	
Strategic Planning	Strategic plan, BoD et al. minutes, IT capital budget, feasibility studies, project authorization by IT governance body
Information Requirements	Information requirements documentation, systems analysis report
Conceptual Design	Diagram or documentation of design, summarized data flow diagram (DFD), systems flowchart, programming flowchart
Alternative Systems Evaluation	Documentation of process, PMO et al. minutes, feasibility study, cost-benefit analysis, system selection report
Detail Systems Design	Design schematic, normalized data documentation, systems design process documentation: detailed DFD, entity-relationship (ER) diagram, relational model diagram, data dictionary
Build/Buy	RFP, purchase order, SLA/contract with SO, authorization for internal IT for AppDev, documentation of meeting(s)
Testing	Testing checklist/plan, testing results documented, user testing signoff, testing results approval/signoff by project sponsor and/or project manager, project plan
Systems Implementation	Implementation plan, documentation of implementation, post implementation review, user acceptance report
"Gateway" Process	Approval of project required before goes to development Development and personal testing signed off, senior programmer or analyst, before goes to QA/QC QA/QC test and sign off, integrated testing where feasible User testing documented and signed off, user acceptance report, before going to production
Monitoring & Maintenance	Maintenance approval documents, support services documentation, IT help desk documents (tickets and results, especially performance charts)

Thus one way to gain an understanding of change management is to ask for the documentation from one or more major IT projects and evaluate it/them:

(1) Does it appear the project was properly authorized, initiated, and tested?
(2) Does it seem to include all of the SDLC phases?
(3) Does the (AppDev/SysDev) process seem to be formal, structured, and repeatable?
(4) Does the overall process seem to be effective in mitigating risks associated with change management?

In fact, the presence of SDLC best practices IS a control in and of itself. For example, following best practices in SDLC will minimize IT risks associated with change management.

3.2.2.5 – Vulnerability Management

CITPs would want some assurance that the infrastructure as a whole, and the components thereof, are functioning at a level sufficient to minimize IT, business, and financial reporting risks associated with applications. The same is true for the financial reporting process.

Some aspects of the infrastructure will be subject to vulnerabilities that arise from time to time. Effectual vulnerability management involves proactively watching for announcements of new vulnerabilities (e.g., SANS) and timely patching vulnerabilities that exist or arise. Objects that may need vulnerability control include operating systems, general use commercial software, and certain internet technologies (routers, browsers, etc.). Exhibit 3.10 illustrates some of the common objects of vulnerabilities (and coincidentally vendor management).

Vulnerability also exists in things that overlap with information security (e.g., malware), unauthorized access, and similar security risks. Vulnerabilities could even exist in COTS software where upgrades are made to correct some vulnerability (e.g., email software and malware, and DBMS and SQL injections).

For instance, one advantage of a DBMS is the fact data can be shared across users and units that need to share data. However, the same feature presents one of the key risks of DBMS. The fact data is centralized means an unauthorized access potentially could lead to access to almost all of the enterprise's data. Vulnerabilities in the DBMS, by their nature, allow unauthorized access and provide a way, albeit often a limited one, for malicious activities to be perpetrated.

3.2.2.6 – Vendor Management

Sound vendor management practices are pertinent across much of ITGC and many of the individual aspects already mentioned, such as servers, network equipment, operating systems, COTS, etc. Reliance and assurance of ITGCs depends to some degree on the reliability of the vendor supplying the product or service. Therefore, employing best practices in vendor management supports assurance of ITGC in many areas. Exhibit 3.10 illustrates some of the examples where vendor management would apply to ITGC.

Standard equipment from reliable vendors is a mitigating factor for risks of IT components such as servers. Likewise wiring, routers, and similar devices benefit from reliable vendors and standard IT components.

EXHIBIT 3.10: IT VULNERABILITY & VENDOR MANAGEMENT OBJECTS	
Servers	Network backbone servers, email server, DBMS server, etc. ADD'L RISKS: Unauthorized access to CENTRALIZED IT assets (programs and data), effective pre-implementation testing
Network Infrastructure	Wiring/cabling, wireless connectivity, routers et al., firewalls ADD'L RISKS: Unauthorized access to IT assets, transmission of data, workstations (desktops, laptops, smart phones)
Operating Systems	Networks, desktops, servers
DBMS	(where applicable) ADD'L RISKS: Unauthorized access to CENTRALIZED data
Commercial Applications	COTS, productivity/office apps,
Email, Browsers, etc.	Viruses, worms, key loggers, and other malware.
Online Sales & Transactions	Payment, collection, theft of credit card data, ID theft, etc.

3.2.2.7 – Portfolio of Systems & Technologies

It is important for management to actually manage the IT portfolio rather than allow it to grow and evolve by happenstance. Without the proper management, IT will be in the portfolio that is no longer necessary, or out of date, or ineffective, or inefficient.

Therefore, effective management has a formal structure and process to evaluate its IT portfolio regularly. Such a process allows management to minimize risks associated with volatile items in the portfolio (i.e., items that are outdated, no longer needed, or need updating).

3.2.2.8 –Systems Implications

Some aspects of systems and technologies have particular IT risks, or are critical aspects of IT risks in other parts of the IT environment.

3.2.2.8.1 – Accounting & Financial Reporting Systems

For the CITP auditor, the accounting and financial reporting systems are a critical element of any IT audit, IT engagement, or IT review. For instance, in a financial audit, using the top-down approach used in RBA, once material account balances, transactions, or disclosures have been identified, usually the next step is to identify what systems and technologies "touch" the data flow inputs, processes, and outputs of that audit object. Those systems and technologies identified in this approach are included in the scope while others are scoped out.

The B&I CITP would likely be concerned with all of the systems and technologies, at least over time, and thus would take a different perspective and approach. However, it would still be a risk-based and top-down approach. It would likely lead to more of the IT space being part of the activities of the CITP, depending on the objectives. Yet even in B&I, the accounting and financial reporting systems that generate the GL and financial reports is likely to be the most significant IT risk of the entity.

3.2.2.8.2 – COTS versus Custom AIS Packages

One IT risk that is generally considered to be a high inherent risk across all entities is customized software, especially where the customizing is done by the entity's own employees. The theory is that bugs (which usually cause errors) are highly likely in custom software, and it is very difficult for seasoned veteran programmers to write code that has no bugs/errors on the first attempt. Thus it is likely that custom software, when implemented, will have bugs and errors.

Years ago, the IT profession came up with controls to minimize this risk and these controls include heavy duty testing, SDLC best practices, and project management principles. Testing, for example, includes unit testing of the specific program, module testing with that program integrated with the accounting function (e.g., payroll), system testing with that program integrated into a system (the accounting system including the GL), and enterprise testing with the AIS integrated with all other packages (including the financial reporting system if different). This process is best done offline; e.g., in a staging area. It should include IT QA/QC and end users as part of the testing. These factors reduce the high inherent risk associated with customized software.

Conversely, COTS can have a low inherent risk, depending on several factors. First, is the software vendor a reliable vendor (e.g., SAGE, Microsoft, etc.)? Second, does the vendor have a substantial market share in the vertical market or particular software market? Thirdly, has the software been in existence for several years, and is it now on a version number much higher than 1.0? If the answer to those questions are all 'yes', and the entity is using a recent version, then the IT inherent risk associated with that AIS package is generally viewed as relatively low. The assumption is if the software is provided by a reliable vendor, and been around for years, used by a large number of entities, and went through a large number of successful upgrades, then the controls in the applications are probably sufficient in scope and reliable in assurance, and thus the risk is relatively low.

3.2.2.8.3 – Enterprise & ERP Systems

Enterprise systems and ERP systems have a similar implication on IT risks; that is, they generally raise the level of risk associated with the AIS. The reason for this is multifaceted but is associated with the size and integration. By definition, enterprise systems and ERP systems incorporate and integrate all, or almost all, of the applications and systems of the entity. The broad scope of integration raises risks for errors and problems.

For COTS ERP systems, there is a need to meet the various needs of customers, so vendors have sophisticated configuration tables that allow standard software to have customized features such as which account to debit and credit for various standard transactions, or which user has authorization privileges for certain accounting transactions (see 3.2.2.1.1, Configuration Management).

Thus the CITP realizes that while the use of COTS ERP can reduce risks in certain ways, the integration and configuration aspects have particular IT risks and those risks need to be addressed and mitigated. Sound configuration practices, and sound audit trails for changes are necessary to mitigate them.

3.2.2.8.4 – E-Business Systems & Applications

The implication for e-business systems is the fact the nature of those systems involves billing and collecting. These systems use electronic payment systems (e.g., PayPal), shopping carts, and other features that are often outsourced to third parties. Thus the reliance of the online shopping or sales system as a whole is reliant on third-party applications and controls. The same principles of sound vendor management apply here as mentioned above.

3.2.3 – Logical Access

Risks associated with logical access have grown as entities have become more and more reliant on systems and technologies, and more and more those systems have expanded their connectivity (e.g., remote access, world-wide web and internet).

Thus a thorough understanding, analysis, and evaluation of logical access is generally something every IT audit would include, and at some point internal IT reviews would as well.

There are a number of tools used to implement logical access controls. In general, the more sensitive and risky a specific access is, the greater the scope or strength of the control; that is, access control is generally multifactor. For example, if the access is of a high risk, the employee may be assigned a separate set of login credentials for that particular access. Or that access may be controlled by a temporary PIN, swipe card, biometric, or other secondary access control mechanism.

A fact about access control effectiveness is: the closer the access control is to the data, the more effective the access control. This fact is true because there are layers to access and access controls could be implemented in more than one layer. Based on Exhibit 1.6 from the Risk Assessment chapter, access can be viewed by these layers (see Exhibit 3.11 here that replicates that exhibit).

EXHIBIT 3.11: Data Focused Financial Statement Risk Assessment

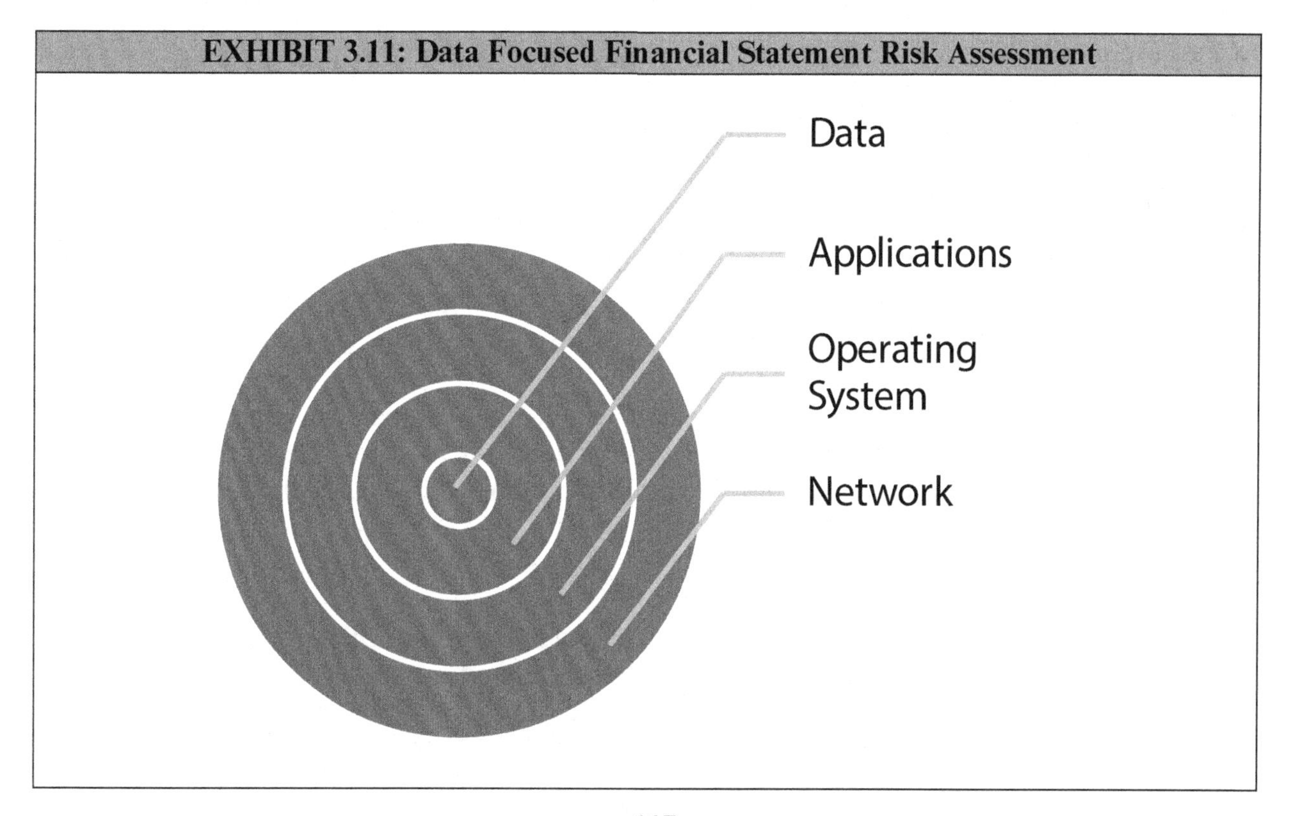

Logical access represents a significant IT risk but it also represents a significant IT control that can provide assurance about accounting transactions.

3.2.3.1 – Segregation of Duties

Logical access can be the tool whereby management provides logical segregation of duties (SoD) to mitigate risks virtually identical to physical SoD. That is, employees are granted restricted rights to applications and data based on their job description – role and responsibilities. Or put another way, critical functions such as authorization is controlled by allowing a limited number of designated employees access to those functions, applications, and/or data.

3.2.3.2 – Data Level

The most effective layer for logical access control is the data layer. Access controls above this layer can be effective, but generally less effective simply because they exist in layers above the data.

3.2.3.2.1 – Access to Data through the Application

The most common access to the data would be the application that uses a particular data file or database. Some applications provide separate access controls (e.g., Microsoft Dynamics) and some do not. Based on the premise above, the most effective access control to data is to have application access controls, and use sound access control principles in managing the application access controls. This access if often referred to as "front door" access.

Those principles would include restricted access for each user (based on his/her job description, for example), as well as formal processes and procedures for adding, changing, and deleting employee access. Employees who have no responsibilities for a certain application should of course have no access.

3.2.3.2.2 – Access to Data through the O/S et al.

Another manner of access to the data is through administrative (admin) rights of the operating system (O/S). All O/Ss provide access controls for administrative rights, and restricted rights for other access. Thus the CITP would be concerned with the number of employees who have admin rights and whether those individuals have roles and responsibilities commensurate with access being granted. Ideally, there should be a reasonably limited number of employees with admin rights. This access if often referred to as "back door" access.

The risk is that a person could access the raw data files or databases, make unauthorized changes, and thus cause problems with information being generated. It is also possible that person could sabotage the data (delete it for example), or steal it for some purpose. Each of these risks is usually significant enough to require mitigation.

3.2.3.2.3 – Access to Data by the DBA

A very similar situation and risk exists for the database administrator (DBA). This person knows a lot of information about the DBMS and data being housed, so much that this person/role represents a significant inherent risk. The DBA not only knows how to gain access to the data files, but knows enough about the data to do a tremendous amount of damage, if so inclined.

There are some tools today that prevent the DBA from accessing the database directly, but rather have the DBA manage the DBMS and have limited access to it (e.g., access to the data definitions but not the raw data itself). Thus the CITP would want some satisfaction that there is a mitigating control in place and operating effectively in order to have adequate assurance about access to the data.

3.2.3.3 – Application Level

Controls at the application level are some of the most important controls in the IT environment. SoD application controls were discussed above, as well as the axiom that logical access controls closest to the data are the more effective ones. But the application level is also the level at which most automated controls operate. And automated application controls are one of the most important aspects of controls and the CITP.

3.2.3.3.1 – Evaluate and Test Application Controls

If the ITGCs are reliable, and if the audit is going to rely on certain application controls, then testing of application controls is critically important in a financial audit. For B&I objectives, application controls are key to fulfilling managements P&P, and thus management will likely want to have them tested and evaluated for operating effectiveness by the IA function or other applicable group.

For those controls that are tested, the CITP would evaluate the relative effectiveness of those controls. For those that are deemed to be reasonably reliable, the financial audit could rely on those controls, which would affect the nature, timing, and extent (NTE) of audit procedures.

That test could be a test of one instance, a sample of one. Both the PCAOB and AICPA have stipulated in standards that under the right set of circumstances a test of one could be sufficient. One way those circumstances would be met is if the control objective has a dichotomous outcome: for example, the transaction was approved or not approved. Regardless, the CITP will need to develop a testing procedure that will result in sufficient evidence to evaluate the automated control.

3.2.3.3.2 – Evaluate and Test Logical SoD

Logical SoD can provide the same kind of assurance that a manual SoD provides; either in the gathering of financial audit evidence, or in evaluating the effectiveness of controls by B&I for internal purposes.

Testing them can begin with something as simple as verifying there is logical access controls of some kind. This test can be done by simply bringing up the critical application and seeing if there is a login, and if so, typing ENTER, ENTER to see if any passwords have been established. A review of the application technical manual should also reveal whether logical access is part of that application.

Once the CITP determines the application has logical access controls, the CITP would want to find a way to determine if there is SoD within the system. Sometimes that can be done by reviewing the access table where data is stored for granting access rights and comparing that to job descriptions or some other relevant information that describes who should be accessing what (i.e., who has the authority to be using that application or the function of that application, and at what level (no access, Read-Only access {RO}, or Read-Write access {RW}). The objective of whatever test is chosen is to determine whether evidence exists that the proper SoD has been implemented in the application (or the determination that the application does not have its own logical access controls).

The CITP might also be interested in password policies, if the application/system provides for its own[15]. The objective is to determine if standard best practices were followed in establishing password policies in the system.

3.2.3.3.3 – Evaluate and Test Spreadsheet Controls
A special case of application level controls is that associated with office productivity applications such as electronic spreadsheets or DBMS. There is a significant degree of use of electronic spreadsheets in financial reporting processes and thus controls over that spreadsheet are just as important, possibly more, than the controls in the AIS applications.

Generally, this situation involves a transfer of data from one or more internal AIS data files to a spreadsheet where some kind of manipulation will be made for financial reporting purposes: e.g., generate a trial balance, consolidation, post year-end journal entries, calculate depreciation, etc.

Controls would involve access and accuracy. For access, the softcopy of the electronic spreadsheet needs to be protected from unauthorized access, or put another way, limited to a minimum number of people in terms of employees' ability to access the file. This restricted access could be accomplished by putting the electronic document in a separate folder which is not shared to network users, but accessed by a separate login credential. Secondly, the spreadsheet itself needs to be protected – formulas in the cells etc. – by locking and password protecting cells and the spreadsheet. This feature would prevent the spreadsheet from errors due to accidental changes in the formulas or data.

Accuracy would involve testing the formulas formally and independently of the person building the spreadsheet, and some formal control to reconcile the final results with the appropriate external information or data. Documenting the independent testing (QA function) would be valuable to the CITP.

3.2.3.4 – Operating System Level
Operating systems (O/S) provide access to the files it houses. Because that access is to raw data, databases, data files, and application files, O/S access has a particularly high inherent risk.

The admin function should also set up a sufficient level of logs to provide information in case of an intrusion, fraud, and other relevant calamities where management or the auditor needs to understand who got in, where they got in, and what they had access to. Logs are critical to

[15] Some systems use the O/S access rights and password policy either by default or by admin's choice at setup. For instance, Microsoft Dynamics and other products use Active Directory factors when Microsoft's SQL Server and network O/S is being used to house the Dynamics applications.

investigating fraud and intrusions and thus testing for adequacy of logs is normally an important issue for management. Thus all servers should all be using tracking logs, especially Virtual Private Networks (VPNs) and other sensitive access servers.

3.2.3.4.1 – Limited Access

As is always the case with logical access, the goal is to limit or restrict the rights of users to the minimum – the access required to do their jobs. Thus sound logical access at the O/S level focuses on limiting access, especially admin access rights, to users. Therefore one key issue is limiting the number of personnel who have admin rights to a minimal number (depends on the size of the entity but probably at least two, and no more than a handful). Another key issue is to remember that when something goes wrong, it is helpful to review access rights at the O/S in case someone is abusing access.

There are tools available to the CITP to read the access rights in the O/S. Sometimes the O/S itself has an admin tool that will allow a user to view the access rights table/information. Tools like dump-sec are able to print out the access rights information in a digestible, readable form. Password policy should also be reviewed for adequacy of the various policy options – when relevant to the audit or review. Usually, the O/S allows admin rights to access the password policy options and set up things like the length of a password, how long it remains active before the user is forced to change it, and factors to "strengthen" the password[16].

3.2.3.4.2 – Admin Rights

The broadest access is reserved for "admin" (administrator) who can essentially view and access any file or folder contained in the O/S – for purposes of managing the O/S (e.g., making patches) and correcting mistakes, flaws, and other minor changes to files or folders. The admin access usually also assigns logical access credentials to the O/S to all other personnel.

For instance, a person can commit a fraud and if he/she has O/S admin rights, files can be deleted, accessed and raw data changed, or other activities to hide a fraud or destroy evidence. It is equally risky if too many users have admin rights because of the increased opportunity for someone to make a mistake using admin access.

3.2.3.5 – Network Level

The network level generally resides above the O/S and application and thus needs to provide adequate access control to users. Similar to the operating system, access rights and administrative rights to the network are critical aspects to control; or put another way, are usually assessed at a relatively high IR. There is also a concern for external unauthorized access risk.

3.2.3.5.1 – Firewalls

Firewall controls basically address the information security (InfoSec) triangle of major points: availability, confidentiality, and integrity. So an effective firewall will provide for adequate availability of its services and functionality, adequate confidentiality of the data it stores and

[16] Generally, mixing lower and upper case, forcing at least one number, and forcing at least one special character are all means of "strengthening" the password.

processes, and adequate integrity over the results produced as information. Integrity and confidentiality are at risk from external hackers, and internally for the entity's own employees. Some hacker tools are aimed at bringing systems down (e.g., denial of service), so even availability is also at risk from external or internal malicious attacks.

Firewall technology provides tools that can effectively reduce the risk of external unauthorized access and other external risks. Firewalls usually have configurations that allow various settings to filter traffic and establish connectivity rules. Thus the CITP would be interested in examining the settings of the firewall, which exist in hardware or software. There are a variety of types of firewalls including packet filtering firewalls, inspection firewalls, and proxy firewalls (especially related to applications). Wireless networks present additional risks as communications are easier to intercept than wired ones if not encrypted or protected.

One problem with firewalls and threats or risks is the fact that most malicious activity is actually perpetrated by insiders, such as employees, contractors, etc. After all, anyone inside the entity is generally treated as a trusted source by networks, because they have legitimate login credentials. A way to overcome that problem is to put a second firewall between the network and back-end systems to filter who gains access to critical systems such as financial reporting systems.

One major control is to patch vulnerabilities with due diligence. Potential intruder types are constantly studying and attempting to break into systems, probing for weaknesses in software and technologies. Vendors become aware of these vulnerabilities and issue patches to keep the "bad guys" from breaking into systems. Entities need to have sound policies and procedures to be aware of relevant patches, and to effectively implement them timely to reduce the risks associated with those vulnerabilities. The current preference is to build automated systems to respond to alerts and automatically update patches to the system.

Another major control area is encryption of data at rest or in transit (e.g., over the Internet) when that data is extremely sensitive (e.g., payroll data, credit card data) or there is a high risk of interception in communications. Encryption tools have various strengths, and encryption is not always needed or the only control solution. For example, Virtual Private Networks (VPNs) can securely transmit data over the Internet.

Putting a combination of effective tools and controls into place for protection of networks is referred to as "hardening" the system. Some other controls to implement would include controls in the following areas: buffer overflow, adware/spyware, anti-virus, certain Internet ports, and intrusion detection. The latter uses patterns of known exploitation to try to recognize an unauthorized attack, an intrusion. Intrusion detection systems are vitally important for entities that have a lot of public exposure, name recognition, or other factor that attracts malicious attacks by these types of cyber criminals.

A key to providing reasonable assurance over network security is to have a current, well-documented network diagram. Trust is more easily seen and addressed with this diagram than without it. Best practices generally state InfoSec BEGINS with this diagram.

3.2.3.5.2 – Network Access Controls

Access controls are based on limited or restricted access. That is, each person or group of persons is granted the least amount of privileges on the network as possible. For example, Active Directory (Microsoft) provides settings to establish access rights to individuals or groups, and do so with a relatively high degree of granularity. Access rights would include privileges for access to applications, folders, files, and other objects. Regardless of the tool or methodology, the CITP would examine and evaluate network access control based on the principle of restricted access.

3.2.4 – Backup & Recovery

Backup and recovery involves the appropriate backup of data, a suitable business continuity plan, and an effective disaster recovery plan. Just like all other ITGCs, the specific scope of this control is dependent on the entity and its proprietary risk associated with backup and recovery.

3.2.4.1 – Data Backup

The entity should have policies and procedures that are effective in enabling the entity to recover fully its data should the data be destroyed or lost. There are some principles, or best practices, associated with backup and recovery of data. The minimum P&P would be:

- Regular backups of data
- Offsite storage of data
- Testing of recovery

Regular backups include timely backups; whatever would be considered timely to the entity. For some, that might be once a week. For other entities it might be every day, and even some every hour.

Data backups can also be created manually or automatically. The latter is considered to be more reliable. Using software, data backups can be created with specific criteria (what data is subject to the current backup) and at specified times. This operation is also fairly easy to test or observe (e.g., a walkthrough).

Data backup could be to a physical media such as tape or disk. It could also be online to a remote server or media. There are a growing number of service providers who offer data storage (e.g., cloud services). The latter has the advantage of reduced costs (especially transporting physical media) and easier access. Because it is usually accessible by an Internet connection, retrieval of data backups from the cloud is simple and fast. The type of media could affect the reliability of the backup/recovery process. For example, CDs, DVDs, and tape are subject to ease of loss versus online servers, and subject to transport risk. Tape is subject to being corrupted or erased by strong magnetic objects.

The data backup procedures should minimize risk or recovery by using multiple backups. The traditional grandfather-father-son methodology illustrates this risk minimizing process. For example, the entity backs up data every day on one set of media or to one digital source ("son"). Then at the end of week, a backup is made to a second set of media or to a second digital source ("father"). Then at the end of the month, a backup is made to a third set of media, or third digital source ("grandfather"). This process reduces the risk that if a restoration fails, the entity is stuck with some kind of manual restoration that is high risk. That is, if during the restoration of yesterday's backup (son), the media fails to be able to restore properly, then the entity can fall back on the weekly backup (father). Likewise if that restoration fails, there is one more backup media to try to restore (grandfather, end of month). This methodology can be part of the criteria for backups; e.g., when data is backed up, the system only backs what has changed, and puts together disparate backups that can quickly be restored based on the date for which to restore.

The data should be stored at a reasonable distance from the entity's operations. That distance is necessary in the case of a natural disaster such as a tornado, hurricane, or flood, so that the disaster does not destroy the operational data, operational computers, and the data backups simultaneously.

Lastly, the entity needs to test the recovery of data at least once a year. That test should be robust enough to provide assurance that data can be effectively recovered if a disaster or other event occurs and causes loss of operational data. The test should be adequately documented to provide assurance to the auditors that it was restored properly. For simpler systems and lower risks, that evidence could take the form of a screen shot that is converted into hardcopy or softcopy document. The CITP would want assurance of the successful testing in some substantive, adequate evidence.

3.2.4.2 – Disaster Recovery/Business Continuity Planning

Some deleterious IT events only require a restoration of data backups, followed by any recovery of events, transactions, and data that occurred in the short interim between the backup and recovery. But some events are more catastrophic and include severe damages to the operational IT and systems.

For instance, some system crashes or malicious attacks cause systems to be down a lengthy time. In those cases, the entity needs more than just restoration of data; they need a Business Continuity Plan (BCP). These plans take into account sever interruptions, a lengthy interruption, and the need to not only restore data but fix/restore computers, O/Ss, and other components affected by the pandemic event.

Worse yet, the entity could be the victim of a catastrophic event such as a fire, flood, tornado, or hurricane where technologies, systems, and data are completely destroyed, as well as the facilities and supplies needed to properly operate and function. In this case, a Disaster Recovery Plan (DRP) is needed to address the scope of the event. A DRP provides for not only restoring the data but all aspects of the systems, should they be destroyed or effectively become unavailable for an unaccepted length of time.

The scope of what the CITP does regarding BCP/DRP depends on the dependency of the entity upon its IT for operations, and the objective. For financial audits, the audit objective involves the degree to which a disaster or significant event can lead to the RMM. Sometimes it will potentially lead to the RMM and sometimes it will not. The procedures the CITP would need to perform in a financial audit is directly associated with the level of risk assessed at the RMM. The higher the RMM, the more in-depth ("stronger") the procedures to test DRP would need to be.

For B&I, the scope is likely to be management's desire to know the BCP or DRP is reliable for sake of operations, because the entity relies upon IT to some significant degree. In this case, the CITP would have a more in-depth set of procedures in order to gain adequate assurance the BCP or DRP would work effectively when called upon.

Some of the steps or items that a thorough BCP/DRP would cover include:

- A written plan
- A predefined ranked list of applications in the order of optimal restoration
- A recovery team, with identified roles and responsibilities
- A backup facility, including building, power, desks, etc.
- A backup of infrastructure/platform
- A backup of O/S(s)
- A backup for computers and workstations
- A backup copy of all applications
- A reliable, relatively current backup of data
- A backup for technical and operational manuals
- A backup of supplies (checks, invoices, paper, etc.)
- A formal, structured test of the full plan
- A regular test of the plan (probably at least once per fiscal year)

The recovery team aspect should include the specific steps by specific personnel in recovery operations. Who starts the process? Where do they meet as a team initially, or where does each one report? What role does each member play in restoring operations?

Some types of backup provisions cover multiple steps. For example, a "hot site" is a building with power on and a computer (main server or mainframe) running that an entity can contract for backup services. Thus a hot site would provide for the building/power/desks/etc., the infrastructure, O/S, and at least some of the computers (especially the servers).

A mutual aid pact is one where another entity uses the same mainframe, or server, and O/S. An example would be a retail chain where each location has its own systems and some excess capacity. In the mutual aid pact, each party agrees to have excess capacity on its server and allow the other party to use its system for BCP/DRP needs. Naturally, the agreement works both ways. Like the hot site, it provides multiple aspects of DRP needs.

A "cold site" provides only a building with power. So when an entity employs a cold site, it still needs to find a way to provide for the infrastructure, O/S, and computers.

The CITP would need to reconcile the risks associated with disasters and/or major business interruptions and determine whether the plan properly mitigates the risks and assessed level of risk. The higher the risk of downtime, the greater the scope and reliability of the BCP/DRP needs to be.

3.2.4.3 – Contingency Planning

Management will likely need to provide for contingency planning other than disaster recovery and business continuity for its IT and systems. Other damaging events that carry any substantial risk should have been identified in the IT risk assessment (see Dimension 1). For instance, risks associated with errors in applications, mistakes in installing hardware, bugs in coding applications, security of data in storage, errors in communications, risks in data integrity during transfers, and other similar risks associated with IT.

The internal CITP will want to be aware of the various IT risks associated with the entity and its systems, business processes, IT function, and controls in order to properly address or review those risks. The best way to ensure that information is available is by applying the risk assessment model described in Dimension 1 with due diligence.

3.2.4.3.1 – Incident Response Plan

There are a number of bad things that can happen related to IT that could potentially affect its public image or customer base in a negative manner. For instance, if a company were to experience a malicious attack on its system where data on credit cards of its customers were compromised, and if that information gets to the public, it could not only affect its customers but prospective customers as well (i.e. its ability to maintain its market share, much less grow). The same would be true for most frauds, especially for not-for-profit (NFP) organizations. In order to mitigate these kinds of risks, management should make plans in advance of the incident in order to effectively respond to the negative event. That plan is known as an incident response plan (IRP).

First, the incident response plan would be thoroughly developed and tested in advance of potential negative incidents. Second, it should be written, and become part of the entity's policies and procedures. Third, and like the DRP, it should include a team which would be responsible for carrying out the actual response. Fourth, it should describe the investigation process of the incident (e.g., who or what department specifically is in charge of the incident response investigation, to whom does the team report, etc.). Because incidents could range from fraud to loss of data to very high-tech intrusions, the team needs to be broad enough to handle a variety of incidents.

The purpose of an IRP is to minimize the damages that could happen as a result of the incident. A secondary purpose is usually to provide feedback to management on changes to preventive or detective controls related to the business processes and functions associated with the incident (i.e. how can the entity keep that particular event from occurring again).

3.2.4.4 – Testing

A critical success factor in backup and recovery, incident response, and contingency planning is to adequately test the plans BEFORE they are actually needed in response to a negative event. That testing should be completely thorough, done with realism in mind, and tested often enough to be highly reliable.

The test should include all relevant aspects of the plan. For instance, for DRP, it should include recovering facility, hardware, operating system, applications, and other components – not just recovery of the data backups.

In general, DRP/BCP should be tested at least once a year. Other contingency plans would be subject to judgment as to how often they should be tested, and possibly to what extent (e.g., incident response that requires dealing with the press and public).

In regards to realism, some tests are conducted where the person in charge of the test asks the entire entity to assume the building has burned and report to the disaster recovery site and begin a restoration of operations. Another realism factor is to have essentially a replicated system of the enterprise's full system for the purpose of testing DRP, BCP, and other needs. That in-house facility is referred to as a staging area.

3.2.4.4.1 – Staging Area

A staging area houses a computer platform identical, or nearly identical, to the enterprise's operational system. It also has copies of all of its applications, operating systems, and other primary components for processing data and performing necessary business functions and processes.

Staging areas are not only useful in testing DRP and BCP plans, but also very helpful in testing applications. By using a full replica of the enterprise system, the application can be tested stand alone by programmers, with other applications in that module (accounting function), across all accounting functions with which it interfaces (e.g., general ledger), and even data transfers and other possible middleware or special applications. That is, it provides the most robust of testing arrangements, because it is able to fully simulate actual IT operations.

A staging area is also used to test (sometimes called "burn in") hardware before it is put into operations.

The best situation is for the staging area system to be located at a different site than the operational systems in case it is needed as part of the DRP.

3.2.5 – Service Organizations

Service organizations present unique IT risk in that for the most part, the controls are outside the entity and not under the control of the entity's management. There is a way to minimize or mitigate this risk of controls at the third party provider.

Basically, the need here is twofold: is the vendor reliable, and does the vendor have adequate controls; sufficient and effective controls to mitigate the IT risks associated with the process and data being outsourced?

3.2.5.1 – Outsourcing of IT Services

For the CITP, third-party providers and service organization issues focus on the outsourcing of IT services. Entities might outsource the IT help desk, IT support (e.g., network support), application development, or processing of some accounting process (e.g., payroll). The native risk associated with outsourcing needs to be addressed, specifically the nature and effectiveness of necessary controls at the service organization associated with the service being provided.

3.2.5.2 – Service Level Agreements

One procedure for evaluating the reliability of the vendor, the nature of the services, and the degree of controls being used is to review the service level agreement (SLA) between the user entity and the service organization (SO). That agreement should not only include terms of the contract, but provide for minimal controls to be provided, and how the user expects the SO to respond to auditors and others who need to understand, examine, and evaluate controls at the SO.

3.2.5.3 – Service Organization Control Reports

Another procedure for evaluating the effectiveness of the SO's controls is to review a Service Organization Control (SOC) report resulting from the engagement of a public accounting firm by the SO to examine and evaluate its controls in an agreed-upon procedure (AUP) engagement.

The standards for such reports have been in place for many years at the AICPA as Trust Services – the old Sys Trust principles and generally accepted privacy principles (GAPP). In 2011, these services are combined into Trust Services and the resulting reports are known as SOC2 and SOC3. SOC1 is the new AUP report associated with SSAE No. 16 (replaces service auditors' responsibilities associated with the original SAS No. 70 "audit").

In essence, a SOC report discusses the design effectiveness, implementation, and operating effectiveness of the identified controls being examined at a SO. A type I report only addresses the first two aspects of the controls and a type II addresses all three.

3.2.5.3.1 – SOC1

For the financial audit, a SOC1 report should provide information on the assurance of relevant controls (ICFR). For most user auditors, the type II will be the one needed.

When the SOC1 report is read by the user auditors, they are looking for the controls directly related to the assessed level of risk in the RMM. The user auditors would decide if the SOC1 report properly addressed all of the controls or not, as well as the impact of the results of the procedures of the service CPA performing the AUP, and as described in the written SOC1 report about assurance over the service provided and its associated data.

3.2.5.3.2 – SOC2

A SOC2 report provides assurance over IT controls related to security, availability, processing integrity, confidentiality, and privacy. A type II SOC2 report would express an opinion on the operating effectiveness of the controls evaluated by the user auditor. A SOC2 report is a restricted report and cannot be released to the public. It is an agreed-upon procedure engagement using the attest standards (typically AT101 or AT201).

3.2.5.3.3 – SOC3

A SOC3 provides the same kind of report on controls as SOC2 but can be used as a marketing and promotion tool to the public to demonstrate the sufficiency of the SO's controls, and basic management, of the service related to the customer's service being provided, and the identified controls related to it. The report is slightly different from a SOC2, but its chief distinction is the fact it is NOT a restricted report.

3.3 – APPLICATION CONTROLS

Applications controls are not only important for assessing assurance over critical financial reporting applications and data for external auditors and CITPs, but also for internal auditors and CITPs to get assurance business processes are following management's policies and procedures, the intentions of management. The latter can have implications about operational efficiency, effectiveness, customer satisfaction, effective decision making, and a variety of other relevant issues.

An application control could be defined as a control that occurs automatically, usually through computer systems, based on predefined criteria, circumstances, times, dates, or events. Application controls are embedded and specific to accounting applications. They are intended to provide controls for authorization, approval, delivery of product or service, transactional recording, integrity of data, and audit trail.

Usually, these controls are described as either being preventive, detective, or corrective controls (see 1.3.2.2 for more on P-D-C model of controls). The purpose is to prevent, detect, or correct certain adverse situations from affecting systems, data, and business processes.

Generally, applications controls are developed to provide assurance over financial transaction functions: initiation, authorization, recording, processing, and reporting. Exhibit 3.12 provides some sample application controls for each of these vital functions.

Application controls are of course the subject for tests of controls (ToC) when the external auditors have sufficient reliance upon an application control. The external auditor would identify an application control where that control objective is relevant to the further audit procedures and RMM, and then perform a ToC to assess its operational effectiveness (i.e. does the control perform consistently across time as designed to perform). The ToC would involve some technical knowledge and maybe even technology tools (e.g., CAATs).

EXHIBIT 3.12: FINANCIAL TRANSACTION FUNCTIONS – SAMPLE APPLICATION CONTROLS	
Initiation	– Data transmission controls – Input edits – Validations – Security
Authorization	– Programmed transaction approvals – Restricted access to information/data files
Record	– Database updates – Automated feeds
Process	– Calculations and related tables – File checking – Automated restrictions to sensitive transactions
Report	– Automated posting to subsidiary ledgers or general ledgers – Automated reporting whether commercial application or "user-defined"

3.4 – INFORMATION SECURITY

Information security overlaps with some of the controls mentioned above, especially the discussion on SOC2/SOC3 (i.e. Trust Services), and DRP/BCP. The basic InfoSec "triangle" provides the three primary areas of concern: confidentiality, (data and processing) integrity, and availability.

Confidentiality addresses the data being stored and also data in transit. The objective would be to ensure the confidentiality of systems, its processes, and its data being created, transported, and stored.

Integrity focuses on the accuracy and reliability of data, the systems and processes that generate it, and the information produced from data. A key operational concern of CITPs is the decision making usefulness related to data integrity. That is, the quality of decisions is directly proportional to the quality (i.e. integrity) of the information used to make them. A key external audit concern is the trustworthiness of the data in the financial reports, which is clearly about integrity.

The last leg of the InfoSec triangle is availability. Obviously availability is about the systems, technologies, and associated processes and data being available when needed for business operations. Therefore, availability is primarily an operational and internal concern rather than an external auditor's concern. However, it is conceivable that availability could lead to some reasonable scenario where the RMM would be great enough to need to be addressed.

There are several concepts and procedures the CITP could use to assess the level of assurance over information security.

3.4.1 – Understanding IT Policies, Procedures, and Standards to Ensure Information/Data Security

Like many, if not most, of the assurance projects with which a CITP would be involved, this one begins with a review of policies and procedures in order to gain an understanding about InfoSec. In the IT P&P, there should be a segment dedicated to InfoSec. That segment would address issues that generally would be classified in the triangle components mentioned above.

The CITP would want to gain an understanding of the intended standards that would be followed in developing, deploying, and monitoring InfoSec for the entity. Those standards should be tied to one of the professional organizations (e.g., System Administration Networking and Security {SANS}, International Information System Security Certification Consortium Inc. {ISC2}, International Systems Security Association (ISSA), Computer Security Institute (CSI), ISACA, etc.) or best practices usually also associated with one or more of those professions.

3.4.2 – Understanding Hardware and Physical Controls to Ensure Information/Data Security

Then the CITP would want to perform walkthroughs, observations, and inspections to gain an understanding of the physical controls in place related to IT hardware and infrastructure.

3.4.2.1 – Computer Center

One area where physical controls are essential to InfoSec is the main computer center. Because of the fact the computer center usually houses the main servers and other sensitive IT, controlling physical access is a high risk. Therefore, the CITP would be checking for physical controls such as locked doors, cameras, and monitoring incoming traffic. Monitoring traffic could be done electronically, manually, and even by security guards. Its purpose is to make it difficult to gain unauthorized entrance to the Center, if the risk is high enough to warrant it.

3.4.2.2 – Server Room

In the computer center, the servers that house financial applications and other critical systems or applications are generally the items of highest risk. Appropriate physical controls usually involve not only physical access to the Center as a whole, but a second set of physical controls to the room containing the servers. In fact, the servers SHOULD be in a separate room with separate physical controls. Those controls also would generally be of a higher nature than those used to access the Center. For example, doors to the Center might be accessible by an authorized swipe card, but for the server room access might require both a swipe card and a biometric (e.g., fingerprint).

In addition, it might be useful to have glass walls around the server room so authorized personnel in the Center could visually see an unauthorized person in the server room. The main objective is to provide physical access controls at the same level as the risk and sensitivity, which would be very high for servers.

3.4.2.3 – Sensitive Hardcopy Information

A similar circumstance exists regarding printed reports and information being generated in the Center. If printouts are high risk, highly sensitive, physical access to the printer and/or printouts needs to also be of a high nature. Thus if highly sensitive printouts are being generated, appropriate access controls might involve a separate print room with separate and more elaborate access controls than the Center's access. Data control groups have been used in the past as physical controls to physically handle hardcopy printouts. The persons in data control would be people with adequate SoD, not involved with inputs or processing of data.

3.4.3 – Understanding Software and Other Process Controls to Ensure Information/Data Security

In addition to necessary physical access controls over the Center, servers, and sensitive hardcopies, InfoSec controls involve those associated with data integrity. Data integrity is dependent on controls in the software applications and business processes that create and manipulate data, and in controls associated with data "at rest" (storage). The CITP will want to gain an understanding of what controls are in operations related to this aspect of InfoSec.

Specifically, what is the nature and effectiveness of application controls over the relevant data? What is the nature and effectiveness of business process controls, especially manual ones? For instance, in payroll processing for legacy systems, there is often a checklist to review and reconcile certain information between "runs" of the legacy payroll (i.e. the separate application steps in payroll). Since that checklist is manual, how reliable is the manual process for reconciling information between those runs/steps?

Then once the data is at rest (in storage), what controls are in place to ensure ongoing integrity and security? For instance, restricted access controls discussed earlier could be used to provide security over data, files, and folders. The better the logical access controls, the more assurance there is about data integrity at rest.

3.4.4 – Understanding Concepts of Security Authorization and Authentication

The logical access control effectiveness is somewhat dependent on separate authorization and authentication controls. ***Authorization*** is about the login credentials and restricting the access to that user on a need to know basis. But, authorization controls by themselves are not adequate for higher risks. Specifically, a hacker or intruder will try to obtain or guess login credentials and if successful will be able to gain access to a network, but that is still unauthorized access.

To prevent this scenario, ***authentication*** controls are needed. The objective of authentication controls is the person using those credentials is who he/she claims to be. The ultimate authentication control is biometric and the control is the person (e.g., fingerprint). But authentication could be some form of multifactor access controls such as: additional credentials, temporary PINs, security questions, and biometrics. In this scenario, the user would need the appropriate login credentials to be authorized to use the system, and then the system would authenticate that person with the additional layer of access controls.

The CITP would need to consider the need for authentication (i.e. higher risks) and whether the appropriate access controls are in place, and whether they are operating effectively.

3.4.5 – Understanding Concepts of Encryption

Another set of controls for data at rest or in transit is encryption controls. Like authentication access controls, encryption is necessary when the risks are high. For example, if the entity saves credit card data, and if that file is on a computer connected to the Internet, then the risk is definitely high (on a scale of 1 to 10, probably a 10). One mitigating control for this scenario would be to encrypt the file containing the credit card data.

Similarly, data in transit across the Internet that has high risk is a good subject for encryption. In fact, the more reliable online vendors usually employ encryption for online purchases for the same objective as the credit card data at rest above.

Encryption basically scrambles the data using some algorithm that is sophisticated enough to reasonably prevent a successful translation if someone intercepts the data. There are various methodologies (public keys, private keys), levels of encryption engines (128, 192, 256), and types of authentication (method of encrypting and decrypting) that the CITP will need to understand should he/she need to assess the effectiveness of an entity's encryption. The strength of the encryption is the combination of all three aspects, and explains why some consider 128-bit encryption engines using high levels of authentication as equal or superior to those systems that use 256-bit engines.[17] Currently, 256-bit encryption is the highest level of security as an engine, but 128-bit is often used with reliable results. For example, Secure Sockets Layer (SSL), used by most online vendors, uses a 128-bit encryption engine.

3.5 – PREPARING AN IT AUDIT PLAN

Preparing the further audit procedures of the IT audit plan is dependent on an appropriate understanding of internal controls.

3.5.1 – Scoping of an IT Audit or Review

The above is not intended to be a comprehensive checklist for every IT audit or review, but rather a fairly comprehensive coverage of things that might be relevant for internal controls for engagements or reviews that are performed by CITPs.

One framework for scope consideration includes the objective, level of risk, and the IT space of the entity (see Exhibit 3.13 Venn diagram). The objective segment would be either objectives of an external engagement (e.g., financial audit, or SOC engagement) or the objectives of an internal review (e.g., management's directions to evaluate external threats via the Internet, security of data, or effectiveness of access controls). The level of risk means to incorporate the risk-based approach in the audit or review. The IT space includes all of the elements of the IT function of the entity. Using a Venn diagram illustrates the thought process and judgment that leads to an overlap of these three components that effectively determine the scope of the IT space that should be included in the audit or review.

For instance, the more risk identified, the more the overlap between risk and IT space. Likewise when objectives do NOT overlap with the IT space, then IT is generally irrelevant for that part of the audit or review; conversely, when IT is involved with objectives, it increases the overlap. For example, in a financial audit, when financial systems and automated controls are identified that are linked to audit objectives, more of the IT space overlaps with the objectives. The "sweet spot" is when IT risk is elevated (generally, assessed high), and IT is relevant to the objectives, then the overlapping of all three areas in the Venn diagram will identify the scope of the IT space to include.

[17] See Seagate whitepaper: "128-Bit Versus 256-Bit AES Encryption", 2008, http://www.seagate.com/staticfiles/docs/pdf/whitepaper/tp596_128-bit_versus_256_bit.pdf

EXHIBIT 3.13: FRAMEWORK FOR SCOPING IT

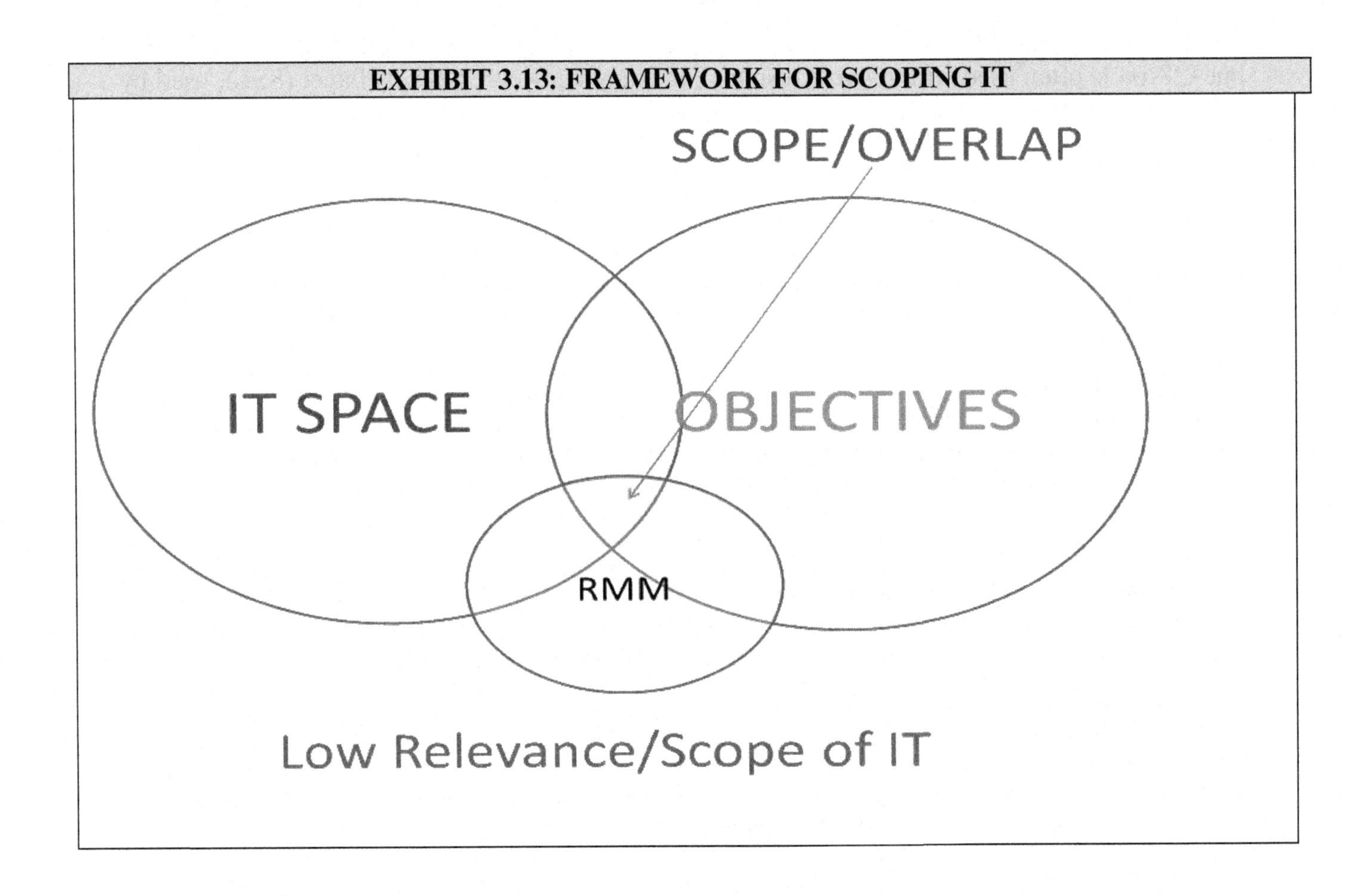

Advanced Reading Recommendations:

AICPA/ITEC. "Information Technology Considerations in Risk-Based Auditing" (discussion paper). 2007. AICPA: online.

AICPA. SAS No. 104-111.

AICPA, Trust Services (2010).

COSO. "Internal Control over Financial Reporting – Guidance for Smaller Public Companies", Volume I, II and III. 2006.

Moeller, Robert R. "IT Audit, Control, and Security". 2010. Wiley: Hoboken, NJ.

PCAOB, AS5.

Weber, Ron. "Information Systems Control and Audit". 1999. Prentice Hall: Upper Saddle River, NJ.

GLOSSARY:

Application Controls

Application controls are internal controls, whether automated or manual, which operate at the transaction-level with the objectives of ensuring that:

- Proper authorization is obtained to initiate and enter transactions;
- Applications are protected from unauthorized access;
- Users are only allowed access to those data and functions in an application that they should have access to;
- Errors in the operation of an application will be prevented or detected and corrected in a timely manner;
- Application output is protected from unauthorized access or disclosure;
- Reconciliation activities are implemented when appropriate to ensure that information is complete and accurate; and
- Ensuring that high-risk transactions are appropriately controlled.

Assertion Level Risks

Assertion level risks are risks that are limited to one or more specific assertions in an account or in several accounts, for example, the valuation of inventory or the occurrence of sales. Assertion level risks are addressed by the nature, timing, and extent of further audit procedures, which may include substantive procedures or a combination of tests of controls and substantive procedures.

The risk of material misstatement at the assertion level has two components:

- Inherent Risk (IR), which is the susceptibility of an assertion to a material misstatement, assuming that there are no related controls. Inherent risk is greater for some assertions and related account balances, classes of transactions, and disclosures than for others.
- Control Risk (CR), which is the risk that a material misstatement that could occur in an assertion will not be prevented or detected by the entity's internal control on a timely basis. Control risk is a function of the effectiveness of the design and operation of the entity's internal control.

Automated Control

Controls automation involves leveraging technology to build and enforce internal controls with the least manual intervention possible. It can take many forms, including better use of available system configuration options of the kind common in enterprise resource planning (ERP) systems, to using workflow and imaging technologies to automate and drive processes from start to completion.

Control Risk

Control Risk is the risk that a material misstatement will not be detected or prevented by the entity's internal control on a timely basis. The auditor must consider the risk of misstatement individually and in aggregate with other misstatements.

Detection Risk
Detection Risk is the risk that the auditor will not detect a material misstatement in the financial statements of the entity being audited.

End-user Computing
In the context of this paper, end-user computing is a function developed using common desktop tools like spreadsheets that are used in financial processes for purposes of determining amounts used for accounting and financial reporting purposes.

Electronic Commerce
Electronic business applications or processes that facilitate commercial transactions. Electronic commerce can involve electronic funds transfer, supply chain management, e-marketing, online marketing, online transaction processing, electronic data interchange (EDI), automated inventory management systems, and automated data collection systems.
Source: Wikipedia; http://en.wikipedia.org/wiki/Electronic_commerce

Emerging Technologies
Changes or advances in technologies such as information technology, nanotechnology, biotechnology, cognitive science, robotics, and artificial intelligence.

Financial Statement Level Risks
Financial statement level risks are risks that may affect many different accounts and several assertions. Financial statement level risks typically require an overall response, such as providing more supervision to the engagement team or incorporating additional elements of unpredictability in the selection of your audit procedures.

Further Audit Procedures
SAS 110 defines further audit procedures that include tests of the operating effectiveness of controls, where relevant or necessary, and substantive procedures, whose nature, timing, and extent are responsive to the assessed risks of material misstatement at the relevant assertion level.

Inherent Risk
Inherent risk is the susceptibility that a relevant assertion could be misstated assuming that there are no other related controls. The auditor should consider the risk of misstatement individually as well as in aggregate with other misstatements, assuming there are no related controls.

Internal Control
Internal control is a process, effected by an entity's board of directors, management and other personnel, designed to provide reasonable assurance regarding the achievement of objectives in the following categories:

- Effectiveness and efficiency of operations
- Reliability of financial reporting
- Compliance with applicable laws and regulations

Key Concepts:

- Internal control is a process. It is a means to an end, not an end in itself.
- Internal control is affected by people. It's not merely policy manuals and forms, but people at every level of an organization.
- Internal control can be expected to provide only reasonable assurance, not absolute assurance, to an entity's management and board.
- Internal control is geared to the achievement of objectives in one or more separate but overlapping categories.

Source: COSO; http://www.coso.org/IC.htm

For additional resources on internal control over financial reporting visit www.cpa2biz.com for:

- *Internal Control—Integrated Framework* (product no. 990012kk), a paperbound version of the COSO report that established a common definition of internal control different parties can use to assess and improve their control systems. [http://www.cpa2biz.com/AST/Main/CPA2BIZ_Primary/InternalControls/COSO/PRDOVR~PC-990009/PC-990009.jsp]
- *Financial Reporting Fraud: A Practical Guide to Detection and Internal Control* (product no. 029879kk), a paperbound publication for CPAs in both public practice and industry. [http://www.cpa2biz.com/AST/Main/CPA2BIZ_Primary/FinancialManagement/Finance/FinancialReporting/PRDOVR~PC-029879/PC-029879.jsp]
- In July 2006, COSO released its guidance, "Internal Control over Financial Reporting—Guidance for Smaller Public Companies," which may assist companies and auditors to understand the applicability of the COSO Framework to smaller entities. This publication can be ordered from the www.cpa2biz.com or through any of the sponsoring organizations. [http://www.cpa2biz.com/AST/Main/CPA2BIZ_Primary/InternalControls/COSO/PRDOVR~PC-990017/PC-990017.jsp]

Internal Control, Five Components of (COSO)

The Committee of Sponsoring Organizations of the Treadway Commission (COSO) outlines internal control in their *Internal Control-Integrated Framework*, as consisting of five related components that must be present for an entity to achieve effective internal controls. These five components are:

- The control environment
- Risk assessment
- Control activities
- Information and communication
- Monitoring

IT Auditor

A professional possessing the necessary knowledge and skills to understand and audit an entity's IT environment, systems, or applications, in support of a financial statement audit, internal audit, or other form of attestation engagement. The IT Auditor often has deep domain-specific knowledge or specialized skills (e.g. in use of computerized tools) that makes them particularly competent to understand the IT environment (and its associated risks) or perform IT-specific audit procedures.

IT Control Risk
IT control risk is a type of control risk where the source of risk is related to the use of IT in the processing of transactions or security of underlying data.

IT General Controls
IT general controls are internal controls, generally implemented and administered by an organization's IT department. The objectives of ITGC are to:

- Ensure the proper operation of the applications and availability of systems;
- Protect both data and programs from unauthorized changes;
- Protect both data and programs from unauthorized access and disclosure;
- Provide assurance that applications are developed and subsequently maintained, such that they provide the functionality required to process transactions and provide automated controls; and
- Ensure an organization's ability to recover from system and operational failures related to IT.

Logical Access Controls
Logical access controls are policies, procedures, and automated controls that exist for the purpose of restricting access to information assets to only authorized users.

Material Weakness
A material weakness is a significant deficiency, or combination of significant deficiencies, that results in more than a remote likelihood that a material misstatement of the financial statements will not be prevented or detected.
Source: AICPA; http://www.aicpa.org/download/members/div/auditstd/AU-00325.PDF

Materiality
Materiality is "the magnitude of an omission or misstatement of accounting information that, in the light of surrounding circumstances, makes it probable that the judgment of a reasonable person relying on the information would have been changed by the omission or misstatement." Materiality is influenced by the needs of financial statement users who rely on the financial statements to make judgments about the client's financial position and results of operation and the auditor must consider audit risk and must determine a materiality level for the financial statements.

Operating Effectiveness
Operating effectiveness is concerned with determining if "controls operate with sufficient effectiveness to achieve the related control objectives during a specified period." This is a function of how control is applied, the consistency with which it is applied, and by whom it is applied.

Risk Assessment Procedures

Risk assessment procedures are audit procedures performed to obtain an understanding of the entity and its environment, including its internal control, to assess the risk of material misstatement at the financial statement and relevant assertion levels.

Risk assessment procedures include:

- Inquiries of management and others within the entity
- Analytical procedures
- Observation and inspection.

Risk-Based Approach

The methodology which provides assurance that significant risks associated with audit objectives have been identified, and that audit procedures address them to adequately gain assurance about the objectives of the audit, and the mitigation of those risks or nature of residual risk that exists.

Risk of Material Misstatement

The risk of material misstatement is defined as the risk that an account balance, class of transactions or disclosures, and relevant assertions are materially misstated. Misstatements can result from errors or fraud.

The RMM consists of two components:

- **Inherent Risk** is the susceptibility that a relevant assertion could be misstated assuming that there are no other related controls. The auditor should consider the risk of misstatement individually as well as in aggregate with other misstatements, assuming there are no related controls.
- **Control Risk** is the risk that a material misstatement will not be detected or prevented by the entity's internal control on a timely basis. The auditor must consider the risk of misstatement individually and in aggregate with other misstatements.

Using the audit risk model to illustrate this concept: Inherent Risk x Control Risk = RMM

Auditors describe RMM as the combined assessment of inherent risk and control risk. However, auditors may make a separate assessment of inherent risk and control risk.

Significant Deficiency

A significant deficiency is a control deficiency, or combination of control deficiencies, that adversely affects the entity's ability to initiate, authorize, record, process, or report financial data reliably in accordance with generally accepted accounting principles such that there is more than a remote likelihood that a misstatement of the entity's financial statements that is more than inconsequential will not be prevented or detected.
Source: AICPA, http://www.aicpa.org/download/members/div/auditstd/AU-00325.PDF

Substantive Procedures

According to SAS 110, substantive procedures, "...are performed to detect material misstatements at the relevant assertion level, and include tests of details of classes of transactions, account balances, and disclosures and substantive analytical procedures. The auditor should plan and perform substantive procedures to be responsive to the related assessment of the risk of material misstatement."

Test of Controls

When the audit strategy involves relying on the operating effectiveness of the controls for some assertions in the design of substantive procedures, or when substantive procedures alone do not provide sufficient appropriate audit evidence at the assertion level, the auditor should design and perform tests of the operating effectiveness of controls. Additionally, they will perform procedures to evaluate the design of internal controls and determine whether they are implemented.

CASE & STUDY QUESTIONS:

ABC Company has 340 employees, is a provider of information storage equipment, and maintains its fixed assets in the form of computer and network equipment. There are a significant number of fixed asset acquisitions, retirements, and disposals, with transactions recorded by a staff accountant. The accountant records the transactions in a spreadsheet designed as a property ledger, posts the related entries to the general ledger, and monthly reconciles the two ledgers. The controller spot checks the entries and reviews the monthly reconciliations. The controller also includes a budget-to-actual analysis of capital expenditures and summary of fixed asset changes in monthly reports provided to senior operating managers who are positioned to question information at odds with the knowledge of business activities.

1. Based on the information provided in the ABC case, what situation has the highest IT risk?
   (A) The fact its fixed assets are IT
   (B) The fact compensating controls are manual
   (C) The fact transactions are recorded in a spreadsheet
   (D) The fact there is no SoD for the property ledger

Key: C
Section Name: Evaluate and test spreadsheet controls (3.2.3.3.3), General axioms about controls (3.1.1.1.3)
Bloom's Taxonomy category: 2. Comprehension, 3. Application, and 4. Analysis
Reference: "IT Audit, Control, and Security", Robert R. Moeller, pages 88–93. "ICFR – Guidance for Smaller Public Companies", COSO, page 61. ITEC White Paper, pp. 8, 12, 13, and 22.
Solution:
Stem (C): *The aspect of this case that demonstrates IT risk is the use of a spreadsheet to perform a significant accounting class of transactions: property ledger.*
Option (A): The fact the fixed assets are IT is not IT risk.
Option (B): The fact the controller performs manual procedures is an example of "downstream" compensating control. It is not an IT risk but rather a compensating control for the lack of SoD.
Option (D): The lack of SoD is not IT risk.

2. Based on the lack of SoD by the staff accountant, how would you assess the IT risk associated with this case?
   (A) The high IT risk in this case is NOT adequately mitigated by any activities described
   (B) The high IT risk in this case is adequately mitigated by the IT controls described as deployed
   (C) The high IT risk in this case is adequately mitigated by the reconciliation of the two ledgers
   (D) The high IT risk in this case is adequately mitigated by the controller's activities

Key: D
Section Name: General axioms about controls (3.1.1.1.3)
Bloom's Taxonomy category: 2. Comprehension, 3. Application, and 4. Analysis

Reference: "IT Audit, Control, and Security", Robert R. Moeller, pages 88–93. "ICFR – Guidance for Smaller Public Companies", COSO, page 61. ITEC White Paper, page 22.

Solution:

Stem (D): *The high IR due to lack of SoD is adequately mitigated by downstream manual controls executed by the controller. This conclusion is based on the design of those controls to detect any errors timely, and the operating effectiveness of the manual control.*

Option (A): The IT risk associated with the spreadsheet is adequately mitigated by the controller's downstream controls.

Option (B): There are no IT controls described as being deployed.

Option (C): The reconciliation of the two ledgers is performed by the same person doing the rest of the property ledger. That is, there is still a SoD problem if that is all that is taken into account, and the risk is NOT mitigated.

3. During ancient times, a written communication from royalty was sealed on the outside of the envelope using a unique ring of the royal person and wax. Which of the following is the **BEST** type of control being used in this instance?
   (A) Access control – authorization
   (B) Access control – authentication
   (C) Access control – both authorization and authentication
   (D) Output control – data control group

Key: B

Section Name: Understanding concepts of security authorization and authentication (3.4.4) and Sensitive Hardcopy Information (3.4.2.3)

Bloom's Taxonomy category: 3. Comprehension, 3. Application, and 6. Analysis

Reference: "Risks, Controls, and Security: Concepts and Applications", Raval & Fichadia, John Wiley & Sons, 2007, page 59.

Solution:

Stem: (B). *Authentication is a control that says the person is who they say they are. This unique ring constitutes a control that identifies the sealed communication as coming from the person it portends to be – the royal person identified by the unique ring.*

Option (A): Authorization says the person is authorized to access something. The seal is about who the person is, not who is authorized to open the seal.

Option (C): See A and B. It cannot be both.

Option (D): Control data groups are controls involving independent persons who are responsible for control over output such as printed checks. There is no independent person responsible for the communication in this analogy.

4. An application control that ensures data entered by a data-entry operator is complete is an example of _______?
   (A) Preventive control
   (B) Detective control
   (C) Corrective control
   (D) Access control

Key: B

Section Name: Understanding Frameworks: P-D-C (3.1.1.4.4) and Logical Access (3.2.3)

Bloom's Taxonomy category: 1. Knowledge

Reference: "Information Systems Control and Audit", Ron Weber, Prentice Hall, 1999, pp. 60, 65.

Solution:

Stem (B): *The purpose of the described control is to detect incomplete data. Therefore, this control is a detective one.*

Option (A): A preventive control would prevent an error from occurring and is generally not intended to make sure data is complete.

Option (C): Corrective controls address data after it is entered, and an error has been detected. Therefore this scenario is not corrective in nature.

Option (D): Access controls apply to access to networks or applications, and not the completeness of data entered.

5. Suppose you have a conventional Debit Card. You go to an ATM machine and withdraw cash from your account. The ATM will not process your request without the card and it's PIN. Which of the following **BEST** describes this type of control?
    (A) Multifactor access control
    (B) Logical access control
    (C) Application level control
    (D) Data level control

Key: A

Section Name: Logical Access (3.2.3) and Understanding the concepts of security authorization and authentication (3.4.4)

Bloom's Taxonomy category: 2. Comprehension, 3. Application, and 4. Analysis

Reference: "Risks, Controls, and Security: Concepts and Applications", Raval & Fichadia, John Wiley & Sons, 2007, page 59.

Solution:

Stem (A): *This situation demonstrates multifactor access control where it takes more than just an authorization (the debit card) but also some separate level of authorization or authentication to gain access (the PIN).*

Option (B): This situation is not about simple access control or else it would only ask for login credentials, such as the card's mag strip.

Option (C): While the ATM software is programmed to ask for both the card and a PIN, the question is about the card and PIN as inputs, authorization. and authentication type functions.

Option (D): While the data in the system would verify the card number, and PIN, in combination, the question is about the card and PIN as inputs.

6. ABC Co. is a large utility that has an IT staff including programmers. The programmers write all of the code (applications) being used in all financial systems using COBOL. Assume that as IT auditor, you have gained an understanding of the ITGC related to application

development. By virtue of interviews of the CIO, Director of Application Development, and a senior programmer, you believe the staff uses a set of standard operating procedures for developing software. You also believe the programmers actually use those standards in a consistent manner. Which of the following is the BEST next step for you as the IT auditor?

(A) Assess ITGCs as reasonably reliable
(B) Ask for documentation on a staging area and examine it
(C) Assess control environment as reasonably reliable
(D) Ask for documentation of a sample of programs and examine it

Key: D
Section Name: Control Environment (3.2.1), ITGC (3.2), Testing: Staging Area (3.2.4.4.1), SDLC (3.2.2.4)

Bloom's Taxonomy category: 2. Comprehension and 3. Application
Reference: "Information Systems Control and Audit", Ron Weber, Prentice Hall, 1999, page 52.
Solution:

Stem (D): *The next thing the IT auditor needs to do is to verify the operating effectiveness by taking a sample of programs and examining the documentation. This process would confirm or disaffirm the fact staff are following best practices in SDLC regarding application development.*

Option (A): ITGC is the body of general controls. This situation is involving only one area SDLC within Change Management. Therefore it is not appropriate to assess the entire body of ITGC based on this information.

Option (B): The operating effectiveness of the staging area is not directly relevant to the presence or absence of SDLC and application development controls regarding the other phases of SDLC. Those could not be assessed by only examining the testing aspect and staging area.

Option (C): The Control Environment is actually a different segment of ITGC from Change Management and SDLC. Therefore it would not be appropriate to make a judgment on the effectiveness of the control environment based on SDLC practices.

EVALUATE, TEST, AND REPORT

Dimension 4

Provide assurance to the public on financial statements, a client service, or a specific segment or piece of an entity's operations.

LEARNING OBJECTIVES

1. To understand the financial statement audit, especially IT considerations
2. To understand attest services for service organizations, both conducting the attest and using the resulting report
3. To understand techniques and procedures used in IT assurance services and internal IT reviews, including tests of controls, gathering evidence, the use of CAATs, and the use of sampling
4. To understand how to assess IT-related controls, how to identify and report on deficiencies and adverse impacts of deficiencies in controls
5. To understand information assurance for accuracy, integrity, security, presentation, timeliness and auditability

4.0 – INTRODUCTION

The main objective of evaluate, test and report is to provide assurance to the public on financial statements, a client service, or a specific segment or process of an entity's operations about the reliability of the subject matter. With the proper consideration of risk, fraud, and internal controls, the CITP would be in position to evaluate the subject matter, test it for assurance, and report on the results of the tests and other procedures.

This dimension of the CITP will provide an overview of these steps, relevant regulations and standards, techniques and tools used for effective design and execution of testing procedures, concepts on information assurance, and the role and responsibilities of the CITP related to this topic, whether in public accounting or Business and Industry ("B&I").

4.1 – TYPES OF AUDIT & ASSURANCE SERVICES

There is a variety of assurance services with which the CITP in public accounting may become involved. This section addresses the different types and something about the standards related to them. The internal CITP will also want to be aware of these services as well, and even perform similar reviews for management.

4.1.1 – Financial Statement Audit

Financial statement audits ("audit") provide management of an entity a creditable assessment of its financial health. Independent experts, CPAs, review the financial statements and their underlying transactions, associated procedures, associated IT, and controls, to determine the relative accuracy of financial information. The primary purpose of the audit is to provide reasonable assurance that the statements being audited are not materially misstated. Users of the financial statements depend on the opinion of the auditors in making major decisions, such as investing in a company.

Guidelines for performing and reporting on audits are governed by regulatory and standard setting bodies.

4.1.1.1 – Regulatory Bodies

Financial statement audits are currently regulated by three different bodies: the Securities and Exchange Commission (SEC), the American Institute of Certified Public Accountants (AICPA), and the Public Companies Accounting Oversight Board (PCAOB).

4.1.1.1.1 – SEC

The financial reporting environment in the U.S. was basically unregulated, although financial statement audits were being performed, up until 1933. The Securities Act of 1933 created the Securities Exchange Commission and gave it federal authority over financial reporting in the public arena. As part of the Act, the law required public companies to have their financial statements audited each year by an independent expert (i.e. a CPA). Thus the SEC has legal authority to regulate financial reporting which was given to it by virtue of the 1933 Act.

However, that did not result in the SEC setting all financial reporting standards, or all financial auditing standards. Rather the SEC, for the most part, allowed the profession to set generally accepted accounting standards (GAAP) for financial statement reports, and allowed the profession to set generally accepted auditing standards (GAAS) for auditing financial statements.

4.1.1.1.2 – PCAOB

The passage of the Sarbanes-Oxley Act of 2002 (S-OX) reshaped the hierarchy of GAAS. A new body was formed, the Public Companies Accounting Oversight Board (PCAOB) to answer to the SEC, and partner with the SEC as the ultimate authority over auditing regulation for public companies ("issuers"). Public accounting firms are required to register with the PCAOB as prerequisite to auditing issuers. Those firms are also required to follow all standards, principles, rules, and interpretations issued by the PCAOB.

4.1.1.2 – Standard Setting Bodies

In addition to the regulatory bodies created by the federal government, there are also standard setting bodies that are the authoritative bodies for developing, issuing, maintaining, and monitoring audit standards, especially what would be considered GAAS.

4.1.1.2.1 – ASB

The AICPA began issuing guidance to auditors in 1917. Since then, the auditing standard setting body at the AICPA has changed names and forms up until 1978 when the AICPA created the Auditing Standards Board (ASB) to become the authoritative body in establishing GAAS, consolidating all previous technical committees and bodies.

The SEC established a requirement for public auditors to include a representation in the audit opinion that the audit was performed in compliance with GAAS. To meet this requirement, the Committee on Auditing Procedure (CAP), one of the predecessor forms of the ASB, issued a booklet entitled *Generally Accepted Auditing Standards – Their Significance and Scope* to facilitate adoption of the SEC requirement. Since then, GAAS is not only a requirement of the SEC for all audits of issuers, but has been the body of standards and principles that guide audits of financial statements. Since 1972, these standards have been issued as Statements on Auditing Standards (SAS).

4.1.1.2.2 – PCAOB

The PCAOB is not only a regulatory body, but also a standard setting body as noted above. The PCAOB began its work after the passage of S-OX by adopting all of the ASB's auditing and attest standards as temporary auditing rules in 2003 as Auditing Standard 1 (AS1). Since 2003, the PCAOB has been issuing Auditing Standards (AS) for GAAS related to public companies.

In 2004, the AICPA recognized this new hierarchy by designating the PCAOB as the authoritative body for GAAS related to issuers, while the ASB was designated as the authoritative body for GAAS related to non-issuers (non-public companies).

4.1.1.3 – Risk-Based Auditing Standards[1]

The financial audit has involved IT since the 1950's, but the audit process, and the role of IT in a financial audit, changed in 2006. In March 2006, the Auditing Standards Board (ASB) issued eight new statements of auditing standards related to risk-based auditing (RBA). These standards, outlined in the AICPA *Audit Guide Assessing and Responding to Audit Risk in a Financial Statement Audit*, represent a significant shift in the way a financial audit must be performed.

One of the key changes from previous audit practices is that the standards require auditors to obtain a more in-depth understanding of the entity and its environment, including its internal controls (see SAS No. 109). This understanding includes the auditor's responsibility to identify both IT general controls (ITGC) and application controls during the audit planning and risk assessment process. The new standards recognize the pervasive nature of IT in financial processes and that IT increasingly represents both a primary source of financial control risk and financial controls. Understanding the impact of IT on inherent risk (IR) and control risk (CR) can lead to a more effective and efficient audit plan.

These standards require auditors to identify and assess the risks of material misstatement (RMM) at the financial statement level and assertion level as the basis to perform further audit procedures (test of controls {ToC} and substantive procedures). The RBA standards stipulate that CR cannot be set to maximum as a default without considering internal controls. Effective application of a risk-based audit approach requires the auditor to:

- Understand risks represented by IT and to link these risks to financial statement assertions
- Incorporate IT risk assessment and IT control tests into audit plans

These Statements of Audit Standards (SAS) provide guidance about the concepts underlying the Standards of Fieldwork, which require the auditor to:

- Gather information on the entity's environment, including internal control, to assess the risks of material misstatement
- Evaluate that information to assess risks at the assertion level
- Design and perform further audit procedures based on those risks
- Evaluate the audit evidence obtained
- Reach conclusions

The Standards of Fieldwork clarify the requirements of the auditor in relationship to the IT control environment. For example:

- ***First Standard of Fieldwork*** – Requires adequate planning of the audit, which includes understanding the entity, its IT environment, and IT-related internal controls.
- ***Second Standard of Fieldwork*** – Requires assessing the RMM, including the risk from the use of IT.

---

[1] Much of this section is taken from the AICPA's ITEC White paper: *IT Considerations in Risk-Based Auditing: A Strategic Overview*, July 26, 2007.

- ***Third Standard of Fieldwork*** – Requires that the auditor obtain "sufficient appropriate audit evidence by performing audit procedures to afford a reasonable basis for an opinion regarding the financial statements under audit." This process should include obtaining an understanding about IT controls and may include testing of IT controls and the use of CAATs (computer-assisted audit tools) as part of further audit procedures.

The primary objective of the RBA Standards is to enhance the auditors' application of the audit risk model in practice by specifying, among other things:

- More in-depth understanding of the entity and its environment including its internal control, to identify the risks of material misstatement in the financial statements and what the entity is doing to mitigate them
- More rigorous assessment of the risks of material misstatement of the financial statements based on that understanding
- Improved linkage between the assessed risks and the nature, timing, and extent of audit procedures performed in response to those risks

Although the impact of IT and the entity's control environment is pervasive throughout the audit process, there is greater emphasis related to the impact of IT in five of the new SASs: 106, 107, 108, 109, and 110. The following sections briefly explore each of the standards and their relevance to the IT risks, controls, and testing elements of an audit.

4.1.1.3.1 – SAS No. 104-111

The risk-based standards changed the nature of the financial audit significantly, including IT considerations.

SAS No. 104 – Amendment to Statement on Auditing Standards No. 1, Codification of Auditing Standards and Procedures ("Due Professional Care in the Performance of Work")

To apply SAS No. 104, one must plan and perform the financial audit in a way that obtains sufficiently appropriate audit evidence to reduce audit risk to a low level so that the financial statements are free of material misstatement, whether caused by error or fraud. Although reasonable assurance is a high level of assurance, it is not absolute assurance. An absolute level of assurance is not attainable because of the nature of audit evidence and the characteristics of fraud. An auditor does not examine 100 percent of the entity's transactions or events and because of the limitations of the entity's internal control, absolute assurance cannot be achieved. This fact is a foundational premise for the other new standards.

SAS No. 105 – Amendment to Statement on Auditing Standards No. 95, Generally Accepted Auditing Standards

SAS No. 105 expands the scope of the Second Standard of Fieldwork from "understanding of internal control" to "understanding the entity and its environment, including its internal control." In addition, this standard emphasizes the quality and depth of the understanding to be obtained by amending the purpose from "audit planning" to "assessing the RMM of the financial statements whether due to error or fraud and to design the nature, timing, and extent of further audit procedures."

By stating that the purpose of the understanding of the entity and its internal control as more than an element of audit planning but rather is now a part of assessing the RMM, this standard essentially considers the auditor's understanding of the entity, its environment and its internal control as providing audit evidence that ultimately supports the audit opinion on the financial statements.

This standard also emphasizes the link between understanding the entity, assessing risks, and the design of further audit procedures. "Generic" audit programs are not an appropriate response for all engagements because risks vary between entities.

This standard clarified the term "further audit procedures," which consists of test of controls and substantive procedures, replacing the term "tests to be performed" in recognition that risk assessment procedures are also performed. SAS 105 also replaced the term "evidential matter" with the term "audit evidence."

SAS No. 106 – Audit Evidence

SAS No. 106 provides the auditor with a definition of audit evidence, relevant assertions, and guidance on designing audit procedures. The standard also re-categorized assertions by classes of transactions, account balances, and presentation and disclosure; expanded the guidance related to presentation and disclosure; and describes how the auditor uses relevant assertions to assess risk and design audit procedures. It includes the requirement that for each significant class of transactions, account balance, and presentation and disclosure, the auditor should determine the relevance of each of the Financial Statement Assertions.

To identify relevant assertions, the auditor should determine the source of likely potential misstatements in each significant class of transactions, account balance, and presentation and disclosure. In determining whether a particular assertion is relevant to a significant account balance or disclosure, the auditor should evaluate:

- The nature of the assertion
- The volume of transactions or data related to the assertion
- The nature and complexity of the systems, including the use of IT, by which the entity processes and controls information supporting the assertion

When the information is in electronic form, the auditor may need to use CAATs to obtain audit evidence. For example, the auditor may use CAATs to help perform recalculation (checking the mathematical accuracy of documents or records). Recalculation can be performed by obtaining an electronic file from the entity and using CAATs to check the accuracy of the summarization of the file.

SAS 106 also identified risk assessment procedures as audit procedures performed to obtain an understanding of the entity and its environment, including its internal control, to assess the RMM at the financial statement and relevant assertion levels. The standard provides that evidence obtained by performing risk assessment procedures, as well as that obtained by performing tests of controls and substantive procedures, is part of the evidence the auditor obtains to draw reasonable conclusions on which to base the audit opinion, although such evidence is not sufficient in and of itself to support the audit opinion.

SAS 106 also introduced the concept that risk assessment procedures are necessary to provide a basis for assessing the RMM. The results of risk assessment procedures, along with the results of further audit procedures, provide audit evidence that ultimately supports the auditor's opinion on the financial statements.

The standard describes the types of audit procedures that the auditor may use alone or in combination as risk assessment procedures, tests of controls, or substantive procedures, depending on the context in which they are applied by the auditor. Risk assessment procedures include:

- Inquiries of management and others within the entity
- Analytical procedures
- Observation and inspection

SAS 106 states that the auditor must compile "sufficient appropriate audit evidence by performing audit procedures to afford a reasonable basis for an opinion regarding the financial statements under audit."

SAS 106 includes guidance on the uses and limitations of inquiry as an audit procedure and indicates that inquiry alone is not sufficient to detect a material misstatement at the relevant assertion and to test the operating effectiveness of controls.

SAS No. 107 – Audit Risk and Materiality in Conducting an Audit

SAS No. 107 is the cornerstone of the risk-based standards in that it states that the auditor should have and document an appropriate basis for the audit approach. The standard states that the auditor must consider audit risk and determine materiality, and it describes the basis for the audit approach or further audit procedures (also discussed in SAS No. 110 below), as the RMM.

The RMM is defined as the risk that an account balance, class of transactions or disclosures, and relevant assertions are materially misstated. Misstatements can result from errors or fraud or both. Examples of IT-related errors that could result in a misstatement that may be material include an inaccuracy in gathering or processing of data from which financial statements are prepared, complex transactions that are performed using IT systems and/or end-user computing (e.g. spreadsheets). The RMM consists of two components:

Inherent Risk (IR) is the susceptibility that a relevant assertion could be misstated assuming that there are no other related controls. The auditor should consider the risk of misstatement individually as well as in aggregate with other misstatements, assuming there are no related controls.

Control Risk (CR) is the risk that a material misstatement will not be detected or prevented by the entity's internal control on a timely basis. The auditor must consider the risk of misstatement individually and in aggregate with other misstatements.

Using the audit risk model to illustrate this concept:

$$RMM = IR \times CR$$

Audit risk is a combination of the RMM, described below, and detection risk (DR), which is the risk that the auditor will not detect material misstatements. In the audit risk model, the various risks are illustrated as follows:

$$Audit\ Risk = RMM \times DR$$

To reduce audit risk to a low level the auditor will assess the RMM and then, based on that assessment, design and perform further audit procedures to reduce overall audit risk to an appropriately low level. Risks of material misstatement may reside at either the financial statement level or the assertion level.

Financial statement level risks potentially affect many different assertions. For example, an organization's lack of qualified personnel in financial reporting roles (an element of the entity's control environment) may affect many different accounts and several assertions. An example of when IT could represent an inherent RMM at the financial statement level is when an entity uses financial applications that are highly customized and/or subject to frequent or significant modifications. To assess CR at the financial statement level, the auditor would determine if the entity has controls (policies and procedures) that, if deployed and operating effectively, could limit access to financial data and financial programs to authorized personnel under authorized circumstances. Control risk would be lowered by the existence of controls over administrative access to the IT environment, and controls over the process where changes are authorized, developed, and deployed to financial applications.

Assertion level risks are limited to one or more specific assertions in an account or in several accounts, for example, the valuation of inventory or the occurrence of sales. An example of when IT could represent an inherent RMM at the assertion level is if the entity uses a customized application for service provisioning and billing, that the entity also relies on to determine revenue recognition. To assess control risk at the assertion level, the auditor would determine if the entity has controls (policies and procedures) to limit access to all aspects of this application (database, program code, and user applications). Examples of controls to lower control risk for assertion level risk include:

- Controls over administrative access to the server(s) for this application
- Controls to limit user access to this application
- Controls over how changes are authorized, developed, and deployed to this application

The auditor's specific response to assessed risks may differ depending on whether the risks reside at the financial statement or assertion level.

Financial statement level risks typically require an overall response, such as providing more supervision to the engagement team or modifying the selection of your audit procedures.

Assertion level risks are addressed by the nature, timing, and extent of further audit procedures, which may include substantive procedures or a combination of tests of controls and substantive procedures.

Because the RMM exists at two levels, the financial statement level and the assertion level, the auditor should assess the RMM at both of these levels separately and in aggregate.

In assessing the RMM, the auditor should have an appropriate, documented basis for their assessment of audit risk. Therefore, the auditor must now consider audit risk, which would include assessing IT control risk. The auditor cannot "default" control risk to maximum and avoid assessing and documenting what the risks are for the entity. When assessing IT controls, the auditor may want to consider whether or not to test the controls, potentially decreasing the amount of substantive procedures required to reduce the audit risk.

SAS 107 also indicates that all known and likely misstatements identified during the audit must be communicated to the appropriate level of management.

There are two significant IT implications in SAS 107. In order to fulfill the requirements of this SAS, the IT auditor must take the appropriate steps to understand (1) if any IT risks lead to the RMM, and (2) whether there are sufficient controls in existence to timely prevent and detect any potential errors or fraud.

SAS No. 108 – Planning and Supervision

SAS No. 108 provides the auditor with guidance on how to plan the audit. Key components of SAS 108 include defining:

- The overall audit strategy
- The audit plan
- Determining the extent of the involvement of a professional possessing specialized skills

When developing an audit plan, the auditor must have a thorough understanding of the entity being audited. This understanding includes how the entity uses IT to capture, store, and process information – information that is critical to assessing the RMM, especially as RMM relates to IT.

The use of professionals possessing IT skills (IT auditor, such as a CITP) can be a significant aspect of many audit engagements in order to properly determine the impact of IT to the audit, to understand the IT controls, to design and perform tests of IT controls, and/or to design and perform substantive procedures (e.g. using CAATs).

In determining whether such a professional is needed on the audit team, the auditor should consider such factors including:

- The complexity of the entity's systems and IT controls, and the manner in which they are used in conducting the entity's business
- The significance of changes made to existing systems, or the implementation of new systems
- The extent to which data is shared among systems
- The extent of the entity's participation in electronic commerce
- The entity's use of emerging technologies
- The significance of audit evidence that is available only in electronic form

Based on the foregoing considerations, the more complex the entity's systems and IT environment, the more likely that an IT professional should be an integral part of the audit team during the planning process and may need to be involved in planning the audit. The same is true regarding the nature of IT (i.e. its inherent risk – for example, in-house programming). In these cases, an IT professional with sufficient understanding of audit objectives and methodology (e.g. the AICPA Certified Information Technology Professional {CITP} and ISACA Certified Information Systems Auditor {CISA}) should participate in determining the need to use additional professionals possessing a sufficient understanding of the technologies being used by the entity in support of its financial processes to understand the effect of IT on the audit.

The auditor should determine whether specific IT audit skills are necessary to support the audit, and, if so, which functions the IT auditor should perform. As a result, it is appropriate to include an auditor with IT skills in a dialogue or brainstorming session to establish an audit plan that includes the IT audit objectives, resources required, and timeline. Specific objectives that may be established for the IT auditor could include:

- Assessing the entity-level IT functions and controls
- Assessing the role of third parties including inherent risks and adequacy of mitigating controls
- Documenting the role of IT applications used to support one or more financial statement accounts, financial statement preparation, and the reporting process. This process may include the preparation of documentation to depict the flow of financial information from transaction initiation, through various stages of processing and reporting.
- Assessing activity-level inherent risks and the adequacy of mitigating controls for one or more IT applications used to support one or more financial statement accounts, financial statement preparation, and the reporting process
- Identifying relevant IT processes that support the relevant applications and inherent general control risks, and the adequacy of controls to mitigate these risks
- Identifying opportunities to leverage computer-assisted audit tools and techniques in the execution of tests for fraud and IT-related substantive procedures

The auditor should apply these considerations when preparing their audit planning documentation.

Entities undergoing an audit should also consider involving an individual with IT competence in their audit preparation process. Some of the audit preparation tasks this internal or outsourced IT resource may be assigned include:

- Answering inquiries regarding the entity's IT and financial systems, information flow, transaction processing, and internal controls
- Describing how IT is deployed relative to the entity's financial processes and financial reporting
- Documentation of the entity's IT and financial systems, network management, change management, and security management policies and process flow
- Facilitating the test of IT controls
- Providing data for substantive testing using CAATs

SAS No. 109 – Understanding the Entity and Its Environment and Assessing the Risks of Material Misstatement

SAS No. 109 indicates that the auditor is responsible for obtaining an understanding of the entity and its environment, including its internal control. While it is not necessary to understand all of the entity's controls, it is necessary to determine those controls that are relevant to the audit. The nature and complexity of the systems that are part of the control environment must be part of the auditor's understanding.

The purpose of obtaining an understanding of the entity, its environment and its internal control is to gain an accurate assessment of inherent risks and control risks, at both the assertion and financial statement level. In turn, this risk assessment will provide the foundation for the design of further audit procedures to respond to the assessed risk.

The pervasiveness of IT in financial processes means that understanding IT will often be a critical component in gaining an understanding of the entity, its environment, and assessing the RMM of the financial statements.

An entity's use of IT may affect any of the five components of internal control relevant to the achievement of the entity's financial reporting, operations, and compliance objectives, and its operating units or business functions.

The entity's use of information technology can result in RMM, and IT can also represent controls the entity has deployed to mitigate risks. As part of understanding the entity and its environment, the auditor should gather information to understand how IT is deployed relative to financial processes and financial reporting. The role and significance of IT will vary from entity to entity, so there is no one method for gathering information and documenting the understanding to fit every situation.

The auditor should obtain an understanding of the effect of IT on internal control. Information the auditor will gather and consider for risk assessment purposes, will include, but not be limited to, the following:

- ***The role of IT in the initiation, authorization, recording, processing, and reporting of transactions***. The auditor should gather information to understand significant accounts, classes of accounts, or financial reporting and information systems that are, directly or indirectly, the source of financial transactions or the data used to generate financial transactions and financial reporting. Information systems may include packaged applications, custom developed applications and/or end-user computing (e.g., spreadsheets) that are used for accounting functions or transaction cycles (e.g., revenue recognition) that drive accounting data (e.g., revenue and A/R entries).
- ***How the entity manages information technology***. This includes the person(s) and third parties that support the IT infrastructure (applications, supporting networks, and servers), and the person(s) that have responsibility for managing the deployment and integrity of the IT infrastructure. Generally speaking, the auditor would expect to see staffing and skills commensurate with the complexity of the deployed systems and the entity's information systems needs. The more complex the deployed technology and information systems needs, the more likely the auditor will want to have a specialized resource, an IT

auditor, conducting the information gathering about how the entity manages its IT to properly assess the entity's IT staffing and skills, and its impact on financial reporting.

- ***Evaluating the design of internal controls and determining whether they have been deployed to mitigate the risk associated with the use of information technology.*** These controls typically are either IT general controls or application controls (see 3.2.1 for more on ITGC). Examples include:
  - IT General Controls (ITGCs). While ineffective ITGCs do not, by themselves, cause misstatements, they may permit application controls to operate improperly and allow misstatements to occur and not be detected. ITGCs may include:
    - *Change Controls.* How changes are made to information system applications and supporting infrastructure.
    - *Backup and Recovery.* How the entity ensures the continuity of financial data and financial reporting capabilities.
    - *Access Controls.* This ITGC includes logical access controls over IT infrastructure that supports business applications and end-user computing (EUC). For instance, access controls to network(s) used to access financial applications and financial data, and access controls to supporting data files. Access controls also include physical access controls to IT infrastructure components (servers, tapes, etc.).
    - *Control Environment.* How the entity manages its IT function related to the financial systems, including the data center, IT support, systems development, application development, IT projects, and similar roles of the IT function.
    - *Service Organization.* If the entity outsources IT roles or functions, then this aspect relates to the reliability of that service being provided by the service organization (SO).
  - Application Controls. These controls relate to those embedded in the business applications, including end-user computing. Examples include: user access controls, controls to ensure integrity of calculations and system procedures, edit checks, error handling, etc. Some of these controls may be a combination of system generated reports and manual reviews. The effectiveness of these types of controls, such as reviews of computer-produced exception reports may depend on the accuracy of the information produced by the information system.

In certain circumstances, the absence of effective logical access controls (e.g., access rights to the financial database, or access rights to the general ledger) could increase the RMM so significantly that a prudent IT auditor would assign a CR of maximum for all of the associated output.

The auditor should consider using a combination of methods to gather information such as obtaining and reading written policies and procedures, survey questionnaires, interviews, walk-through reviews of processes, walk-through reviews of data centers, network closets, and other observable aspects of the IT infrastructure. The use of flowcharts to depict the flow of financial information, may (depending on the complexity) provide insight as to the role of technology in financial processes, and may also be useful to identify inherent risks.

Based on their understanding of the role of IT in financial functions and their understanding of supporting control functions, the auditor should assess the risk of material misstatement and document the assessment accordingly. Documentation of the risk assessment process should enable an experienced auditor, having no previous connection to the audit, to understand:

- The audit procedures performed
- The results of the audit procedures and the evidence obtained
- The conclusions reached

Information to be provided in this risk assessment may include, but not be limited to:

- ***Subject***: Identify the source of the risk to be described, for instance, the related-to organization, IT process or procedures, and/or IT infrastructure component (e.g., application, network, database, etc.)
- ***Inherent Risk***: Identify and describe the risk to financial reporting
- ***Type of Risk***: Indicate if the risk is associated with the potential for error, fraud, or both
- ***Risk Level***: Define if at financial statement or assertion level. If at the assertion level, identify specific assertions if possible, like existence or occurrence, completeness, valuation or allocation, accuracy or classification, or cutoff.
- ***Controls Designed to Mitigate this Risk***: Summarily describe the controls designed and placed in operation to mitigate these risks
- ***Control Risk Assessment***: Assess the significance of the risk (for example, using a scale of high, moderate, or low, or a scale of 1 to 5), and provide rationale for the assessment rating. The rationale would be related to the extent to which controls effectively prevent or detect the inherent risk and would consider factors for whether the controls are:
    - Suitably designed to mitigate the inherent risks
    - Whether the controls are placed in operation
- ***Risk of Material Misstatement***: Assess the RMM and provide rationale for the assessment rating. The rationale would for this assessment is the auditor's judgment of the net effect of the inherent risk and control risk.

Control risk assessment: A control is suitably designed if it provides reasonable assurance that the risk it is intended to mitigate will be prevented or detected. A manually performed control can be determined to be placed in operation if it can be determined that the person(s) responsible for execution of the control understands and is capable of fulfilling their responsibilities.

For example, the auditor would conduct a walkthrough review of a standard operating procedure to confirm the person(s) responsible for the control understands their control responsibilities and is capable of fulfilling their responsibilities.

Automated controls can be determined to be placed in operation by gathering evidence that the control is deployed. An example would be a screen shot of the system used to grant administrative access rights and a listing of those individuals who have been granted those rights.

FIGURE 4.1: ILLUSTRATIVE EXAMPLE OF IT & ASSESSING RMM[2]	
#1. Risk Subject:	Inventory Tracking and Reporting and COGS Calculation
Background	The client uses a custom financial application for the purposes of inventory management including inventory valuation and reporting and cost-of-goods sold calculation. The client's technical and financial personnel make frequent changes to this application. Inventory represents approximately 60% or more of the client's asset valuation.
Inherent Risk	Inventory and Cost of Goods Sold (COGS) could be misstated due to errors made as part of authorized changes being made. There is potential for unauthorized changes being made that could affect inventory balances and COGS values. These account balances are very significant to the overall profitability of the entity.
Type of Risk	This risk is both from error and fraud. Program changes are inherently at risk of error. Financial personnel have the ability to make changes to the programs and this could enable them to change inventory balances and cost of goods sold fraudulently.
Risk Level	Assertion level for: • Inventory existence and valuation. • Cost of Goods Sold valuation.
Controls designed to mitigate this risk	*Change Control*: The client has developed and deployed policies and procedures associated with change control (X-Ref W/P #). *Access Control*: The client has developed and deployed policies and procedures for access control over the application, database, and supporting network.
Control Risk Assessment	*Low*: The entity's controls effectively mitigate the inherent risks. *Change Control*: The auditor has determined that the entity has a suitably designed standard operating procedures (SOP) for change management and that the SOP is placed in operation. *Access Control*: The auditor has determined that the entity has a suitably defined SOP for granting and managing logical access rights to the network and applications used for financial functions and that the SOPs are placed in operation.
Risk of Material Misstatement	*Moderate-to-High*: While the CR is low, the IR for this situation is very high.

SAS No. 110 – Performing Audit Procedures in Response to Assessed Risks and Evaluating the Audit Evidence Obtained

The auditor should design and perform audit procedures based upon the assessment of the RMM. SAS 110 indicates that the design of further audit procedures should consider the following:

- The significance of risks and the likelihood that material misstatement will occur
- The characteristics of the class of transactions, account balance, or disclosure
- The nature of specific controls used by the entity and if they are manual or automated

[2] Taken from AICPA ITEC's white paper on RBA, *Information Technology Considerations in Risk-Based Auditing: A Strategic Overview*, June 26, 2007.

- Whether the auditor plans to test controls to modify the nature, timing, and extent of substantive procedures

The purpose of further audit procedures is to perform test of controls and/or substantive procedures and test for the overstatement or understatement of accounts. Whenever audit procedures are performed using information provided by the entity's information system (i.e., accounts receivable aging report), the auditor should obtain audit evidence about the accuracy and completeness of thc information being provided.

According to SAS 110, "the auditor should perform tests of controls when the auditor's risk assessment includes an expectation of the operating effectiveness of controls or when substantive procedures alone do not provide sufficient appropriate audit evidence at the relevant assertion level." The following highlights the role of IT in further audit procedures for the purposes of testing IT-related controls.

Tests of controls would be appropriate when:

- The control(s) mitigates one or more inherent risks that are significant
- Tests of the operating effectiveness of the control(s) could provide a basis for lowering assessed risk levels, enabling the auditor to apply CAATS effectively and/or reduce the extent of substantive procedures
- The increasing probability or likelihood that the controls that an entity uses are going to be automated controls and that the entity will be relying on the system to provide their control structure
- The need to determine that IT-related controls have been implemented properly and to obtain audit evidence about the operating effectiveness of the controls

In addition to your obtaining an understanding of the entity's controls (see SAS 109), the following are examples of tests the auditor may perform to determine the deployment and effectiveness of IT controls (ITGCs and/or application controls):

- ***Inspection***, including:
    - Inspecting change management policies and procedures
    - Inspecting documentation of change management controls
    - Inspecting log files to determine what user access rights were associated with movement of new objects to production environment
    - Review of a system-generated administrative access rights list
- ***Observation***, including:
    - Conducting a walk-through review of the entity's data center to observe physical and environmental controls, and general orderliness of the data center
    - Observing automated controls being performed for situations that are required per the design of the control
- ***Inquiry***, including:
    - Interviewing personnel to determine if responsibilities regarding performance of control procedures are understood and the person(s) are capable of effectively performing the control(s)

- ***Confirmation***, including:
  - Performing a function within an application (usually a test environment) to confirm the existence of an automated control

The following are factors that the IT auditor may consider in determining the extent of tests of controls:

- General computing controls considerations include:
  - The frequency of performance of the control. For instance, the frequency of the event(s) occurring to which the control applies would determine the relevant population for sample or test selection.
  - The length of the period regarding operational effectiveness. For example, the auditor should select tests that cover the entire period relevant for operational effectiveness. Normally this would be the fiscal period, however, it could be less in circumstances when the entity's environment changes during the fiscal period.
  - When multiple general controls affect one or more financially relevant applications, the auditor will need to determine if some combination of ITGCs need to be tested to reduce audit risk to acceptable levels for assertion level risks and financial statement level risks.
- Testing automated controls considerations include:
  - Normally, a test of one specific instance of an automated control is a relevant basis for concluding on the controls' effectiveness. However, to extend forward the conclusions of an automated control, the auditor would also need to confirm the deployment and operational effectiveness of general controls that help ensure the integrity of application controls.
  - When considering whether to use audit evidence for automated control testing from prior audits, the auditor should carefully assess the effectiveness of general controls that help ensure the integrity of application controls. Evidence of highly effective general controls, especially change management, will provide a basis for the auditor to reduce, but not eliminate, tests of automated controls.

There is information in the entity's systems that can be useful in the performance of substantive procedures. The purpose of this section is to highlight the relevancy of leveraging information technology in support of substantive procedures. CAATs may be used to facilitate tests of details of transactions, account balances and disclosures.

The use of CAATs requires the auditor to have comfort that the data has integrity and that there are controls over that data. Once those conditions have been met, CAATs allow the auditor to use the entity's data files to assess transactional and supporting data, and allow the auditor to take vast amounts of normalized data and integrate and analyze that data, creating stratification of data:

- Identification of data that is potentially an outlier or anomaly
- Assist the auditor in sample selection

The following are examples of substantive procedures the auditor may perform using CAATs:

- ***Recalculation*** including the use of CAATs to recalculate report balance
- ***Re-performance***

- Analytical procedures including using ***CAATs*** to test journal entry files for unusual entries (e.g., Benford tests)

CAATs enable the auditor to expand the extent of their use of substantive procedures. For instance, when testing an entity's transactions, of which there may be thousands or more, CAATs allow the auditor to test across the entire population as opposed to being limited to a smaller sample.

In general, the use of CAATs can provide the auditor more flexibility than more traditional substantive procedures. Once they are established, updating CAATs can be done with relative ease because it involves gaining access to current data (transactional information) and perform the audit procedures to cover the remaining time period.

The documentation of all audit procedures should meet the standards of AU Section 339, Audit Documentation, (AICPA, Professional Standards, vol. 1) which states that documentation should be sufficient such that an experienced auditor, with no prior experience with this client, can understand the procedures performed, evidence examined, and conclusions reached.

SAS No. 111 – Amendment to Statement on Auditing Standards No. 39, Audit Sampling
SAS No. 111 addresses the concepts of establishing tolerable deviation rates when sampling tests of controls such as matching and authorization.

Generally, sampling does not apply to tests of controls like automated application controls as they are usually tested only once or a few times when effective ITGCs are present. In addition, sampling is generally not applicable to analyses of controls for determining the appropriate segregation of duties. In addition, sampling may not apply to tests of certain documented controls or to analyses of the effectiveness of security and access controls.

In some circumstances, the auditor may design a sample that will be used for dual purposes:

- Testing the operating effectiveness of an identified control
- Testing whether the recorded transactions are correct

When a dual-purpose sample is used, a preliminary assessment must be made that there is a low risk of exceptions to the control. Generally, the size of a sample designed for dual purposes should be the larger of the samples that would otherwise have been designed for the two separate purposes. In evaluating dual purpose tests, the auditor should assess the risk levels of control exceptions and the possibility of monetary misstatements separately.

4.1.1.3.2 – AS5
The PCAOB issued AS5 to supersede AS2, which was its guidance regarding performing an audit of management's assessment of the effectiveness of internal control over financial reporting (ICFR) for issuers in response to section 404 requirements of S-OX[3]. The PCAOB

[3] S-OX §404 requires management of issuers (public companies) to do an assessment of its (key) internal controls over financial reporting (ICFR) and requires an independent CPA to opine on that evaluation.

states that effective ICFR provides reasonable assurance regarding the reliability of the financial reporting process and financial statements. However, if one or more material weakness in ICFR exists, then the entity's ICFR cannot be considered effective.

The PCAOB further states that the audit of ICFR should be integrated with the audit of the financial statements. In an integrated audit, the internal control audit (S-OX 404 compliance) where ITGC and other controls are examined, usually by an IT auditor, is the cornerstone of the financial audit. The results of the controls audit lead to the identification of IT risks, especially those that can lead to the RMM, and the assessed level of those risks. Because these risks drive the nature, timing and extent of the Further Audit Procedures (FAP), the IT auditor should design procedures to accomplish the objectives of both audits simultaneously.

Like the RBA risk standards, AS5 states that the internal controls audit should use a top-down approach. As part of that approach, the auditor would examine entity-level controls (ELC). The control environment aspect of ELC is similar to the control environment element of ITGC described in Dimension 3. ELC also include period-end financial reporting process, including associated IT risks. Paragraph 36 says:

> *"The auditor also should understand how IT affects the company's flow of transactions. The auditor should apply paragraph 29 and Appendix B of AS12,* Identifying and Assessing Risks of Material Misstatement, *which discusses the effect of IT on ICFR and the risks to assess. The identification of risks and controls within IT is not a separate evaluation. Instead, it is an integral part of the top-down approach used to identify significant accounts and disclosures and their relevant assertions, and the controls to test, as well as to assess risk and allocate audit effort as described by this standard."*

AS5 repeatedly emphasizes the importance of the correlation of RMM and the complexity of the company or business unit (see 4.1.1.4.1 for similar guideline from SAS No. 94, for non-issuers). For example, paragraph 47 states:

> *"A less complex company and business unit with simple business processes and centralized accounting operations might have relatively simple information systems that make greater use of (commercial) off-the-shelf packaged software (COTS) without modification."*

If there are control deficiencies that, individually or in the aggregate, result in one or more material weaknesses, the auditor must express an adverse opinion on the company's ICFR, unless there is a restriction on the scope of the engagement. AS5 uses the same delineation and definitions of control deficiencies[4] as those in SAS No. 115 (see section 4.3.1.1).

---

[4] See Appendix A of AS5 for definitions of control deficiency, significant deficiency, and material weakness of controls.

4.1.1.4 – IT Considerations

The focus of the CITP in the RBA approach to either financial audits or controls audits or IT reviews will be on the considerations of IT risks. Some of the key IT considerations were presented in SAS No. 94 (superseded by SAS No. 109) and AS5.

4.1.1.4.1 – SAS No. 94 (SAS No. 109)

The adoption of SAS No. 94, "The Effect of IT on the Auditor's Consideration of Internal Control in a Financial Statement Audit" (SAS 94) addressed the issues of control risk embedded in IT. The basic IT consideration in SAS 94 was that the auditor was directed to gain an understanding of how IT impacts the system of internal control, much like SAS 109 did later (in fact, SAS 109-110 supersede SAS 94).

One key principle SAS 94 stipulated was the need to audit through systems more often. In regards to incorporating IT-related procedures in the financial audit, SAS 94 states, "*It is not practical or possible to restrict detection risk to an acceptable level by performing only substantive tests.*" SAS 94 states that CAATs are needed to test the automated controls in the relevant information systems, and states when it is not appropriate to use CAATs.

Another key principle is the concept of a sample size of one being sufficient to test an automated control. SAS 94 states that under the right circumstances, a sample size of one may be sufficient to gain assurance over the operating effectiveness of a certain kinds of automated controls. This factor is a key factor in test of controls (ToC). Later, the PCAOB would stipulate the same principle in Auditing Standard 2 (AS2)[5].

SAS 94 made another key statement about IT risk and control risk: that the level of IT risk is directly proportional to the nature and complexity of the IT in the relevant financial systems, and not necessarily the size of the entity. Thus a small size company with complex IT in its relevant systems and business processes has a relatively high IR revolving around IT. Conversely, a rather large company with simple IT in its relevant systems and business processes will likely have a low level of risk related to IT. In the following section, it will be seen that the PCAOB agrees with this concept in its "AS5 Guidance".

4.1.1.4.2 – AS5[6]

Auditing Standard No. 5 (AS5) has the following implications for IT consideration of a controls audit related to a financial audit of an issuer: Assess the nature and complexity of the entity's IT relative to business processes, accounting operations, and information systems (from simple to sophisticated complexity).

---

[5] AS2 was superseded by AS5, which promotes the same basic concept, especially in the PCABOS Staff "AS 5 Guidance" document.

[6] Much of 4.1.1.4.2 is taken from the PCAOB's, "An Audit of Internal Control Over Financial Reporting That Is Integrated with an Audit of Financial Statements: Guidance for Auditors of Smaller Public Companies" (January 23, 2009), Chapter 5 "Auditing IT Controls in a Less Complex IT Environment". The guidance is staff views for AS5.

The complexity of the IT environment has a significant effect on the risks of misstatement and the controls implemented to address those risks. The auditor's approach to the ICFR or financial audit is usually different for a simple IT complexity than for a sophisticated IT complexity.

- Transaction processing
- Software
- Systems configuration and security administration
- End-user computing

Testing of the automated controls in COTS for simple complexity entities could address logical SoD, data input errors, or proper recording of certain types of transactions. Focus on testing these and ITGC that are important in the effective operation of the automated controls.

FIGURE 4.2: COMPLEXITY OF IT[7]		
CONTEXT	*SIMPLE COMPLEXITY*	*SOPHISTICATED COMPLEXITY*
IT Operations Function	• No formal one	• Formal, Structured
Transaction Processing	• Data inputs readily compared or reconciled to outputs • Relies primarily on manual controls • Relies on automated controls of the COTS	• Processing and outputs more complicated, less readily reconciled to inputs • Relies primarily on automated or IT-dependent controls • Relies on controls in COTS, and those developed by the entity in customized software
Software	• COTS • Limited scope of integration to other systems • Little to no configuration to implement	• Some customized software • Enterprise (e.g., ERP) • Moderate to high configuration requirements to implement
IT Configuration	• Centralized • Single location • Limited number of interfaces between IS	• Decentralized • Multiple locations • Many interfaces between IS
System/Platform	• Managed by small number of personnel	• Managed by staff of several IT professionals
End-User Computing	• Relatively dependent on electronic spreadsheets	• Relatively dependent on applications, some downloads of data to spreadsheets
Service Organizations	• Tend to rely on SO for IT operations functions	• Tend to use its own staff for IT operations, but outsources other functions
IT Risks & RMM	• Could identify many of these risks by understanding the COTS being used, how it was installed, and how it is being used	• Various sources, and not readily identified in one single area of IT or a single technology
ITGC: Change Management	• Simple controls designed to make sure software is updated properly	• Complex set of controls for custom software and testing, commercial software and configuration, and hardware

[7] Taken from a combination of the PCAOB's AS5 Guidance document, "*Audit of Internal Control Over Financial Reporting that Is Integrated with an Audit of Financial Statements: Guidance for Auditors of Smaller Public Companies*", January 23, 2009, and the AICPA's IT Audit School materials.

ITGC: Access Control	• Fairly simple controls designed to prevent unauthorized changes to financial data in COTS	• Relatively complex set of controls for physical and logical access over financial data at rest, in transit, and wherever it resides in IT
ITGC: Data Backup & Recovery	• Fairly simple controls designed to address potential loss of data needed in financial statement preparation	• Relatively complex set of controls to restore systems, technologies, and operations as a result of a pandemic event
Application Controls	• Tend to be manual and detective	• Tend to be automated or IT-dependent and preventive

Potential IT risks affecting financial reporting:

- Reliance on systems or programs that are inaccurately processing data, processing inaccurate data, or both
- Unauthorized access to data that may result in destruction of data or improper changes to data, including the recording of unauthorized or nonexistent transactions or inaccurate recording of transactions
- Unauthorized changes to data in master files
- Unauthorized changes to systems or programs
- Failure to make necessary changes to systems or programs
- Inappropriate manual intervention
- Potential loss of data

The nature and extent of these risks are somewhat dependent on the level of "complexity". For example, generally, as complexity increases, the type and number of potential IT risks increase, which could lead the IT auditor to devote more attention to IT controls. After identifying any relevant IT risks, the IT auditor would need to identify any controls that address those risks.

First, the risks in the company's IT processes or systems relevant to financial reporting, and the controls that address those risks are generally lower for simple complexity than for sophisticated complexity.

Second, the reports produced by IT systems that are used by the company for performing important controls over financial reporting are generated by COTS. It is vitally important that those reports be reliable. Some of these reports could end up as part of substantive procedures (e.g., an Accounts Receivable subsidiary list used to confirm A/R).

Third, the automated controls that the company relies upon are important to maintain effective ICFR.

Testing ITGC:

Security and Access[8] – controls over operating systems, critical applications, supporting databases, and networks that help ensure that access to applications and data is restricted to authorized personnel.

[8] In Dimension 3, this aspect of ITGC is referred to as Access Controls.

For entities with simple complexity, security administration is likely to be centralized, and P&P may be informal. A small number of people or even a single person typically supports security administration and monitoring on a part-time basis. Controls for mitigating the risk caused by lack of SoD tend to be detective controls rather than preventive. Access controls tend to be monitored informally.

Tests of security and access controls could include evaluating the general system security settings and password parameters; evaluating the process for adding, deleting, and changing security access; and evaluating the access capabilities of various types of users.

Computer Operations – controls related to day-to-day operations that help ensure that computer operational activities are performed as intended, processing errors are identified and corrected in a timely manner, and continuity of financial reporting data is maintained through effective data backup and recovery procedures[9].

For entities with simple complexity, there may be no formal operations function. There might not be formal P&P regarding problem management or data storage and retention, and backup procedures tend to be initiated manually.

Tests of controls over computer operations could include evaluating the backup and recovery processes, reviewing the process of identifying and handling operational problems, and, if applicable, assessing control over job scheduling.

Systems Development and System Changes – controls over selection, design, implementation, and configuration changes that help ensure that new systems are appropriately developed, configured, approved, and migrated into production, and controls over changes – whether to applications, supporting databases, or operating systems – that help ensure that those changes are properly authorized and approved, tested, and implemented. Although they might be viewed as separate categories, in simple complexity systems, systems development and system change procedures often are combined.

Typically, in the simple complexity environment, the entity uses a single or small number of COTS that do not allow for modification of source code. Any modifications are prepared by the vendor, and updates or patches are sometimes implemented over an Internet connection between the vendor and the entity. Usually, this function is performed by a single individual or small number of personnel.

End-User Computing – variety of user-based computer applications including spreadsheets, databases, ad-hoc queries, stand-alone desktop applications, and other user-based applications. These applications might be used as the basis for making journal entries or preparing other financial statement information. EUC is especially prevalent in simple complexity environments.

[9] NOTE: In Dimension 3, backup and recovery is treated as a separate aspect of ITGC, a different category of ITGC than computer operations (called Control Environment in Dimension 3).

EUC controls are controls over these end-user based applications such as spreadsheets that help ensure these applications are adequately documented, secured, backed up, and reviewed regularly for process integrity. EUC include general and application controls over user-developed spreadsheets and applications.

Tests of controls over EUC could include: assessing access controls to the source application, data, and/or folder to prevent unauthorized access; testing controls over spreadsheet formulas or logic or scripts; testing of controls over the completeness and accuracy of information reported by the EUC application; and reviewing the procedures for backing up the application and its data.

Application Controls – automated or IT-dependent controls intended to help ensure that transaction are properly initiated, authorized, recorded, processed, and reported. For example, the three-way match process (purchase order, receiving report, and vendor invoice) could be done automatically by the application. Management's review and reconciliation of an exception report generated by the system is an example of an IT-dependent manual control.

The general nature of application controls tends to be similar in most IT environments, but in simple complexity environments, the controls tend to be manual and detective rather than automated and preventive.

Testing application controls in the simple complexity environment could include a combination of inquiry, observation, document inspection, and re-performance of the controls. Efficiencies can be achieved through altering the NTE of testing procedures performed related to automated and IT-dependent application controls if ITGC are designed and operating effectively. In some situations, benchmarking of certain automated controls might be an appropriate audit strategy.

4.1.2 – Assurance Services for Service Organizations

The financial audit is not the only assurance service affected by IT risks and IT considerations. CPAs also evaluate and report on service organization controls (SOC). This area has been a key one for both public accounting and B&I CITPs because often IT plays such a key role in providing the relevant service. In the past, the "SAS 70 audit" was the premier example. But over time, the SAS 70 morphed into things not intended in the technical literature, so the AICPA developed an array of assurance services to meet the ever-expanding role and significance of IT in service organizations and establish a framework to prevent misapplication of SAS 70 audits.

In 2011, that array was classified into three different reports; a SOC1[10], SOC2, and SOC3 report (see Exhibit 4.3 below).

Thus one procedure for evaluating the effectiveness of a SO's controls is to review a Service Organization Control (SOC) report resulting from the engagement of a public accounting firm by the SO to examine and evaluate its controls in an agreed-upon procedure (AUP) engagement.

[10] SOC1 report replaces the former "SAS 70 audit" report.

The standards for such reports have been in place for many years at the AICPA as Trust Services – a set of principles regarding systems, security, and generally accepted privacy principles (GAPP). In 2011, the AICPA created a framework (see Exhibit 4.2) to distinguish between the characteristics and usage of the various types of reports that relate to SOs. The resulting reports are known as SOC1, SOC2 and SOC3. SOC1 is the new AUP report associated with SSAE No. 16 (replaces service auditors' responsibilities associated with the original SAS No. 70 "audit"[11]).

In essence, a SOC report discusses the design effectiveness, implementation, and operating effectiveness of the identified controls being examined at a SO. A type I report only addresses the first two aspects of the controls and a type II addresses all three.

FIGURE 4.3: SERVICE ORGANIZATION CONTROLS FRAMEWORK[12]

Factors\SOC Report	SOC-1	SOC-2	SOC-3
Applicable Standard	SSAE 16: AICPA Guide (2011)	AT 101: AICPA Guide (2011)	AT 101: Technical Practice Aid
Relevant Controls	ICFR	Security/Systems, Privacy	Security/Systems, Privacy
Controls Reference	<undefined>	Trust Services Principles/ GAPP	Trust Services Principles/ GAPP
Usage of Report	User auditor, management of SO, management of user	Knowledgeable parties (see AT 101)	Anyone

4.1.2.1 – Trust Services

The AICPA's Trust Services has five basic principles: security, availability, processing integrity, confidentiality, and privacy (see Exhibit 4.4). Each of these is expanded upon to provide details on the characteristics and nature of each one as an effective control by outlining criteria and illustrative controls for each.

[11] It is debatable as to whether the SAS 70 service was ever an audit, but rather an assurance service related to SO controls.

[12] Taken from AICPA's SOC comparison document located at:http://www.aicpa.org/InterestAreas/InformationTechnology/Resources/TrustServices/DownloadableDocuments/10957-378%20SOC%20Whitepaper.pdf, last viewed June 27, 2011.

FIGURE 4.4: TRUST SERVICES PRINCIPLES FRAMEWORK[13]	
Principle 1: Security	The system is protected against unauthorized access, both physical and logical
Principle 2: Availability	The system is available for operation and use as committed or agreed
Principle 3: Processing Integrity	System processing is complete, accurate, timely, and authorized
Principle 4: Confidentiality	Information designated as confidential is protected as committed or agreed
Principle 5: Privacy	Personal information is collected, used, retained, disclosed, and destroyed in conformity with commitments in the entity's privacy notice and with criteria set forth in GAPP

Attest criteria, for those except privacy, include policies, communications, procedures, and monitoring (see Exhibit 4.5). Each criterion is then subdivided into several segments with illustrative controls.

Attest procedures are also described as principles, criteria, and controls. The attest report is either a type I or type II.

FIGURE 4.5: TRUST SERVICES ATTEST FRAMEWORK[14]				
Criteria/Principles	*Security*	*Availability*	*Processing*	*Confidentiality*
1.0 – Policies				
2.0 – Communications				
3.0 – Procedures				
4.0 – Monitoring				

4.1.2.2 – Generally Accepted Privacy Principles

The generally accepted privacy principles (GAPP) are an international[15] set of principles related to the fifth element of Trust Services. GAPP is made up of ten criteria (see Exhibit 4.6). Each of these is expanded upon to provide details on the characteristics and nature of each criterion as an effective control by outlining details and illustrative controls for each.

[13] Taken from the AICPA's Trust Services web site materials located at: http://www.aicpa.org/INTERESTAREAS/INFORMATIONTECHNOLOGY/RESOURCES/TRUSTSERVICES/Pages/default.aspx, last viewed June 27, 2011.

[14] *Ibid.*

[15] GAPP was jointly developed by the AICPA and Canadian Institute of Chartered Accountants (CICA).

FIGURE 4.6: GAPP ATTEST FRAMEWORK[16]	
Management	The entity defines, documents, communicates, and assigns accountability for its privacy policies and procedures
Notice	The entity provides notice about its privacy policies and procedures and identifies the purposes for which personal information is collected, used, retained, and disclosed
Choice and Consent	The entity describes the choices available to the individual and obtains implicit or explicit consent with respect to the collection, use, and disclosure of personal information
Collection	The entity collects personal information only for purposes identified in the notice
Use, Retention, and Disposal	The entity limits the use of PI to the purposes identified in the notice and for which the individual has provided implicit or explicit consent. The entity retains PI for only as long as necessary to fulfill the stated purposes or as required by law or regulations and thereafter appropriately disposes of the PI
Access	The entity provides individuals with access to their PI for review and update
Disclosure to Third Parties	The entity discloses PI to third parties only for the purposes identified in the notice and with the implicit or explicit consent of the individual
Security for Privacy	The entity protects PI against unauthorized access, both logical and physical
Quality	The entity maintains accurate, complete, and relevant PI for the purposes identified in the notice
Monitoring and enforcement	The entity monitors compliance with its privacy policies and procedures and has the procedures to address privacy related complaints and disputes

4.1.2.3 – SSAE No. 16/SOC1 Assurance

A SOC1 report should provide information on the assurance of relevant controls (ICFR). Both the original SAS 70[17] and the SSAE No. 16 standard specifically limit the use of the associated services and reports to controls over financial reporting (ICFR). However, SAS 70 reports were

[16] Taken from the AICPA's Privacy web site materials located at: http://www.aicpa.org/privacy, last viewed on June 28, 2011.

[17] See sections of SAS 70/AU324 where it is clear the standard **ONLY** addresses ICFR: AU324.03: "The classes of transactions in the entity's operations that are significant to the entity's financial statements." "The procedures, both automated and manual, by which the entity's transactions are initiated, authorized, recorded, processed, and reported from their occurrence to their inclusion in the financial statements." "The related accounting records, whether electronic or manual, supporting information, and specific accounts in the entity's financial statements ..." "How the entity's information system captures other events and conditions that are significant to the financial statements." "The financial reporting process used to prepare the entity's financial statements including significant accounting estimates and disclosures."

issued for a variety of other controls purposes. Care should be taken by CITPs that the SSAE No. 16/SOC1 service/report not be misapplied to other controls needs – such as those identified in the Trust Services literature (and related SOC2, SOC3 reports).

The service is an AUP under the attest standards, AT801.

For most user auditors, the type II report will be the one needed.

In the SSAE No. 16 standard, management of the SO is required to document its controls in the form of assertions, which becomes the object of the AUP procedures and subsequent report.

When the SOC1 report is read by the user auditors, they are looking for the controls directly related to the assessed level of risk in the RMM. The user auditors would decide if the SOC1 report properly addressed all of the controls or not, as well as the impact of the results of the procedures of the service CPA performing the AUP, and as described in the written SOC1 report about assurance over the service provided and its associated data.

4.1.2.4 –SOC2 Assurance

A SOC2 report provides assurance over IT controls related to: security of data and processes; availability of data, systems, and automated processes; processing integrity; confidentiality of data; and privacy issues related to personal information (i.e. Trust Services principles). A type II SOC2 report would express an opinion on the operating effectiveness of the controls evaluated by the user auditor. A SOC2 report is a restricted report and cannot be released to the public. It is an agreed-upon procedure engagement using the attest standards (typically AT101 or AT201).

The user of the SOC2 report is looking for a reliable provider (CPA firm), the correct application of SOC2 (such as users and relevant controls), and relevant information (about user's relevant controls).

4.1.2.5 –SOC3 Assurance

A SOC3 provides the same kind of report on controls as SOC2 but can be used as a marketing and promotion tool to the public to demonstrate the sufficiency of the SO's controls, and basic management, of the service related to the customer's service being provided, and the identified controls related to it. The report is slightly different from a SOC2, but its chief distinction is the fact it is NOT a restricted report.

The user of the SOC3 report is looking for a reliable provider (CPA firm), the correct application of SOC3 (such as users and relevant controls), and relevant information (about user's relevant controls). A SOC3 report is the ONLY SOC report that is available to the public (e.g., posted on web sites, distributed to prospects, or otherwise used as a marketing piece).

4.1.3 – Other IT Assurance Services and IT Reviews

There are other relevant assurance services with which CITPs in public accounting might become involved, and a number of different reviews and reports with which CITPs in B&I might become involved. For public accounting, that would include an IT-related AUP (similar to SOC2 and SOC3 engagements), or specialized consulting engagements. For B&I CITPs, tasks other than those related to financial audits and SOC reports would probably include various IT reviews and reports, or specialized compliance audits for management.

One key common element to these other types of IT-related engagements and reviews is that they follow much of the premises and procedures described in this Dimension and Dimension 1 (risk) and Dimension 3 (Internal Controls).

4.1.3.1 – Agreed-Upon Procedures

There is a wide variety of IT-related engagements that could end up as an AUP using attest standards AT101 or AT201 related to IT, including the sufficiency of IT, the operational effectiveness of IT, and other similar engagements.

For IT controls, the best standard to follow if the controls are ICFR, or are associated with the financial statement, might be AT501, "*Reporting on the Entity's Internal Controls Over Financial Reporting.*". Examples of AT501 engagements include:

- Examining the suitability of the design of ICFR
- Examining the design and operational effectiveness of ICFR (i.e., providing a private company the equivalent of an AS5 audit for public company)
- Examining the design and operational effectiveness of a selection of the entity's ICFR
- Examining the design and operational effectiveness of ICFR based on criteria established by a third party (regulatory agency, business partner, etc.)

One condition of AT501 is that the opinion of the AT501 AUP has to be issued at the same time as the opinion for the financial statements. The types of opinions are basically the same as those of financial audit (adverse, disclaim, qualified, and unqualified).

4.1.3.2 – Consulting Engagements

When the scope of the IT engagement or procedures are not clearly defined, something necessary in AUP, the engagement to examine IT-related objectives might best be conducted using the consulting standards – *Statement on Standards for Consulting Services* (SSCS). For instance, an engagement to determine the effectiveness of an entity's IT function where the client does not stipulate the procedures or controls to examine but rather wants the CPA (CITP) to determine what areas are at risk. Another example might be an IT risk assessment that results in a report the entity plans to use, with or without edits, as its IT risk assessment document. Sometimes, a fraud investigation takes on the nature described above and is performed as a consulting engagement (relevant when the investigation includes digital evidence or CAATs to be used).

4.1.3.3 – IT Compliance

There are also a growing number of specialized IT compliance engagements that are needed.

4.1.3.3.1 – PCI

One specialty IT compliance assurance service is PCI. The Payment Card Industry (PCI) covers credit cards, debit cards, prepaid cards, e-purse, ATMs, and Point of Sale (POS) cards. The PCI Security Standards Council (PCI SSC) has developed a body of security standards for these financial services known as PCI Data Security Standards (PCI DSS) but often referred to as just

PCI. PCI SSC even provides its own certification for auditors, the key one being qualified security assessor (QSA).

PCI presents the opportunity for CITPs to provide needed assurance services; specifically the degree to which end-point retailers employ the PCI DSS. Merchants who comply with the standards via qualified standards assessments receive a compliance certification along with a listing on the PCI SSC web site. Thus, it is of great value for merchants to be PCI certified.

CITPs would measure and evaluate the compliance on the 12 requirements and provide a report on the results. Most often, this service would come in the form of an AUP engagement using the 12 PCI requirements as the procedures.

4.1.3.3.2 – HIPAA

Another specialty is Health Information Portability and Accountability Act (HIPAA) compliance (1996). HIPAA established national standards for electronic health care transactions and data for patients. The Administrative Simplification (AS) section (Title II) also addresses the security and privacy of health data. Since HIPAA defines violations relating to its provisions, and sets civil and criminal penalties for those violations, and since it is a federal regulation, all health care entities have a need for a HIPAA compliance assurance service.

Because this assurance service is about data, privacy, and security, the CITP is perfectly positioned to be the key provider of that assurance.

<u>4.1.3.4 – IT Reviews</u>

Internally, there is a broad scope of IT reviews that management may wish to see performed. These reviews could cover such issues as efficiency and/or effectiveness of:

- E-commerce system
- Supply chain system
- Computer-aided manufacturing system
- Financial reporting system
- Application development
- Transfers/middleware/interfaces
- Critical spreadsheets (privacy, security, etc.)
- Purchase of any key or significant technology or system
- Major changes to systems (e.g., switching from one vendors' applications to a new one)
- ERP conversions or operations
- Sufficiency of Disaster Recovery Plan / Business Continuity Plan
- Sufficiency of third-party IT service organizations, etc.

The CITP would use knowledge, skills, abilities, tools, and techniques described in the Dimensions to properly provide these reviews effectively. That is, those things needed to adequately perform these kinds of reviews use the same kinds of skills etc. as other types of IT-related engagements or reviews mentioned in the Dimensions.

4.2 – AUDITING TECHNIQUES & PROCEDURES

IT-related assurance services and IT reviews follow a similar process in performing the associated "audit" program. The techniques and procedures include planning for tests of controls (ToC) for both application controls and ITGC, gathering sufficient evidence related to program objectives, sampling considerations (if applicable), and using IT tools and techniques to gain efficiencies and/or effectiveness. The latter has generally become a beneficial option because of the expansion of computerized applications and business processes, digital data, and the increased ease of using the tools. Computer-assisted audit tools (CAATs) have become a valuable asset in audits, assurance services, and IT reviews for a variety of program objectives. Exhibit 4.6 shows an example of the overall process using a financial audit as the illustration.

The first phase of this process is the planning of the audit or review. The second phase depends on the type of audit or review being conducted, but generally follows the RBA. Once the CITP gains a thorough understanding of the target systems, technologies, and/or data, the CITP would usually perform some sort of risk assessment related to the audit or review objectives. From the information gained during the understanding step, combined with the information gained from the risk assessment step, the CITP then would design the appropriate tests and procedures of the audit or review. Those procedures would be directly linked to the risk. That is, the greater the risk, the more powerful the procedure and the more persuasive the evidence needs to be. The second phase concludes with the execution of those tests and procedures. Analyzing the evidence gathered from the tests and procedures, the CITP would use professional judgment to determine if the audit or review objectives had been satisfactorily met. If not, the IT auditor would return to the first phase of planning and iterate the first two phases. If they have been met, then the CITP proceeds to phase three which is to complete the evaluation of audit or review findings, compile evidence to support decisions or conclusions, and conclude with some kind of report on the results of the audit or review, and the report or a separate report generally includes some recommendations.

EXHIBIT 4.7: IT AUDIT PROCESS – Financial Audit Illustration[18]

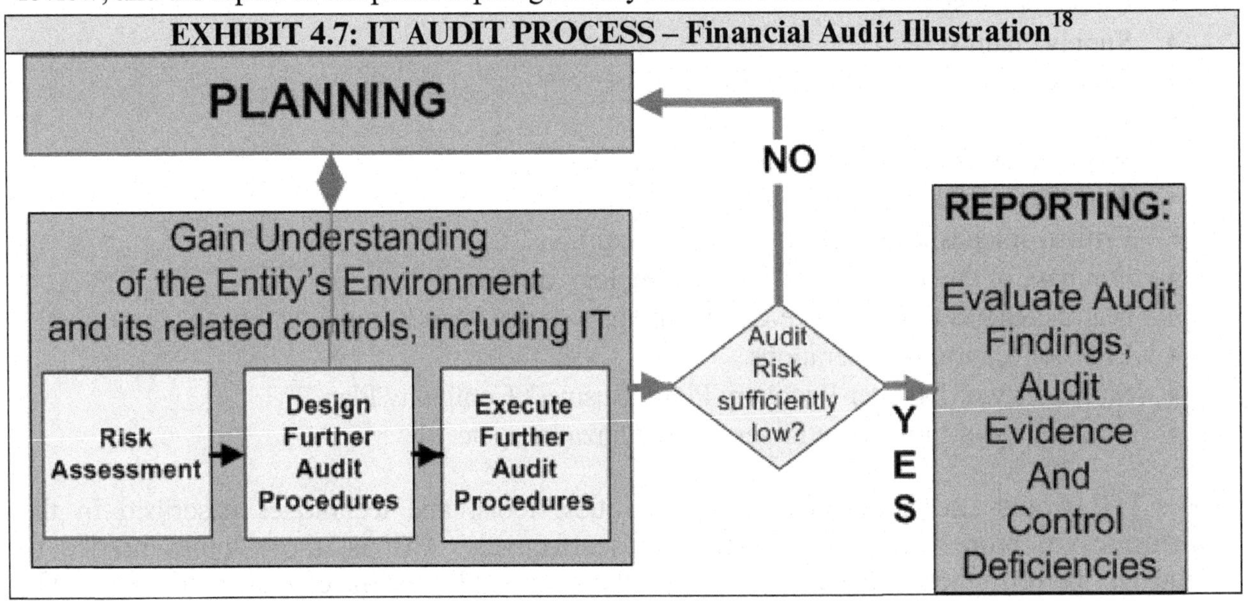

[18] Taken from AICPA ITEC's white paper on RBA, "*Information Technology Considerations in Risk-Based Auditing: A Strategic Overview*", June 26, 2007.

4.2.1 – Planning for Tests of Controls

Automated controls should be tested when there is an expectation of operating effectiveness for them, when substantive procedures alone do not provide sufficient evidence, and when there is a lack of audit trail other than through IT or digital data. Controls must be tested when required by law (e.g., S-OX), when no paper audit trail exists (e.g., EDI), and when substantive procedures alone do not provide sufficient audit evidence (e.g., high volume of routine transactions).

In addition, it is likely to be beneficial to conduct ToCs when it is a continuing client, when controls are stable (i.e. do not change) during the year, when there is effective ITGC, when walkthroughs have shown the design of a control is effective, when there is good SoD, and when reliance on internal audit is acceptable.

Planning for tests of controls (ToC) for application controls is reliant upon several factors. First, the ToC can ONLY be conducted if the relevant ITGCs are reliable. Second, ToC must be related to the audit objectives. Third, the objective is operational effectiveness, not simply the appropriate design of the control, or the implementation of the control. That consideration involves how controls were applied during the period under consideration, the consistency with which they were applied, and by whom they were applied.

One approach to determining the benefits of testing application controls versus manual substantive procedures is to look for overlaps. This overlap is the key to audit/review efficiency and effectiveness. This overlap scenario is when the audit objective and the control objective are virtually the same. For instance, if an audit objective is to gain assurance that disbursements were properly approved, and if there is an automated control or set of controls whose purpose is to make sure all disbursements are properly approved, and if the ITGC are reliable, then that audit situation should be ripe for efficiency gains by employing ToC over the set of approval controls. Typically, if the ToC results indicate the automated control is reliable, then the manual substantive procedures can be reduced substantially by relying on the automated control and reducing the scope of substantive procedures by increasing the cutoff or reducing the sample size. Another key factor is that it may be possible to test this particular kind of control with a sample/instance of one transaction (probably two transactions at the most given there are two outcomes: approved, disapproved).

Besides ToC over automated controls, ToC could be associated with ITGC such as application or systems testing.

4.2.1.1 – Application Control Testing

Application testing is a vital component of ITGC and auditing procedures. Application testing should follow basic System Development Life Cycle (SDLC) guidelines for customized code (applications written by the enity's own IT staff). That includes the testing of new or revised applications by the programming team. This testing should be a hurdle for which no change to applications can be performed without first successfully passing through the internal programming test.

Next, the IT function should have a quality assurance testing whereby an independent party in the IT function tests the application. Again, the application cannot be moved to the next stage without passing through this stage properly in an ideal SDLC environment.

After that process, the application should be tested by the end users and the internal sponsor in particular. Once this stage is passed, an end user acceptance agreement should be signed to provide evidence the application was properly tested by the end users.

Finally, the application is tested by being interfaced to all potential applications and modules in the entity's system, offline, to ensure integration errors do not occur. This integration testing is best performed within a staging area.[19]

The CITP would perform the application testing by interviewing key personnel and asking about the testing processes, reviewing the chain of relevant documents (e.g., end user acceptance report), observing the processes in operations, and/or other relevant procedures. Observation might be particularly useful in staging or project management meetings. The purpose of those procedures would be to gain assurance that the testing of applications follows the proper procedures and employs adequate controls to ensure minimal probability of errors, fraud or operational problems in deploying new or revised applications.

4.2.1.2 – System Testing

System testing follows the same processes as above but with some additional controls and best practices due to the scope of a system versus a single application. That is, a new or revised system should go through all of the above. The use of a staging area is much more important in system testing than application testing because of the increased risk of a system change versus an application change.

The system testing would proceed from the new or revised application layer mentioned above to integration with relevant financial reporting or accounting applications or systems, all the way up to and including the GL. It also would include an enterprise test where the new or revised system is integrated with all components of the enterprise system. Obviously, this last step is key for ERP or systems that are essentially fully integrated from customized and/or COTS systems.

Because of the increased risk, system testing usually includes a "war room" approach to the switch over from the old system to the new (including major revised) system. The staging area is usually a good place to centralize the switch over and be prepared for any and all types of integration or application failures.

When it is relevant to the assurance service or IT review, the set of procedures would be similar to ones described for application testing above.

---

[19] A staging area is a simulated enterprise system environment where all of the relevant applications and systems are present as they are in real operations, including the same type of hardware and connectivity. Only in this manner can an application or system be tested to the highest effectiveness. Applications can work properly when isolated but have errors or create problems when interfaced with other applications or systems.

4.2.2 – Evidence Gathering

The primary strategy in gathering evidence is to ***reduce audit risk*** to a sufficiently low level, and to provide sufficient evidence for the various audit objectives. For instance, evidence must be gathered for each relevant assertion of each material account balance or class of transactions or disclosure in a financial audit.

In the RBA, one driving factor behind evidence gathering is that the ***power of the tests*** used to gather evidence must be aligned with the level of assessed risk to the audit objective (e.g., the specific assertion(s) of a material account balance). That is, the higher the assessed level of risk, the more powerful the test required in order to gather sufficient evidence. Different types of tests have different levels of power and thus provide different evidence strategies (see Exhibit 4.8).

EXHIBIT 4.8: EVIDENCE STRATEGY	
Level of Reliance on Test Results	**Types of Tests**
Little	Inquiry
Moderate	Observation
High	Inspection or Re-performance

For instance, in a financial audit, if the assessed level of risk is moderate, inquiry alone is ineffective in gathering sufficient evidence[20], and inspection or re-performance is over-auditing. Observation is generally the optimum level of procedure to gather the appropriate evidence. Likewise when the assessed level of risk is high, observation alone is inadequate to gather sufficient evidence. It should be noted that combining two or more types of procedures has an additive effect on the end result of power.

Then there is the dynamic determination of the ***nature, timing, and extent*** (NTE) of audit procedures. For financial audits, generally, the lower the detection risk needs to be in order to achieve an acceptable level of audit risk, the more persuasive and reliable the evidence needs to be. Exhibit 4.9 describes some useful ways to determine the NTE of procedures needed.

[20] **NOTE**: Technical standards from the PCAOB and AICPA state that inquiry alone does not provide adequate evidence for audit procedures period.

EXHIBIT 4.9: EVIDENCE AND NATURE, TIMING & EXTENT OF PROCEDURES[21]		
Nature of Evidence (Source)	**Timing of Evidence (When)**	**Extent of Evidence (How Much)**
More Persuasive & Reliable When: • Directly obtained by the auditor • Obtained from independent and knowledgeable outside sources • Internally obtained when controls are effective • Exists in documentary form rather than oral representation • Provided by original documents rather than photocopies or facsimiles	***More Persuasive and Reliable When:*** • Obtained closer to the time of the transactions or valuations • Obtained on an unannounced or surprise basis • Obtained through use of cut-off periods • Obtained throughout the audited period for sampling procedures	***More Persuasive and Reliable When:*** • Testing involves more individually significant items • Larger sample sizes are used • Lower acceptable analytical variances are established • More disaggregation is used in analytical procedures • Inquiries or confirmations are corroborated

4.2.3 – Sampling Considerations
Sampling can be an asset to the audit or review. However, care must be taken in choosing the proper statistical methodology and an optimal sample size. Sampling is also important in examining ITGCs.

4.2.3.1 – Sampling Methodologies
There are four methodologies for statistical sampling.

Attribute sampling estimates the rate of occurrence of certain characteristics of the population. Attribute sampling is particularly useful for examining deviations in the performance of a control, and is thus useful in ToC. Any failure of the control to function properly would be treated as a deviation.

Discovery sampling is designed to identify a small number of ***critical*** deviations or exceptions in the population. It is most often used to detect a fraudulent transaction. If there is a single deviation in the sample (i.e. a fraudulent transaction), then the auditor must examine the entire population.

Classical variables sampling (CVS) provides an estimate of a numerical quantity, such as a dollar balance of an account. It is used by auditors primarily to perform substantive tests. CVS includes mean-per-unit estimation, ratio estimation, and difference estimation. Thus, CVS is useful in confirming accounts such as accounts receivable.

[21] Taken from the AICPA's IT Audit School materials.

Probability-Proportional-to-Size Sampling (PPS) develops an estimate of the total dollar amount of misstatement in a population. PPS uses dollar-unit sampling or monetary unit sampling (MUS). In PPS, the higher the dollar value of a sample transaction, the more likely it is to be included in the sample. MUS is often used in fraud detection.

One other sampling approach is a "directed sample". In this approach, the sampler determines sample size based on professional judgment. For instance, if the table suggests a sample size of 66, the sampler may choose to add a cutoff factor of all transactions above a certain figure. The sampler may also use professional judgment to simply reduce the sample size of 66 if the ToC proved to be reliable, where the assumption is there is low risk of deviations or misstatements because the ToC are reliable.

4.2.3.2 – Sample Size

Sample size is determined by the size of the population, the deviation (error) rate, and statistical methodology. Tables have been created to assist the IT auditor in determining sample size easily. For instance, if the population is 10,000 transactions and the objective is anti-fraud control effectiveness, with a 95% confidence interval, discovery sampling tables indicate a sample size of 483. Using the same criteria, attribute sampling tables indicate a sample size of 66 (7% tolerable deviation rate, one allowable deviation). This comparison shows the fact that sample size is dependent on the methodology and other factors.

It also demonstrates "power". Simply put, the larger the sample size, the more transactions a CITP will examine, and the greater the probability anomalies or exceptions will be found. Thus, discovery sampling has more "power" in its sample size than attribute sampling in the case above.

In choosing the sample, effect size is another factor. If the deviation is measured in dollars or amount, then the sampler can determine the size of the deviation. For example, in medical research, a statistical test for the effects of smoking on males 40-50 years of age, it may be assumed that smoking reduces the life span of the smoker. The question is, how much of a reduction is big enough to be important? Perhaps one year is not significant, but five years may be. The determination of that number of years is size effect. Obviously size effect has everything to do with materiality and tolerable misstatements.

4.2.3.3 – Sampling ITGCs

When examining ITGCs, the CITP will often rely on samples and review as the procedure of choice. For example, if the entity writes some of its own relevant applications, then the entity will need controls to ensure those applications are materially free of bugs, errors, and fraud. One way to provide this kind of control is to adhere to SDLC principles (basically, best practices). In order to gain an understanding of the entity's controls over application development, the CITP could review a list of all relevant applications, eliminate those that are not relevant, and eliminate those that are considered minor (impact, risk, size), and take a directed sample of what is left. Examination of the documentation on those relevant major IT projects should provide the CITP with evidence as to whether application development controls are operating effectively or not. A relatively easy way to make that determination is to simply compare the documentation and processes described with the principles of SDLC.

Other ITGCs could be sampled. For example, IT support operations (sample support tickets and audit them), logical access controls for terminated employees (sample terminated employees during the period), authorization and sound vendor management of IT change management (sample of IT purchases from the period), and proper testing procedures for change management or application development or systems development (sample changes in IT, review testing documentation). Some ITGCs are better suited for a full review (e.g., minutes of the BoD, steering committee, change management committee, and PMO – which are few in number and therefore not too cumbersome).

4.2.4 – Technical Tools & Techniques (CAATs)

CAAT is an acronym for computer-aided audit tools, or computer-assisted audit techniques. In general, it is the employment of computers and technologies to automate one or more audit procedures or processes. CAATs have the potential to change the audit from routine documentation of the audit trail (numbers and documents) to analysis of the evidence (in digital form). IT auditors actually make this switch often without realizing it.

4.2.4.1 – Why CAATs?

CAATs can be used for three basic purposes: to replace or supplement substantive procedures in an audit plan, to gain audit efficiencies or effectiveness, and to obtain value-add recommendations for management or the client. The primary advantage of CAATs is that it evaluates 100% of the transactions, and is not limited to examining samples of data or transactions.

It is likely that if a reasonably experienced CITP participates in the audit planning for assurance services that he/she would be able to find ways to employ CAATs as an alternative to extensive manual substantive procedures in such a way as to create audit efficiencies. Sometimes it is simply quicker to gather evidence using a CAAT rather than manual procedures. But even if in the first year if efficiencies are not obtained, in the second and following years, the CITP might gain significant efficiencies because the efforts to develop the data extraction process and CAAT procedures can be turned into automated processes saving time in future audits and reviews.

An increase in audit effectiveness might also be obtained by the use of CAATs. Part of this is associated with the fact that CAATs are examining 100% of the population and not a sample. Another aspect of it is the fact that CAATs usage naturally leads to analysis of transactions versus the temptation to get into rote documentation of the audit trail. But the greatest opportunity for audit effectiveness is when high risks are present. Again, high-powered tests are needed to gather sufficient evidence when high risk exists. One way to effectively perform inspection and re-performance is by using CAATs. Combined with the fact of 100% examination, this approach may be the most powerful of all choices. So when audit risk or RMM is assessed at a very high level, CAATs should be carefully considered.

Another key advantage is the statistical analyses that can be performed to turn an audit trail set of procedures into more of an analysis of the transactions. CAATs provides statistical analyses that are unavailable in manual substantive procedures, and provides for improved sample selection using directed samples combined with techniques such as stratification, identification of outliers, etc.

It is fairly common for the results of tests and procedures performed with CAATs to lead to value-added recommendations for management of the client. It is likely that the use of CAATs will improve the quantity and quality of those recommendations. In addition, IT recommendations seem to be more appreciated by client and management.

Regulatory requirements also affect the need for CAATs. For instance, it is difficult to comply with S-OX section 404 audits without the use of CAATs. Some government agencies required CAATs as part of their request for proposals (RFPs). Some international audits also require CAATs.

CAATs may also provide the solution to solving a problem in the audit. For example: assessing the extent of bad debts or bad loans, inventory problems, assessing the performance of collecting cash, and speeding up time prove certain calculations (e.g., extending inventory value).

There are other reasons for using CAATs related to certain internal analyses needed, or external reporting pressures.

4.2.4.2 – How to Effectively Use CAATs

In a financial audit, a CAAT could be used to identify the most efficient and effective financial audit procedure. When the audit objective of substantive procedures is the same as an automated process or output of CAATs, then that procedure is a good subject for IT-related procedures using CAATs. Generally, an experienced CITP can identify multiple opportunities for CAATs in an audit or review of a large entity or an entity with a high level of nature and complexity of its IT.

4.2.4.3 – Ways to Use CAATs

There are numerous ways to use CAATs in an audit or review. For instance, the CITP could use CAATS to check automated controls by re-performing edit checks, matching, and other controls or business processes. Then, based on the results, the CITP can draw an inference about the effectiveness of automated controls and business processes. For example, if no errors exist in the results, then controls were working effectively – because tests included 100% of transactions – and we can infer they were effective throughout the period under review or audit. Vice versa, if a large number of exceptions are identified, controls are likely to be deficient.

CAATs are also helpful in gathering evidence related to the relevant assertions for material account balances, classes of transactions, or disclosures.

- ***Technical accuracy and valuation assertions***: Total records in a file, recalculate totals in a file, prove accuracy of calculations, aging (debt, AR, AP, re-perform automated calculations)
- ***Existence and validity assertions***: Exception testing to identify unusual items and anomalies (for example, a relationship between two data sets that do not correlate correctly)

4.2.4.4 – CAATs-Techniques

The following is an illustrative list of possible techniques:

- Compare or combine data from different sources
- Compare or combine financial and non-financial data
- Duplicates testing: payments, inventory sold, issued, or received, payroll checks
- Gaps testing: AR, sales invoices, checks, inventory tickets
- Matching: cross check a master file with its transaction file (e.g., vendors to disbursements, employees to payroll checks)
- Use of other commands within the tool (e.g., classify or group, Benford's Law, etc.)
- Statistical sampling
- Cutoff: year-end GL and JE, inventory transactions, test for dates or sequence numbers at year end

CAATs are also useful in examining thresholds and cutoffs associated with approvals. Approval levels include: purchase orders, dual approval, check approval. The process would include a test of data just below an approval threshold to recognize the abuse of approval level or test data for leading digit anomalies (both to identify excessive number of transactions just below the approval level).

CAATs are beneficial when certain analyses are needed. For example, risky transactions and anomalies might be identified with the use of the stratification technique. Trend analysis is another useful technique to identify anomalies, and is especially useful in fraud detection.

4.2.4.5 – CAATs-Tools

CAAT tools are available in a wide variety of technologies and software packages. They provide technology for data extraction, data mining, and data analysis.

4.2.4.5.1 – Simple Tools

The simple tools include technologies such as: database queries, database report writers, electronic spreadsheets, and spreadsheet plug-ins[22]. Simple tools are useful for small data sets and simple procedures (e.g., extracting a suitable sample). They are affordable and relatively simple to use.

However, most of these tools are susceptible to error and caution should be exercised in using them for evidence gathering. That is, controls and steps should be implemented to ensure data integrity both at data extraction and throughout testing usage of the data.

4.2.4.5.2 – Sophisticated Tools

The sophisticated tools include technologies made by vendors such as ACL, IDEA, Arbutus, and PanAudit. Their usefulness includes specialized testing, use of very large data sets, and the need

[22] Plug-ins are tools that become embedded with the host technology usually as a menu option. Active Data is one such example, and is designed for Excel. It becomes part of Excel as a menu/tab option.

for sophisticated procedures. When higher risks exist in the audit or review plan, they are likely to be more appropriate than simple tools. They also are more costly.

4.2.4.6 – CAATs Considerations

Before using CAATs, some considerations will need to be made. They include:

- What data is involved (type, format, consistency, large data set or small)
- What types of systems are involved (COTS, custom)
- Where is the data located (local or remote; single or multiple sources)
- Contact for data extraction

A primary requirement is how to ensure data integrity. First, at the data extraction point, the CITP needs to have assurance that the data set extracted is **exactly** the data set on the operational computer. One methodology is to use something similar to the batch control total approach[23] to data processing. Second, the CITP must ensure data integrity throughout the process of testing and reporting. That means locking down spreadsheet data, or using read-only (RO) data in a CAAT tool.[24]

Perhaps the most difficult part of using CAATs is to extract the data successfully and effectively from the operational computer to the CAAT tool. There is an ideal format that looks like a spreadsheet: the first row is column headings, all rows are contiguous (no subtotals, no breaks, etc.), each row beginning with the second contains data, and usually no cell is empty. The file formats easiest to import are dBASE, delimited text/ASCII, Excel files, print to file, and pdf (not scanned). Other options usually are fairly time consuming to effectively import. The last option is to hand key all of the data, and that clearly is a time consuming, last resort, approach.

4.2.4.7 – Digital Data Considerations

There are some other and unique considerations for digital data when fraud is involved. Legally, the data must be subject to proper chain of custody. The CITP needs to understand the broad scope of possible digital sources beyond the entity's computer systems and data. The fourth amendment (expectation of privacy) must be observed carefully. The different types of data should be considered. That is, data exists in relatively extractable form but also in metadata (data about data such as the formula in a spreadsheet or email headers), and in latent form (not easily extractable, usually requires a SME). See Dimension 2 for more of fraud and data.

4.3 – ASSESSMENT OF CONTROLS

In an audit, the assessment of controls is an important part of audits of ICFR (e.g., SOX audits). In an IT review, assessment of controls may be THE purpose. Either way, control matters will

[23] A total of number of records being extracted, the total of an amount column, and a total of a numeric but non-dollar amount column. Reconcile these to those of the operational computer data when n extracted. Some CAATs have this process built into it.

[24] Most CAATs use RO for imported data for this reason.

come to the attention of the CITP or IT auditor that should be evaluated as to whether or not the control is an impairment to data integrity or effective business processes. There is a standard manner of rating control problems as to their deficiency, if one exists.

4.3.1 – Deficiency Evaluation of IT-Related Controls

While the technical literature for financial audit does not contemplate expressing an opinion on controls for private companies, there is a requirement for auditors when they detect control deficiencies. There is technical literature that does require expressing an opinion of controls for public companies (issuers).

The technical literature on control definitions evolved in response to the Sarbanes-Oxley Act of 2002 (SOX). Section 404 of SOX requires management of financial statement issuers to evaluate the entity's system of internal controls, and for the auditor to opine on that evaluation. In response to that, the PCAOB and AICPA converged on definitions about control deficiencies.

That is, the technical literature focuses not on controls per se, but rather on control deficiencies of "key" controls. Control evaluation is not described as dichotomous (either "good" or "bad") but as types of deficiency. CITPs must be familiar with these terms, definitions, and the application thereof. Because of the convergence of technical standards, there is a common set of definitions for three types of control deficiency.

These definitions are included in SAS No. 115, "Communicating Internal Controls Related Matters Identified in an Audit". The severity of such deficiency is further defined as a combination of magnitude (of misstatement caused by the Control Deficiency {CD}) and probability (that such control will actually fail). There is also a list of material weakness (MW) indicators, and a list of CDs that would at least be significant deficiencies (SD).

The PCAOB has identical definitions and information in AS5, "An Audit of Internal Control Over Financial Reporting that is Integrated with an Audit of Financial Statements."[25] Obviously, CITPs in B&I, where the entity is an issuer, will be concerned with the issues related to these terms. Because of the prevalence of this definition, all CITPs need to know and understand them.

<u>4.3.1.1 – Deficiencies Definitions</u>

Control deficiency definitions have been made congruent by the various relevant parties (PCAOB and AICPA primarily). They are as follows:

4.3.1.1.1 – Control Deficiency

Control Deficiency (CD): The design or operation of the control does not allow management or employees, in the normal course of performing their assigned functions to prevent, or detect and correct misstatements in a timely basis.

[25] See Section 2.F for definitions of control deficiencies. AS5 also includes identical lists of SDs and MWs, and the same severity formula as SAS No. 115.

4.3.1.1.2 – Significant Deficiency

Significant Deficiency (SD): A significant deficiency is a deficiency, or a combination of deficiencies, in internal control that is less severe than a material weakness, yet important enough to merit attention by those charged with governance.

4.3.1.1.3 – Material Weakness

Material Weakness (MW): A material weakness is a deficiency, or combination of deficiencies, in internal control, such that there is a reasonable possibility that a material misstatement of the entity's financial statements will not be prevented, or detected and corrected in a timely basis.

4.3.1.2 – Aggregation of Deficiencies

One key factor in assessing deficiencies is to aggregate them, for much the same reason and in much the same way as financial auditors aggregate misstatements. A single deficiency may not represent a significant impact on assurance of certain audit objectives. However, if several control deficiencies of small risk are found to be present, they should be aggregated to determine if in the aggregate they represent a SD or MW.

4.3.2 – Materiality/Impact to the Entity

SAS No. 107 and 109 were discussed about, complete with an illustration on how to assess the RMM (see exhibit 4.1). Documentation is required of the risk assessment and resulting materiality for each relevant account, class of accounts, and disclosures. That includes the relevant assertions on those objects.

4.3.2.1 – Risk of Material Misstatement

For the CITP, the RMM begins with the identification of IT risks where the IR is beyond some threshold of tolerance (e.g., moderate or high IR). Then the CITP would examine CR related to that IT risk to determine if management has adequately reduced the RMM to an acceptable level. That is:

RMM = IR x CR

4.3.2.2 – Operational Deficiencies

Assurance services and IT reviews may identify operational deficiencies. In fact, for the IT review that may be the review purpose. For assurance services, the CITP would need to consider whether such deficiencies impact the audit program, and whether they should be reported as value-add recommendations to management. In the IT review, they will likely be either an integrated part of the review or a subject of a separate report to management.

4.3.3 – Assessment Reporting

The result of the deficiency evaluation described in 4.3.1 may lead to the need to report on the deficiency.

4.3.3.1 – SAS No. 115

The current technical literature related to evaluating and reporting control deficiencies is SAS No. 115, "*Communicating Internal Control Related Matters Identified in an Audit*". SAS 115 uses the definitions given in 4.3.1.1. Misstatements are evaluated on both magnitude and probability (see Exhibit 4.10).

Magnitude of misstatement is generally limited to the amount of the account balance recorded in the financial system. The materiality level is the driving force behind measuring magnitude. Factors that affect the magnitude of a misstatement resulting from a deficiency include the financial statement amounts or total of transactions exposed to the deficiency, and the volume of activity in the account class of transactions exposed to the deficiency.

Probability of misstatement refers to the likelihood that a control could have failed to prevent or detect a misstatement in the financial statements. SAS 115 uses the term "reasonable possibility". The determination of reasonable possibility may be made without quantifying the probability (e.g., an estimated range). In many cases, the probability of small misstatements will be greater than that of a large misstatement.

EXHIBIT 4.10: ASSESSING SEVERITY OF CONTROL DEFICIENCY

Probability of Misstatement

Magnitude*	Reasonably Possible	Remote
Material**	Material weakness	Could be significant deficiency, but not a material weakness
Less than material	Could be significant deficiency, but not a material weakness	Could be significant deficiency, but not a material weakness

** Magnitude of misstatement that occurred, or could have occurred*
*** Quantitatively or qualitatively material*

While there are no listed indicators of SD in SAS 115, some indicators of MW are:

- Ineffective oversight of financial reporting and internal controls by those charged with governance
- Restatement of previously-issued financial statements to reflect the correction of a material misstatement due to error or fraud
- Identification of fraud, whether or not material, on the part of senior management
- Identification by the auditor of material misstatement of the financial statement under audit in circumstances that indicate that the misstatement would not have been detected by the entity's internal control

Further, deficiencies in the design of control or failures in the operation of internal control may be deficiencies, SD, or MW.

The auditor is required to communicate SDs or MWs in writing to those charged with governance. The communication should be made by the report release date.

4.3.3.2 – Other Reporting

Assessment reporting is also valuable and needful for engagements other than the financial audit, and for IT reviews internally. The reporting is generally proprietary to the special assurance service or IT review. In that report, controls identified as not functioning properly and/or causing relatively high risk of operational failure or financial misstatement would be reported along with a summary of test results and recommendations for improvements to that internal control. For AUP associated with internal controls, the reporting is dictated by the respective attest standard (e.g., AT101, AT201, etc.).

4.4 – INFORMATION ASSURANCE

Information assurance is similar to other assurance but limited to the presentation of data. Some of the more important factors are quality, presentation, timeliness, and auditability.

4.4.1 – Information Quality

Information quality is related to data integrity. That is, the quality of information presented in a report or screen only has quality if the data used to generate it has integrity. It also has quality if the information is useful for decision making (i.e. effectiveness), delivered with integrity, and the cost is reasonable.

4.4.1.1 – Effectiveness

Primarily, information quality effectiveness is related to the usefulness of the information in making decisions. It also refers to information being relevant and pertinent to the business processes affected by it. Information needs to be timely, correct, consistent, and usable to be effective. If the information enables the manager and/or user to make sound, productive decisions, then the information is effective. If the information is not helpful in making decisions, then that information would be considered ineffective.

4.4.1.2 – Delivery

The delivery of the presentation of that information must get to the right place at the right time in order to have quality. Thus, delivery also plays a role in making information effective. If the information gets to the wrong person, or late, then that information is likely to be ineffective in making sound decisions.

4.4.1.3 – Cost

The cost of the information is related to the efficiency of information. If the information is cost-beneficial, then it will generally be efficient.

4.4.2 – Information Presentation

Data is raw numbers and words that are converted into something meaningful and useful, which is information. Therefore, information is by its nature presented in some form, usually a report or screen output.

4.4.2.1 – Relevance

The information being presented needs to be relevant to the task or purpose at hand.

4.4.2.2 – Fitness for Use

Decision making has a set of criteria and circumstances. In order for information presented to be valuable, it must fit the use determined by the set of circumstances surrounding the situation or decision.

4.4.2.3 – Disclosure

Proper disclosures should be presented with information to provide the user any supplemental information. For example, if the data came from different internal sources, or if some data is internal and some external, then the information presentation should identify those sources.

4.4.3 – Information Timeliness

Timeliness is usually a critical factor for information usefulness. That means all of the relevant data should be used, and should be current when presented.

4.4.3.1 – Latency

Data should be designed with its usefulness in mind. Management should also have a formal process to ensure valuable, useable data does not lay dormant in data files. Thus, usefulness of data and information benefits should be considered during change management, application development, and system development processes, and all of the data should be properly documented.

4.4.3.2 – Currency

For information to be useful and valuable, it necessarily needs to be current. The older information is, the less useful it tends to be. Controls should be in place to ensure that information is current.

4.4.4 – Information Auditability

In order to verify the veracity and reliability of information, information being presented needs to have an audit trail back to the original data. Thus information should be auditable as part of assurance of information quality.

4.4.4.1 – Source Traceability

Information used for decision making and in business processes needs to be able to be traced back to the original data used to create that information. This traceability is necessary to ensure the integrity and reliability of the information. That is, the information being reported is indeed a presentation of the data it claims to present.

Source traceability is usually “audited” by using data mining or CAAT tools. Controls should be in place to make sure data can be traced from source to output. This tracing is usually a function of data, application, and systems design.

4.4.4.2 – Transformation Traceability

When data is transformed into information, there is a need to trace the data through that process – usually an automated one. Thus the design of middleware and transfer systems need to be tested to ensure transformation traceability which will ensure the integrity auditability of the information.

Advanced Reading Recommendations:

AICPA/ITEC. "Information Technology Considerations in Risk-Based Auditing" (discussion paper). 2007. AICPA: online.

AICPA. SAS No. 104-111, 115.

AICPA, Trust Services (2010).

COSO. "Internal Control over Financial Reporting – Guidance for Smaller Public Companies", Volumes II (Guidance) and III (Evaluation Tools). 2006.

Moeller, Robert R. "IT Audit, Control, and Security". 2010. Wiley: Hoboken, NJ.

PCAOB, AS5.

Weber, Ron. "Information Systems Control and Audit". 1999. Prentice Hall: Upper Saddle River, NJ.

GLOSSARY:

Application Controls

Application Controls are internal controls, whether automated or manual, which operate at the transaction-level with the objectives of ensuring that:

- Proper authorization is obtained to initiate and enter transactions;
- Applications are protected from unauthorized access;
- Users are only allowed access to those data and functions in an application that they should have access to;
- Errors in the operation of an application will be prevented or detected and corrected in a timely manner;
- Application output is protected from unauthorized access or disclosure;
- Reconciliation activities are implemented when appropriate to ensure that information is complete and accurate; and
- Ensuring that high-risk transactions are appropriately controlled.

Assertion Level Risks

Assertion level risks are risks that are limited to one or more specific assertions in an account or in several accounts, for example, the valuation of inventory or the occurrence of sales. Assertion level risks are addressed by the nature, timing, and extent of further audit procedures, which may include substantive procedures or a combination of tests of controls and substantive procedures.

The risk of material misstatement at the assertion level has two components:

- Inherent Risk (IR), which is the susceptibility of an assertion to a material misstatement, assuming that there are no related controls. Inherent risk is greater for some assertions and related account balances, classes of transactions, and disclosures than for others.
- Control Risk (CR), which is the risk that a material misstatement that could occur in an assertion will not be prevented or detected by the entity's internal control on a timely basis. Control risk is a function of the effectiveness of the design and operation of the entity's internal control.

Automated Control

Controls automation involves leveraging technology to build and enforce internal controls with the least manual intervention possible. It can take many forms, including better use of available system configuration options of the kind common in enterprise resource planning (ERP) systems, to using workflow and imaging technologies to automate and drive processes from start to completion.

Control Risk

Control Risk (CR) is the risk that a material misstatement will not be detected or prevented by the entity's internal control on a timely basis. The auditor must consider the risk of misstatement individually and in aggregate with other misstatements.

Detection Risk

Detection Risk (DR) is the risk that the auditor will not detect a material misstatement in the financial statements of the entity being audited.

End-user Computing

In the context of this paper, end-user computing (EUC) is a function developed using common desktop tools like spreadsheets, that are used in financial processes for purposes of determining amounts used for accounting and financial reporting purposes.

Electronic Commerce

Electronic business applications or processes that facilitate commercial transactions. Electronic commerce can involve electronic funds transfer, supply chain management, e-marketing, online marketing, online transaction processing, electronic data interchange (EDI), automated inventory management systems, and automated data collection systems.
Source: Wikipedia; http://en.wikipedia.org/wiki/Electronic_commerce

Emerging Technologies

Changes or advances in technologies such as information technology, nanotechnology, biotechnology, cognitive science, robotics, and artificial intelligence.

Financial Statement Level Risks

Financial statement level risks are risks that may affect many different accounts and several assertions. Financial statement level risks typically require an overall response, such as providing more supervision to the engagement team or incorporating additional elements of unpredictability in the selection of your audit procedures.

Further Audit Procedures

SAS 110 defines further audit procedures (FAP) that include tests of the operating effectiveness of controls, where relevant or necessary, and substantive procedures, whose nature, timing, and extent are responsive to the assessed risks of material misstatement at the relevant assertion level.

Inherent Risk

Inherent Risk (IR) is the susceptibility that a relevant assertion could be misstated assuming that there are no other related controls. The auditor should consider the risk of misstatement individually as well as in aggregate with other misstatements, assuming there are no related controls.

Internal Control

Internal control is a process, affected by an entity's board of directors, management and other personnel, designed to provide reasonable assurance regarding the achievement of objectives in the following categories:

- Effectiveness and efficiency of operations
- Reliability of financial reporting
- Compliance with applicable laws and regulations

Key Concepts:

- Internal control is a process. It is a means to an end, not an end in itself.
- Internal control is affected by people. It's not merely policy manuals and forms, but people at every level of an organization.
- Internal control can be expected to provide only reasonable assurance, not absolute assurance, to an entity's management and board.
- Internal control is geared to the achievement of objectives in one or more separate but overlapping categories.

Source: COSO; http://www.coso.org/IC.htm

For additional resources on internal control over financial reporting visit www.cpa2biz.com for:

- *Internal Control—Integrated Framework* (product no. 990012kk), a paperbound version of the COSO report that established a common definition of internal control different parties can use to assess and improve their control systems. [http://www.cpa2biz.com/AST/Main/CPA2BIZ_Primary/InternalControls/COSO/PRDOVR~PC-990009/PC-990009.jsp]
- *Financial Reporting Fraud: A Practical Guide to Detection and Internal Control* (product no. 029879kk), a paperbound publication for CPAs in both public practice and industry. [http://www.cpa2biz.com/AST/Main/CPA2BIZ_Primary/FinancialManagement/Finance/FinancialReporting/PRDOVR~PC-029879/PC-029879.jsp]
- In July 2006, COSO released its guidance, "Internal Control over Financial Reporting—Guidance for Smaller Public Companies," which may assist companies and auditors understand the applicability of the COSO Framework to smaller entities. This publication can be ordered from the www.cpa2biz.com or through any of the sponsoring organizations. [http://www.cpa2biz.com/AST/Main/CPA2BIZ_Primary/InternalControls/COSO/PRDOVR~PC-990017/PC-990017.jsp]

Internal Control, Five Components of (COSO)

The Committee of Sponsoring Organizations of the Treadway Commission (COSO) outlines internal control in their *Internal Control-Integrated Framework*, as consisting of five related components that must be present for an entity to achieve effective internal controls. These five components are:

- The control environment
- Risk assessment
- Control activities
- Information and communication
- Monitoring

IT Auditor

A professional possessing the necessary knowledge and skills to understand and audit an entity's IT environment, systems, or applications, in support of a financial statement audit, internal audit, or other form of attestation engagement. The IT Auditor often has deep domain-specific knowledge or specialized skills (e.g. in use of computerized tools) that makes them particularly competent to understand the IT environment (and its associated risks) or perform IT-specific audit procedures.

IT Control Risk
IT Control Risk is a type of Control Risk where the source of risk is related to the use of IT in the processing of transactions or security of underlying data.

IT General Controls
IT general controls are internal controls, generally implemented and administered by an organization's IT department. The objectives of ITGC are to:

- Ensure the proper operation of the applications and availability of systems;
- Protect both data and programs from unauthorized changes;
- Protect both data from unauthorized access and disclosure;
- Provide assurance that applications are developed and subsequently maintained, such that they provide the functionality required to process transactions and provide automated controls; and
- Ensure an organization's ability to recover from system and operational failures related to IT.

Logical Access Controls
Logical access controls are policies, procedures, and automated controls that exist for the purpose of restricting access to information assets to only authorized users.

Material Weakness
A material weakness is a significant deficiency, or combination of significant deficiencies, that results in more than a remote likelihood that a material misstatement of the financial statements will not be prevented or detected.
Source: AICPA; http://www.aicpa.org/Storage/Resources/Standards/DownloadableDocuments/AU-00325.PDF

Materiality
Materiality is "the magnitude of an omission or misstatement of accounting information that, in the light of surrounding circumstances, makes it probable that the judgment of a reasonable person relying on the information would have been changed by the omission or misstatement." Materiality is influenced by the needs of financial statement users who rely on the financial statements to make judgments about the client's financial position and results of operation and the auditor must consider audit risk and must determine a materiality level for the financial statements.

Operating Effectiveness
Operating effectiveness is concerned with determining if "controls operate with sufficient effectiveness to achieve the related control objectives during a specified period." This is a function of how control is applied, the consistency with which it is applied and by whom it is applied.

Risk Assessment Procedures

Risk Assessment Procedures are audit procedures performed to obtain an understanding of the entity and its environment, including its internal control, to assess the risk of material misstatement at the financial statement and relevant assertion levels.

Risk assessment procedures include:

- Inquiries of management and others within the entity
- Analytical procedures
- Observation and inspection

Risk-Based Approach

The Risk-Based Approach (RBA) methodology which provides assurance that significant risks associated with audit objectives have been identified, and that audit procedures address them to adequately gain assurance about the objectives of the audit, and the mitigation of those risks or nature of residual risk that exists.

Risk of Material Misstatement

The risk of material misstatement (RMM) is defined as the risk that an account balance, class of transactions or disclosures, and relevant assertions are materially misstated. Misstatements can result from errors or fraud.
The RMM consists of two components:

- **Inherent Risk** is the susceptibility that a relevant assertion could be misstated assuming that there are no other related controls. The auditor should consider the risk of misstatement individually as well as in aggregate with other misstatements, assuming there are no related controls.
- **Control Risk** is the risk that a material misstatement will not be detected or prevented by the entity's internal control on a timely basis. The auditor must consider the risk of misstatement individually and in aggregate with other misstatements.

Using the audit risk model to illustrate this concept: Inherent Risk x Control Risk = RMM

Auditors describe RMM as the combined assessment of inherent risk and control risk. However, auditors may make a separate assessment of inherent risk and control risk.

Significant Deficiency

A significant deficiency (SD) is a control deficiency, or combination of control deficiencies, that adversely affects the entity's ability to initiate, authorize, record, process, or report financial data reliably in accordance with generally accepted accounting principles such that there is more than a remote likelihood that a misstatement of the entity's financial statements that is more than inconsequential will not be prevented or detected.
Source: AICPA, http://www.aicpa.org/Storage/Resources/Standards/DownloadableDocuments/AU-00325.PDF

Substantive Procedures

According to SAS 110, substantive procedures, "...are performed to detect material misstatements at the relevant assertion level, and include tests of details of classes of transactions, account balances, and disclosures and substantive analytical procedures. The auditor should plan and perform substantive procedures to be responsive to the related assessment of the risk of material misstatement."

Test of Controls

When the audit strategy involves relying on the operating effectiveness of the controls for some assertions in the design of substantive procedures or when substantive procedures alone do not provide sufficient appropriate audit evidence at the assertion level, the auditor should design and perform tests of the operating effectiveness of controls (TOC). Additionally, they will perform procedures to evaluate the design of internal controls and determine whether they are implemented.

CASE & STUDY QUESTIONS:

Management of a provider of material-based solutions for electronic, acoustical, thermal, and coated metal applications has decided to make significant modifications to its inventory management software applications. The IT operations has its own staff and IT director who reports to the COO. The company has offices in Riverside, Midway, and Bluff City, located it two states. The inventory systems is interfaced with the GL system, as is the revenue system (which is a custom application written by its own staff). The inventory account is material to the balance sheet. The company has two applications developers on staff and needs to rely on those individuals to develop, test, and migrate the software to production. As the company does not have an automated code promotion utility to control versions and development processes, the IT manager:

- Identifies and analyzes risk resulting from changes that will be required
- Assigns changes to developers so that each developer works on only those changes assigned to him/her
- Assigns to the developer NOT responsible for a particular change responsibility for testing the change and migration to production
- Reviews any significant changes
- Locks versions following user acceptance testing to prohibit further changes prior to release into production

The IT manager also relies on manual controls to manage the code version and migration. He therefore:

- Creates a manual log listing the version of the code copied to the development environment, along with date and time, and manually tracks the migration to test and then to production
- Separates the review of all version control procedures prior to moving the code to production from those performed by the individual responsible for the IT function

1. Based on the information provided in this case, how would the prudent CITP evaluate the characterization of IT complexity?

    (A) Simple complexity
    (B) Mostly simple with some sophisticated aspects
    (C) Sophisticated complexity
    (D) Moderate complexity

Key: C
Section Name: IT Considerations (4.1.1.4)
Bloom's Taxonomy category: 2. Comprehension, 3. Application, and 4. Analysis
Reference: "ICFR – Guidance for Smaller Public Companies" (Vol. II), COSO, page 72.
Solution:
Stem (C): *Because the entity writes its own applications to relevant financial applications, it is by definition sophisticated complexity.*
Option (A): The fact the entity does NOT use COTS, and writes some of its own applications means it cannot be simple complexity

Option (B): There is NO simple aspects to this case, in regards to IT considerations
Option (D): Because there is no simple aspect of IT considerations in this case, it cannot be moderate

2. Based on the case above, for a financial audit, what is the most likely conclusion of the prudent CITP regarding the audit program?

   (A) Because of the level of complexity, a professional IT auditor is not relevant as an integral part of the audit team during the planning process
   (B) Because of the controls in place, a flowchart of the relevant financial applications is not relevant to the IT audit tasks
   (C) Because of the controls around application development, IR associated with custom software has not been mitigated
   (D) Because of the nature of application development, it is not necessary to test all IT projects, just use a small sample of major projects

Key: D
Section Name: Planning for tests of controls (4.2.1), Evidence Gathering (4.2.2), Sampling Considerations (4.2.3)
Bloom's Taxonomy category: 2. Comprehension, 3. Application, and 4. Analysis
Reference: "IT Audit, Control, and Security", Robert R. Moeller, pages 133-134. ITEC White Paper, page 9, 12, 13.
Solution:
Stem (D): The general process for evaluating controls over application development is to take a sample of major projects and evaluate them.
Option (A): Because it is sophisticated complexity, a professional IT auditor IS needed
Option (B): When application development is present, a flowchart may be helpful (ITEC White Paper, page 12
Option (C): Controls in the case to mitigate the IR in custom software do reduce the audit risk (RMM) considerably.

3. Based on the case above, how would you assess the controls around application development and the fact there is limited SoD?

   (A) There is no control deficiency
   (B) There is a control deficiency
   (C) There is a significant deficiency
   (D) There is a material weakness

Key: A
Section Name: Deficiency Evaluation of IT-Related Controls (4.3.1)
Bloom's Taxonomy category: 2. Comprehension, 3. Application, and 4. Analysis
Reference: SAS No. 115, AS5

Solution:
Stem (A): The compensating controls for lack of SoD include the IT director review, and the process of segregating the two on each project, especially in separating testing. These compensating controls are sufficient to reduce the IR to no control deficiency.
Option (B): See (A), should not be evaluated as a control deficiency
Option (C): Because of the controls mentioned in (A), the controls should not be evaluated as significant
Option (D): There is no indication of material weakness in the case.

4. Based on the case above, for a financial audit, what is a control designed to mitigate the IR of custom applications?

    (A) IT director reviewing significant changes
    (B) Segregating the two employees on a project by development and testing
    (C) Identifies and analyzes risk resulting from changes that will be required
    (D) All of above

Key: D
Section Name: Evaluating Evidence (4.2.2)
Bloom's Taxonomy category: 2. Comprehension, 3. Application, and 4. Analysis
Reference: "IT Audit, Control, and Security", Robert R. Moeller, pages 167-172.
Solution:
Stem (D): Each of these controls has some ability to mitigate the IR associated with application development and limited SoD
Option (A): This control does mitigate some of the IR. The IT director has some probability of identifying or recognizing errors or fraud in significant applications.
Option (B): This control does mitigate some of the IR. Some SoD is better than none.
Option (C): This control does mitigate some of the IR. Knowing the risks that could occur and analyzing them should reduce the occurrence of potential risks.

5. In using CAATs, suppose it is decided that depreciation amounts performed by automated applications should be tested. Which of the following is the BEST category for this test?

    (A) Selecting audit samples
    (B) Summarizing data and performing analyses
    (C) Comparing data on separate files
    (D) Testing calculations and making computations

Key: D
Section Name: CAATs (4.2.4)
Bloom's Taxonomy category: 1. Knowledge, 3. Application
Reference: "IT Audit, Control, and Security", Robert R. Moeller, pages 167-172.
Solution:
Stem (D): This test is re-performance of an automated calculation and is therefore categorized as testing calculations and making computations

Option (A): Although a test could be designed to test a sample of depreciation calculations, using CAATs, and 100% of the transactions, and testing an automated calculation are best suited for testing calculations
Option (B): Although a test might be designed to test depreciation calculations by summarizing data, using CAATs, and 100% of the transactions, and testing an automated calculation are best suited for testing calculations
Option (C): It may be possible to test depreciation calculations using data file comparisons, using CAATs, and 100% of the transactions, and testing an automated calculation are best suited for testing calculations

INFORMATION MANAGEMENT & BUSINESS INTELLIGENCE

Dimension 5

Ensuring that information is managed such that it provides value in decision making and it serves other managerial needs. The management of information includes effectively managing business processes, data analysis and reporting, and performance management.

LEARNING OBJECTIVES

1. To understand information management and how it can provide value to the entity by the appropriate management of information
2. To understand and identify opportunities associated with the value of using IT to create or modify work flows and business processes that have the potential to make more effective use of resources
3. To understand the process of gathering, modeling, and transforming data with the goal of identifying the more useful information, suggesting conclusions, and supporting effective decision making
4. To understand how to apply data analysis and reporting concepts in such a way as to efficiently and effectively analyze enterprise performance, and to help the entity to achieve its accountability goals and objectives, using both financial and non-financial information

5.0 – INTRODUCTION

The main objective of this Dimension is to provide content on *managing* and *utilizing* information for an entity. Information *management* includes managing information from design to destruction. This Dimension also provides familiarity with the business processes and certain software categories in which information is generated, computed, analyzed, changed, or deleted. *Utilization* of information involves data mining and business intelligence whereby business users are empowered to make effective operational and strategic decisions. We include discussion about reporting tools and techniques, and various performance measures in particular.

5.1 – INFORMATION MANAGEMENT

Probably the most important aspect of information management is the ability to recognize transactional data and other relevant data that has the potential to affect the effectiveness of operational and strategic decisions, and the benefits thereof. This recognition would require critical thinking about data, what is valuable, what is not, how best to report it, what purposes it would best benefit, and how to leverage information to gain competitive advantages or long-term business success.

For the purposes of Dimension 5, ***data*** will be defined as a collection of numbers, characters, images, and other outputs from devices or processes that collect data and information. Data is a collection of raw, unorganized alphabetic, numeric, or symbolic representations of objects.[1] ***Information*** is defined as data organized into usefulness, especially for decision-making purposes. Information is data that has been validated as accurate and timely, is presented within a context that gives it meaning and purpose, is specific and organized for a purpose, and can lead to an increase in understanding and decrease uncertainty.[2] The value of information is directly related to its ability to affect positively behaviors, decisions, or outcomes.[3]

5.1.1 – Information Lifecycle Management

The foundation of effective information management is a thorough understanding of the information lifecycle management (ILM). There is a wide range of lifecycle descriptions, but the one presented herein is consistent with the body of ILM models. Our steps will be to: identify, capture, organize/manage, access/share/utilize, archive, and destroy, as seen in Exhibit 5.1.

5.1.1.1 – Identify

For information to serve its optimal benefits, there must be a formal, structured approach to identifying what data to capture that has the potential to significantly assist management in operational and strategic decisions. In the basic information requirements stage of systems development life cycle (SDLC), or systems analysis, the appropriate transactional data should be identified by using standard principles (i.e. meeting with users and business owners, studying business processes, understanding the outputs, etc.). However, end users and business

1 See Business Dictionary definition online: http://www.businessdictionary.com

2 *Ibid*

3 *Ibid*

owners/sponsors often do not realize the full scope of effective data. Thus the entity needs a formal, structured approach to ensure security and business intelligence (BI) needs will also be met with the data being identified. That structure could involve a cross-functional team, some form of IT governance guideline and/or body, a change control committee, or similar structure. The process would include involving end users, business managers, information security specialists, and BI specialists/analysts up front in the project in order to identify a complete body of data, as well as a formal, documented process.

EXHIBIT 5.1: INFORMATION LIFECYCLE

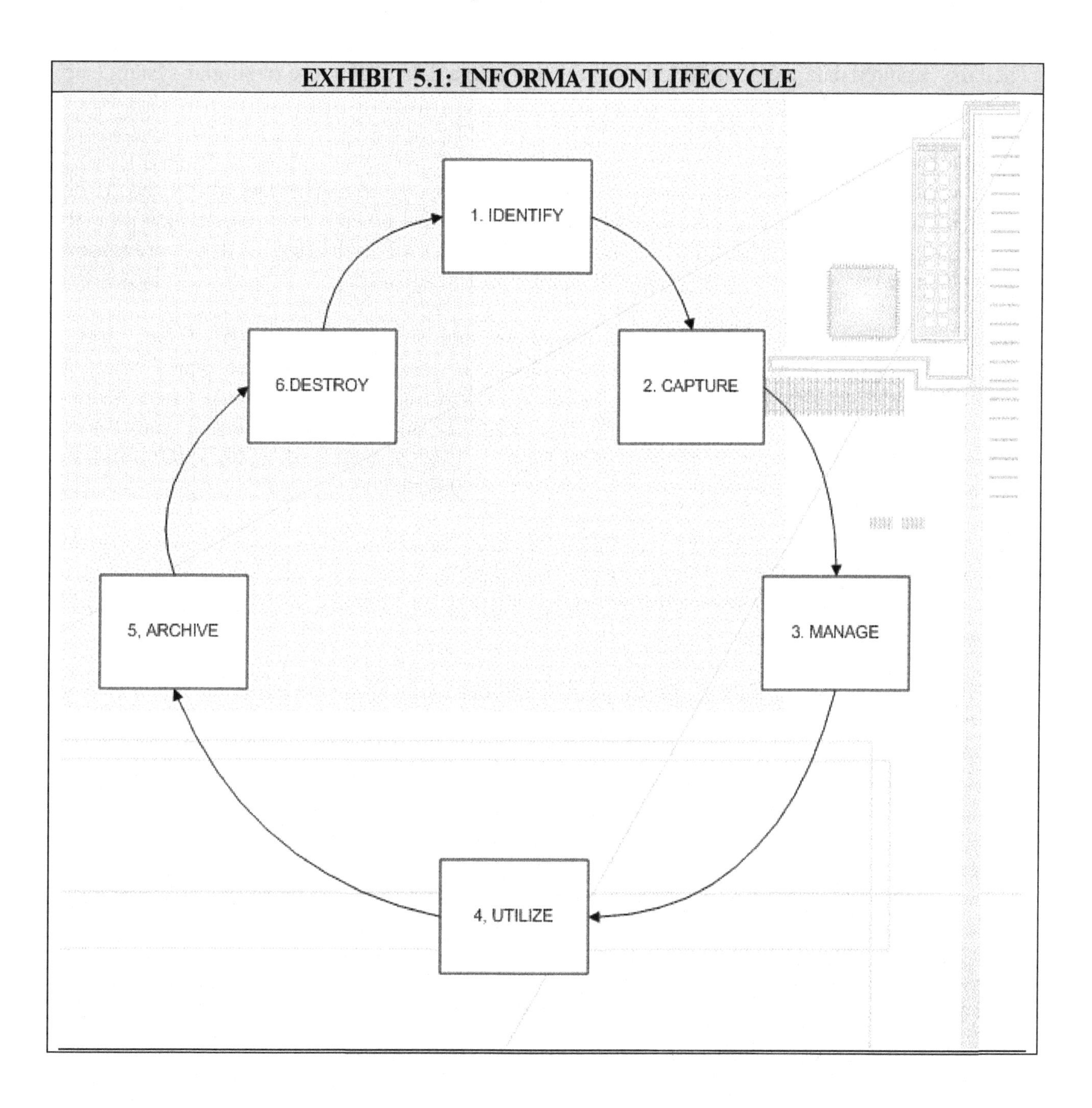

5.1.1.2 – Capture

Whether the data is being created or already has been created, the next step is to capture data in all of the processes that should be able to be captured by transactional processing systems (TPS). Care should be taken, however, to recognize data that might be in manual processes or external systems/locations (external to TPS). Manual processes might involve manually entering data into an electronic spreadsheet or database offline. External data might exist in internal systems other than TPS, such as customer relationship management or supply chain management systems. External data might also exist external to the entity.

Then the captured data would need to be aggregated into a data warehouse or similar system (see 5.3.1.2, Data Warehouse).

5.1.1.3 – Manage

The next step would involve managing the data that is being captured. The data would need to be organized into systems, and eventually organized down to the tables/files. It would also need to be organized at the enterprise level for strategic purposes, such as BI (e.g., a data warehouse). That organization would involve a choice of a platform and software.

The management of the captured data would include several key factors. First, proper management of data should provide appropriate access to users. Data should be shared where it is beneficial and necessary for operations and decision-making, but also restricted where data is NOT necessary. This aspect is referred to as availability and generally means to make sure access to information is given to those who need it. Logical access is a key component in managing data, both in availability and restricted access to data.

Data should be managed to ensure the quality of data. Data integrity is reliant upon adequate controls over data input, processing, storage, and output. Controls at the point of data entry are generally considered more efficient and effective than controls at processing or output phases.

Timeliness of delivery of data as information is another factor in managing data. Whether it is information for supervisors in operations or executives planning strategy, information normally has a time context to it. That is, there is a time window when the information would be useful, and at some point in time, the information becomes less useful, possibly useless. For instance, a scheduling supervisor in operations may need information on human resources available and man hours required for a certain week for planning. That information would be needed far enough in advance of that specific week in order for the scheduler to make effective decisions in scheduling human resources. But once the week begins, and possibly before, the usefuleness of that information will have diminished. Similarly, decisions and tasks of other managers and executives have a time factor, and timeliness means the information gets to the user when they need it. Therefore, information should be presented to users WHEN they want it.

Format is another aspect of managing data, specifically as data is transformed into information and communicated to users. The format needs to be one that suits the task being performed, and the person performing the task. For instance, the further up the corporate structure a user is, the more likely that information needs to be aggregated. Many times graphical presentation is more efficient and effective than tabular data or printed reports. Often a system interface or screen output is more effective. Therefore, information should be presented to users HOW they want it.

5.1.1.4 – Utilize

With proper management of data in place, the next step is to provide proper utilization of that data as information. Users will need access to information, especially users associated with operational or strategic responsibilities. One key benefit of a database approach is the fact data can be shared, as data or as information, with all need-to-know parties. Information management thus would include delivering and reporting information timely to the right person.

5.1.1.5 – Archive

Some data will need to become part of "permanent" data, some semi-permanent, and some temporary. In recent years, entities are capturing and storing more and more data. The key is to identify the life span of data being collected and to provide the appropriate archive system, storage, and management for permanent data. A data warehouse is often employed to archive permanent and semi-permanent data needed for BI or other strategic purposes.

The entity would need to use archival techniques for developing its policy for archiving various types of information and data. The information/data could be categorized by type where useful lives are consistent within each category. For instance, email might consistently have a useful life of 18 months and be archived accordingly. Attachments to email, however, might need to be archived based on the type of document it is, and a different rule applied to the attachment. Similarly, legal documents and work product have special requirements that might require archiving for several years. The Securities and Exchange Commission (SEC) requires data and documents related to audits and reviews of financial statements to be kept for seven years. But informal meeting notes in electronic documents are likely to have short lives.

5.1.1.6 – Destroy

Data that reaches the end of its life span should be recognized as such, and provisions should be in place to appropriately destroy that data. But different types of data have different lives, and some of the life spans differ between entities. Thus data destruction policies need to be developed based on contractual, legal, and other constraints. Data should not be stored infinitely without this consideration. To do so incurs costs and risks, including legal risks (e.g., e-Discovery, see 2.5.2). Therefore each entity should work with legal counsel and as to the specific criteria for the archival and data destruction policy.

5.1.2 – Compliance

Proper information management means the information is in compliance with relevant policies and procedures, laws and regulations, and contractual obligations.

5.1.2.1 – Internal Policy

Management should develop policies and procedures (P&P) related to information, and the ILM above provides a start of items to be considered. Monitoring of compliance with P&P should also have been provided, and compliance monitored through the various processes and measures established by management.

5.1.2.2 – Regulatory

There are a variety of state and federal laws that address the protection and handling of information for which management needs to have considerations in place to ensure compliance.

5.1.2.2.1 – Privacy

There are several federal and state regulations related to personally identifiable information (PII) – information that would potentially allow someone access to financial assets, or personal medical information.

From the federal perspective, there is the ***Health Information Portability and Accountability Act*** (HIPAA) of 1996. The Administrative Simplification provisions of HIPAA require health care entities to provide reasonable privacy and security for PII for health data. Management of health care entities obviously need information P&P and monitoring to ensure compliance with this legal requirement. (See 4.1.3.3.2 for more on HIPAA)

Another key federal law is the ***Gramm-Leach-Bliley Act*** (GLBA) of 1999. GLBA applies to financial institutions such as commercial banks, investment banks, securities firms, and insurance companies. However, some key aspects of GLBA apply to entities that receive PII such as credit reporting agencies, appraisers, mortgage brokers, etc. One of these relevant information-related aspects is known as the Safeguards Rule, and requires financial institutions to design, implement, and maintain safeguards to protect customer information. The requirements include a written information security (InfoSec) plan that describes how the entity plans to protect PII, for consumers past or present. Affected management would need to study how they manage private data and do a risk analysis in order to properly comply with GLBA.[4]

The first and probably most influential state law was California SB-1386, "***California Database Breach Act***" of 2002. Effective July 1, 2003, residents of California whose unencrypted PII was, or is reasonably believed to have been, acquired by an unauthorized person must be notified by the entity with the breach. In other words, any agency, person, or business that conducts business in California, and owns or licenses digitized PII must disclose any security breach to residents affected. Other states have since adopted a similar law. Management must do a risk assessment to determine if they are subject to CA SB-1386, or similar state law, and take action accordingly with P&P and a monitoring process.

Another key state law is the ***Massachusetts Data Privacy Act*** (MDPA), bill 201 CMR 17. Companies who do business with people who reside in Massachusetts or businesses that are located there must comply with this law. MDPA establishes minimum standards for safeguarding PII of any resident of the state by organizations or individuals who own, license, store, or maintain PII. It applies to the collection, storage, or processing of PII. Thus an entity (e.g., data center) that simply stores PII, or processes PII (e.g., credit card processing) may be subject to this law. PII is defined in MDPA as social security numbers, driver's license or state-issued ID numbers, financial account numbers, and credit/debit card numbers (with or without CVV codes, PINs, or passwords). Care should be taken by entities that maintain PII data to make sure whether they are subject to MDPA.

---

[4] Some of this paragraph is taken from http://en.wikipedia.org/wiki/GLBA.

5.1.2.2.2 – Security

All four of these laws cover both privacy and security issues related to data and information, and PII in particular.

Industry requirements can affect the entity. For example, entities that use credit/debit cards have PCI compliance issues in order to accept and process charges (see 4.1.3.3.1, PCI).

5.1.2.3 – Other External Compliance

Other external compliance-related issues would relate to contractual obligations and industry requirements. The PCI compliance above is an example of industry requirements. Banks have other requirements from Federal Financial Institutions Examination Council (FFIEC) which has certain auditing requirements that affect information management.

5.1.3 – Information and Data Modeling

Data can be unstructured or structured. Unstructured data do not have a prescribed format and are captured, stored, and processed in free form (e.g., a text editor and text file, similar to word processing). Structured data have a prescribed format, and data is organized and stored into files, records, and fields with criteria for data entered into that format – such as transaction data stored from the business processes of an enterprise resource planning (ERP) system. In order for computers to process data properly, it must be structured. That process of prescribing data format is known as information or data modeling. Data must be standardized in order for efficient processing to occur across systems and interfaces in the entity. That development process would also incorporate business rules into the data model.

5.1.3.1 – Understanding Data Modeling Concepts

Basically, data modeling provides an effective means for defining and analyzing data needed to support the business processes and other needs of the entity. Data models for different entities, and even different systems within an entity, are necessarily different. The result is interfaces are often problematic, require custom applications or manual rekeying, constrain the business processes, or otherwise present challenging needs.

Data Modeling should be the foundation for reporting. By gathering reporting needs first, data modeling can lead to an effective design of the data that will be captured, stored, and ultimately the information being reported. By following the data modeling approach, the resulting normalized data structure will lead to true process-based reporting and eliminate the limitations of systems-based reporting.

Data Modeling could also lead to more effective controls. The construction of the data models should identify key controls and key integration points. These factors enable management to develop effective controls, especially those associated with data transfers at points of integration as they represent high inherent risk.

These points illustrate the value data modeling can bring to an entity. More than a systems process, it can be an effective approach to improving reporting and controls.

5.1.3.1.1 – Data Structuring Using Schemas
In gathering information requirements, or the identify stage of the ILM, data can be structured using standard schemas: user, conceptual, and physical schema levels.

The data elements referred to in "identify" above (5.1.1.1) are developed into a ***external schema*** with criteria, descriptions, and definitions of the data (see Exhibit 5.2). The external schema is also associated with information requirements, specifically a schema for each user or group of users. This view is also known as the user view or schema. External view means the perspective of the data from external sources, specifically the users of the data. Different users, or groups of users, usually have different needs, use data for different purposes. Thus in order for the eventual system to adequately provide the data and information for all of the users, a composite view must be compiled that represents all of the needs.

These individual user or user group schemas are valuable for CITPs as they define what data a user or group of users need in order to perform their duties and as such are a tool for establishing logical access controls. That is, they provide with some precision what databases, files, records, and fields for which a user or user group should have access, and whether access is read-only (RO) or read-write (RW). It also provides some of the business rules for data integrity.

Once the external schema is complete, a composite of all external views or schemas is developed to represent the entity's view or schema, or the composite users' view, which is known as the ***conceptual schema***. The conceptual schema exists only on paper or in a digital document but prescribes the format of the database(s) with specificity of the data to be captured, stored, and processed at the enterprise level. The conceptual schema is also referred to as the logical schema.

Last, the conceptual schema is implemented via a database management system (DBMS) onto a physical computer, and is known as the ***physical schema***. That is, a database administrator (DBA) or similar technician formats databases, files, and fields to define all of the data to be captured in that particular system properly. This level of schema is also known as the internal view or schema.

Exhibit 5.2 depicts these levels of data abstraction and how they relate to each other.[5]

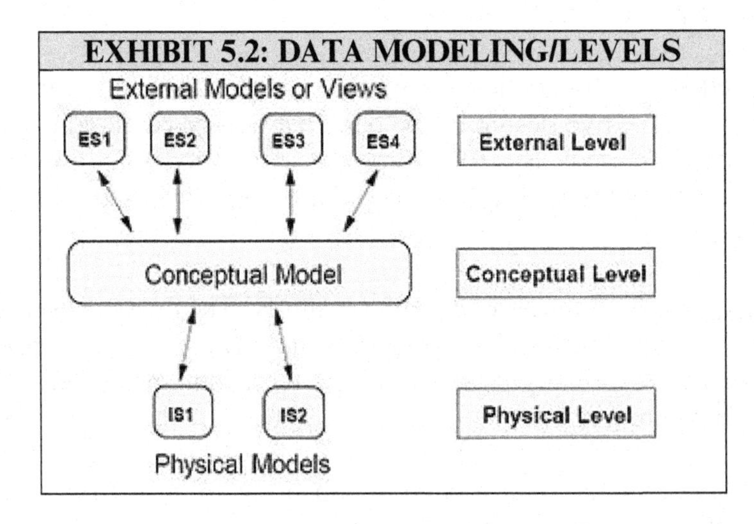

5 Taken from http://en.wikipedia.org/wiki/Data_modeling. Last accessed July 1, 2011.

5.1.3.1.2 – Understanding the Logical Unit / Structure of Data

Data has a ***hierarchical structure*** it follows. The smallest data segment is a bit (0 or 1); that is, data is stored in binary digit form. Eight bits make up a byte, which represents a keystroke on the keyboard (a letter, number, or special character). A field is a stream of sensible bytes (keystrokes) that constitute a data value, as described by the logical schema. A field describes a characteristic or attribute of the thing being tracked. A closely related set of fields makes up a record. A record is the data set for an instance of the thing being tracked by the database. A closely related set of records makes up a file. A file is all of the instances for a thing being tracked (files are persons, places, or things). A closely related set of files make up a database (e.g., payroll database with employees, payroll checks, withholding tables, etc.). A closely related set of databases make up an enterprise database (e.g., financial reporting database including payroll, AR, AP, GL, etc. databases). Exhibit 5.3 recaps the structural hierarchy of data along with synonyms from the relational database terminology, which conceptualizes the structure of data to something similar to an electronic spreadsheet.

EXHIBIT 5.3: DATA HIERARCHY[6]

DATA	***DESCRIPTION***	***RELATIONAL TERM***
BIT	0 or 1	--
BYTE	Keystroke, character	--
FIELD	Data Value, grouping of characters, attribute	Column
RECORD	Set of data values, a collection of attributes	Row
FILE	Group of related records	Table
DATABASE	Integrated collection of related files	--

Data values take on one of a variety of basic ***data types***. Data types can be simplified into three types: numbers, alphanumeric, and dates. Numbers would be used for quantities, amounts, and dollar amounts. Alphanumeric are illustrated by an address, where letters, numbers, and even special characters may be used in the data value. Dates are self-describing, but the data formatting should describe the specific date format (i.e. mm/dd/yy, or yyyy/mm/dd, etc.). Data definitions usually refine the specific nature and format of these data types. For instance, a quantity on hand in inventory may only be whole numbers so it would be defined and formatted to NOT accept decimal numbers. It may also have a lower and upper bound (minimum and maximum amounts).

5.1.3.1.3 – Understanding the Need for Data Normalization

Data files are generally seen as being in two forms: a flat file with all the transactional data in a single record (row), and databases where transactional data is broken down into separate files using a structured process. The latter is the outcome of data normalization.

Normalized data is a transactional flat file that has gone through a formal process where certain factors are eliminated in order to eliminate data anomalies; addition, deletion, and change anomalies. Anomalies are synonymous with errors and the antithesis of data integrity. Thus to

[6] Per Laudon & Laudon, "Management Information Systems: Managing the Digital Firm", 11e, 2009. Prentice Hall" Upper Saddle River, NJ, pp. 144-145.

CITPs, data files susceptible to data anomalies represents a significant IT risk in that system. Likewise, normalized data increases the integrity associated with capturing and managing data.

One of the outcomes of normalized data is to maximize the efficiency of the data model. The steps in the normalization process eliminates unnecessary redundancy of data elements, leaving any specific data field represented only once in the normalized database, except for duplication of fields as key fields to establish the relationships between files.

Integrating data from different systems is usually more efficient if the resulting integration data model is normalized.

5.1.3.1.4 – Understanding the Need for Consistency of Data

In order for computer processing and the actual "reporting" on information to be efficient and correct, data should also follow a consistent form in data entry. With some fields, that constraint is not readily a problem, but string fields (alphanumeric) and date fields should be examined for a need for consistency, and processing and keypunch rules should be established to enforce consistency. For instance, dates should follow the same format in data entry, storage, and processing. If the format is yyyy/mm/dd, then that should be enforced by the data entry and processing applications (that is, force the date entered to be converted into this format). The date entry might be easier and more effective (i.e. less errors) if entered as mm/dd/yy. However, the point is data cannot be correctly sorted, processed, and reported unless there is a consistent format.

A similar situation exists in entering certain string values. For instance, on an address, there should be some data entry rules for entering street as "street" or "st."; post office boxes as "POB", or "P.O. Box #####", or "PO Box #####", etc. Otherwise queries, reports, data mining, and data analytics can be frustrated by too many variable formats of data.

5.1.3.1.5 – Understanding Conceptual Data Modeling

Data structures should be documented and accurately portrayed with one or more of the conceptual data modeling tools available. They include the entity-relationship (ER) model, relational model, and Unified Modeling Language (UML).

The ***ER model*** depicts the relationship between files and records in the various data files in a top-down fashion. The resulting depictions are called ER diagrams. The ER diagram depicts the file, the type of interaction it has with another file (usually diagramed as a verb), and the relationship between records in one file to the other.

The ***relational model*** serves a different purpose. The relational model illustrates the data files as tables with arrows from primary keys to foreign keys to illustrate the relationships between data files (see Exhibit 5.4). The advantage of the relational model is the fact that individual files are depicted as a table, similar to an electronic spreadsheet, and fields are depicted as columns, records as rows. That abstraction is fairly easy for users to see and grasp a general understanding of the data structure.

The most recent data model is the ***unified modeling language*** (UML), which is particularly associated with object-oriented programming (OOP); that is, newer programming languages such as C sharp (C#) and Java. Both static and dynamic aspects can be depicted in a UML diagram, both structural information and types of behavior. UML is much more technical in nature than ER and relational models, and thus more difficult for CITPs to review and use unless they have training or experience in OOP.

EXHIBIT 5.4: RELATIONAL MODEL[7]

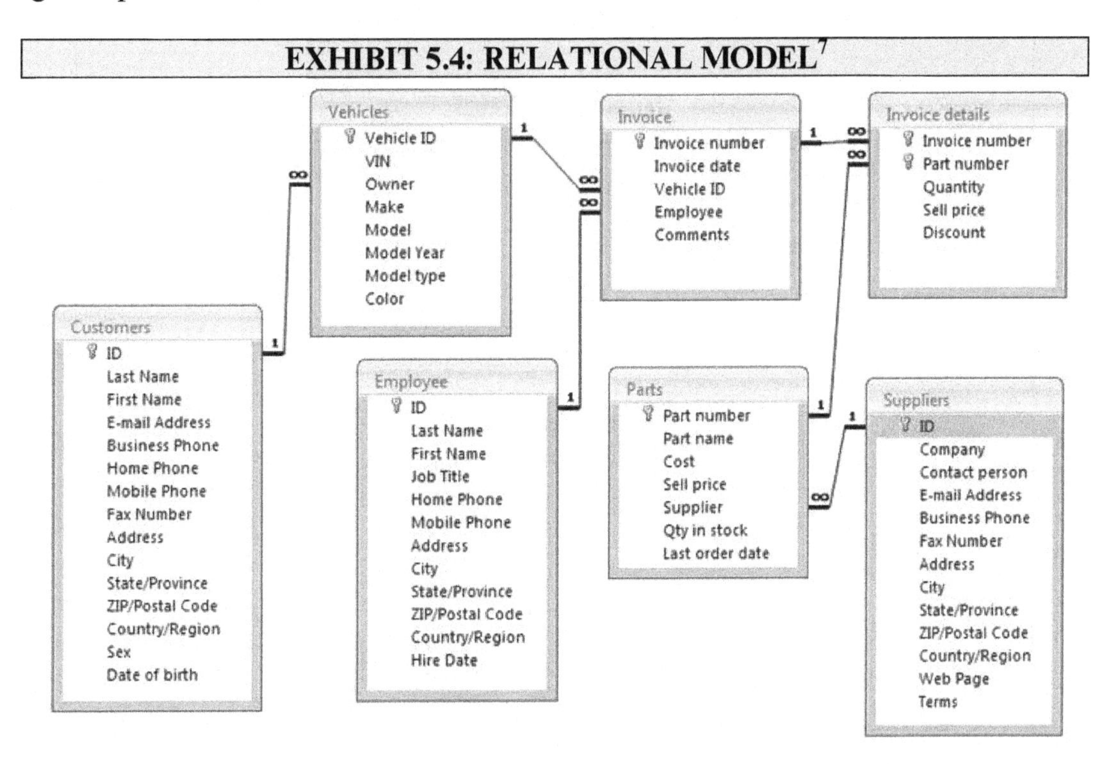

5.1.3.2 – Understanding Information Architecture Concepts

A business architecture is the organization and structure given to the information and IT of the business. The business information architecture should be properly documented, including the documents and diagrams that describe it. An effective design bridges the business model, business units, and business operations into a coherent architecture that facilitates the management and use of the relevant information.

5.1.3.2.1 – Business Information Architecture Components

A thorough business information architecture contains components of the structure of the enterprise information capabilities, IT/information governance structure, business processes, and business information. Capability is what the organization does, and the business processes are the how. Applicable external factors are also included in the components. See Exhibit 5.5 and 5.6 for examples of a business information architecture diagrams.

The architecture necessarily means an integrated view of an enterprise is required. The views included would be a business strategy view, business capabilities view, IT capabilities view, business knowledge view, business processes view, information resources view, and organizational view. The general purpose is to enable management to improve decision-making. Mapping and modeling are key functions and outcomes.

---

[7] Taken from Microsoft.com, illustrates the visualization of the relational model as used in Microsoft Access software.

EXHIBIT 5.5[8]

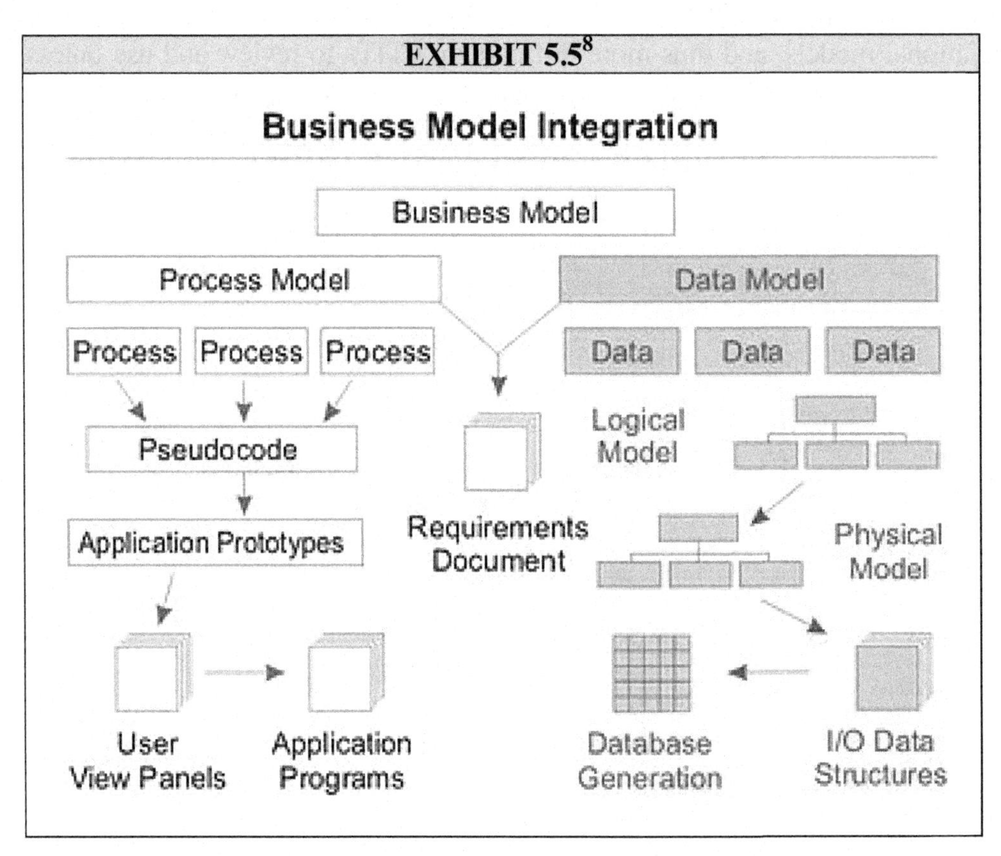

EXHIBIT 5.6: BUSINESS INFORMATION ARCHITECTURE[9]

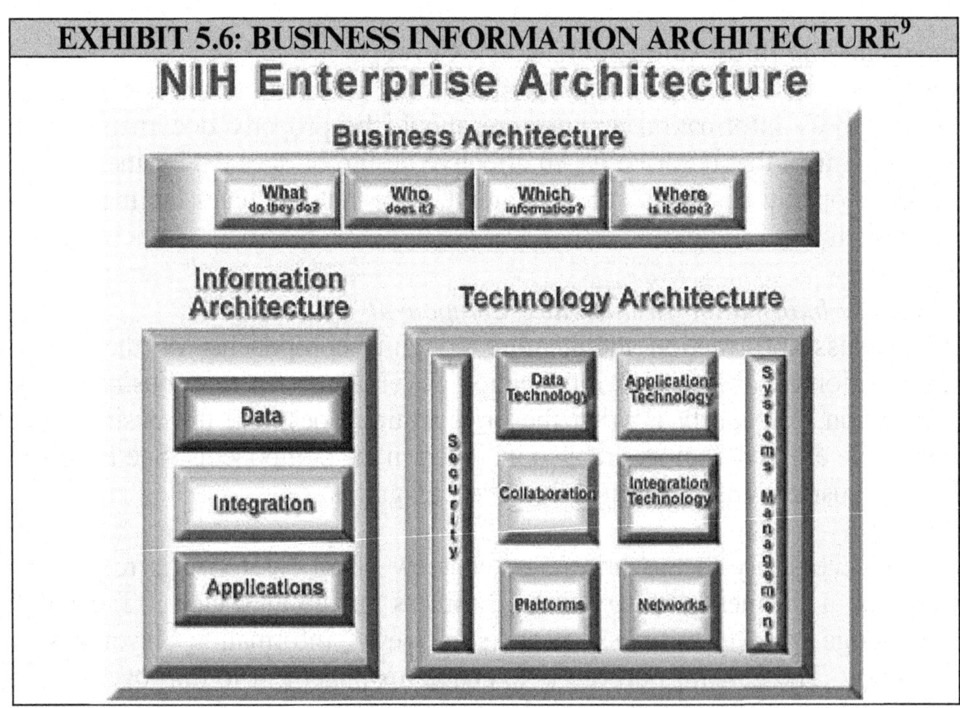

8 Taken from http://en.wikipedia.org/wiki/Business_process_modeling.Llast accessed on July 1, 2011.

9 An example of business information architecture from the National Institutes of Health, accessed at http://en.wikipedia.org/wiki/Business_architecture. Last viewed July 1, 2011.

The business integration model shows how the dual tracks of data and process modeling come together, and their relationship. The Data Model portion of Exhibit 5.5 shows how the information requirements phase ("requirements document") captures the data users need and the processes they perform in carrying out their accounting responsibilities. It also shows the components of data modeling (see Exhibit 4.2) that lead to the physical model, which leads to the data structure, which leads to database generation – including relational database construction where applicable. In the process model side, the processes are automated in application code and pseudo code, where the application and database generation eventually meet. Thus business processes are melded with the data modeling to produce the business model for systems.

Another view is the business architecture. This model shows an extension of the business model. The information architecture illustrates the common occurrence of integration of data from various sources that gets used by applications. This integration represents some level of complexity to that integration, and the more complex it is, or the more data being moved, the greater the risk becomes. Because there is some inherent risk in integration, that box in Exhibit 5.6 represents a need for controls to make sure the risks have been mitigated.

The technology architecture is the parallel structure of technology that houses the data and applications, and allows for processing and integration represented in the information architecture. These boxes will also represent risks, and require mitigating controls. The business architecture section asks four key questions that can help to identify the risks and need for controls, as well as assist in properly mapping data, information, and technologies.

5.1.3.2.2 – Business Information Types

Business information comes for a wide variety of sources and formats. It can be financial or non-financial. Some formal process should be undertaken to obtain a reasonable understanding of the relevant sources of information, which should also be documented. The mapping of that information into the architecture should also be performed and documented. A list of some possible sources of information includes:

- Accounting information systems (e.g.; information about accounting values, customers, vendors, inventory items, bills of materials, etc.)
- Financial reporting systems
- Financial information systems
- Economic data
- News
- Social media: blogs, social communities (e.g., Facebook), professional communities (e.g., LinkedIn), Twitter
- Directories of people
- Research (internal, external)
- Management (strategy, business model, estimates, etc.)
- Electronic spreadsheets
- Desktop/End-User computing (databases, spreadsheets)
- Office productivity documents
- (Certain) email
- Internet/web sites, RSS feeds, wikis

This list illustrates the potential scope and complexity of data integration, and thus represents potential risk and the need for controls for integration.

5.2 – BUSINESS PROCESS IMPROVEMENT

Business process improvement (BPI) has the goal of optimizing business processes to achieve efficiencies and effectiveness, using a structured approach. The approach is generic and can apply equally to commercial, not-for-profits, or government agencies.

According to former IBM president John Akers, "Our studies show that more than 50 percent of the total cost of billing relates to preventing, catching, or fixing errors." IBM became one of the first to focus on BPI in non-production processes. Essentially, BPI attempts to reduce variation and/or waste in processes, resulting in more efficient use of scarce resources. Successful BPI usually results in radical changes rather than incremental changes. The primary goal, however, is to align business processes to realize organizational goals (doing things right). BPI usually involves automating former manual or semi-manual processes, collapsing multiple processes into a single process, or both.

5.2.1 – Business Process Management

Business process management (BPrM) is a profession of its own.[10] BPrM focuses on more than efficiency and effectiveness gains in revising business processes, but rather takes a holistic approach that strives for innovation, more flexibility, and integration with technology. A continuous improvement approach is also key to successful BPrM. Similar to total quality management (TQM), BPrM considers processes as potentially strategic tools that can be better managed, improved, and then deliver value added products and services to the entity's clients. The difference in BPrM and TQM or BPI is the deliberate focus it has on leveraging technology to accomplish the goals and purposes of BPrM. That fact being said, BPrM also depends on human-driven processes, usually parallel to IT, where human judgment is performed in the steps of the business processes.

BPrM tools allow management to:

- Clarify Vision – strategy functions and processes
- Define Processes – baseline the process or the process improvement
- Test/Model Processes – simulate the change to a process prior to implementation
- Analyze Alternative Processes – compare various simulations to determine an optimal solution
- Improve Processes – Select the optimal solution and implement that improvement
- Control Processes – Monitor the improvement in real time, feed results back to simulation model, use for next iteration of improvement (often user-defined dashboards)
- Re-engineer Processes – When necessary, revamp the process completely from scratch

The BPrM Life Cycle uses similar activities and terms (see Exhibit 5.7).

---

[10] See the web site for the BPM Institute at www.bpminstitute.org

The design phase identifies existing processes, and describes the "to be" processes. The process flow is documented along with the relevant actors, alerts, standard operating procedures (SOP), service level agreements (SLA), and manual movement mechanisms.

EXHIBIT 5.7 – BPrM LIFE CYCLE[11]

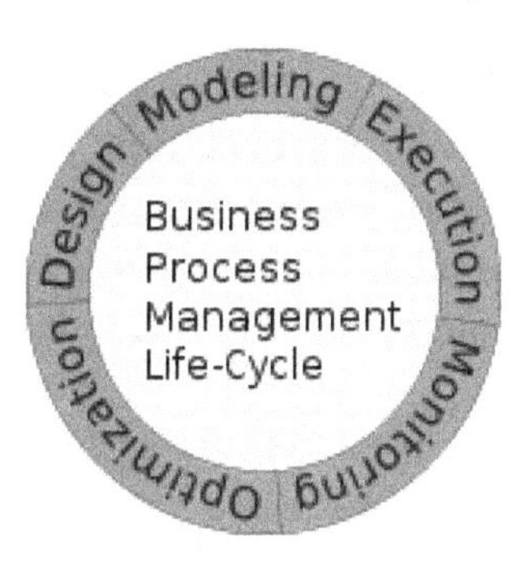

The model phase uses the theoretical design above and introduces new combinations of variables. What-if analysis is performed on those "to be" processes. Next is the execution phase. In it, the entity either develops or purchases a solution that is best suited to execute the required steps of the process determined in the model phase. The monitoring phase can take place in real time, a reasonable time frame, or ad hoc. Monitoring encompasses observation of the individual processes that results in accurate performance statistics. For instance, those measures could include cycle time, defect rate, and productivity. The next phase is optimization. It includes gathering process performance information from the modeling and monitoring phases. That information is used to identify potential or actual problem areas, such as bottlenecks, and potential opportunities for efficiencies or effectiveness improvements. Any improvements recognized herein are taken to the design phase for another iteration.

5.2.1.1 – Understanding of Business Processes that Impact Financial Data

The CITP will be particularly interested in business processes associated with the initiation, authorization, processing, and reporting of financial data, and the processes included in financial reporting functions. The approach to gaining a proper understanding means the CITP will need to know the flow of data and/or the body of processes used in financial transactions and financial reporting.

In understanding the processes that ultimately result in transacted business information, the CITP will want to gain an understanding of the information flows of accounting cycles and other areas of financial transaction management. This understanding can be obtained through walk-throughs, ovservations, interviews, system analysis. Examples of cycles and classes of transaction include:

- Revenues (sales, receivables, cash collections, etc.)
- Disbursements (bills, checks/payments, credits, payroll, etc.)
- Conversion (Inventory, manufacturing, or job cost – where applicable)

---

[11] Image taken from http://en.wikipedia.org/wiki/Business_process_management. Last accessed July 1, 2011.

- Journal Entries
- GL
- Financial reporting

5.2.1.2 – Proper Design and Integration of Internal Controls into Business Processes
Internal control is both a structure and a process. The main goal is to ensure there is expert input into BPrM regarding controls.

Each entity should have a formal structure for designing and implementing the proper level and effectiveness of controls into the body of business processes. That structure could take various forms: a form of IT governance, a change management committee, a cross-functional BP steering committee, an expert on business process change team, etc.

There should also be a formal process for making sure there is a sufficient system of internal controls. The entity should have P&P that ensure the use of expertise in integrating effective controls into all relevant business processes. That expertise could be an independent internal auditor or accountant, a consultant, a change committee function, an IT governance function, an IT steering committee function, etc. The process should also include formal monitoring to close the loop on improvements to controls. [see Dimension 3, section 3.1.1.3, Control Development Life Cycle, for more on this topic]

5.2.1.2.1 – Business Activity Monitoring (BAM) Approach
Business Activity Monitoring (BAM) is software that automatically monitors business activities embedded in information systems. It refers to the aggregation, analysis, and presentation of real-time information about those activities. BAM can also address multiple business processes, including those that span multiple systems or applications.

Typically, the results are displayed in a dashboard style, where real-time results are compared to key performance indicators (KPIs). When performance is in acceptable bounds, within criterion established for a specific KPI, then the dashboard uses a green symbol or some other icon to communicate acceptable performance. If the performance is slightly outside of acceptable bounds, then the symbol is yellow (caution) or similar icon. Finally, if the performance gets to an unacceptable level, then a red symbol, or similar icon, is used to indicate the seriousness of the current performance.

A key distinction of BAM dashboards is the fact they are instantaneous, dynamic, and real-time. Others, such as business intelligence (BI) dashboards, are refreshed periodically and thus have some static nature to them, and are not available real-time continuously.

Due to the proprietary nature, such as the choice and criteria of KPIs, BAM systems could require a great deal of customizing. There are industry standard BAMs, such as banking, manufacturing, and certain service industries, and these require less customization. Usually, BAM systems require a sophisticated implementation and therefore often entities hire a BAM expert who specializes in installing BAM systems.

Modern BAM systems operate, and are independent of, the need for BPrM or other similar tools and techniques. They can process high volumes of underlying technical events and present results dynamically, bypassing the need for intervening systems or tools.

For instance, assume a bank is interested in minimizing the amount of money it borrows overnight from a central bank. Each day, interbank transfers are communicated and executed via automation by a set time. A failure of one or more transactions could cost the bank an excessive amount of interest charged by the central bank. A BAM solution could be programmed to process each transaction message, wait for confirmation, and if within a stated period of time no confirmation occurs, the BAM could send an alert. The alert would cause someone to initiate a manual intervention to either investigate the delay or start a transaction to cover the event before it becomes costly.[12]

5.2.1.2.2 – Continuous Monitoring

Continuous monitoring (CM) is the system of processes and technology that is used to ensure compliance and avoid risk issues associated with an entity's financial and operational systems. CM involves people, processes, and technology that work together to detect weak or poorly designed controls, allowing management to correct or replace them. Continuous monitoring tools usually address one or more of the following types of monitoring: continuous audit, continuous transaction analysis, continuous controls monitoring, or continuous reporting. CM focuses primarily on the quantitative side of controls and risk issues.

Generally, these tools "sit" on the operational system and continually inspect each transaction based on criteria and parameters of what constitutes an anomaly, and usually some degree of failure or error. Low degree alerts are sent to files, or emailed to a responsible party, for resolution. Moderate degree problems would receive greater and more urgent attention. High degree would create an instant alert to someone, and immediate attention would be given to the problem (e.g., identification of a fraudulent journal entry).

Some continuous monitoring examples of interest to CITPs would be illustrated as follows: identify, quantify, and report on control failures such as duplicate vendor records, duplicate payments of same vendor's invoice, and disbursement transactions that fall outside approval criteria. In fact, CITPs are critical to the development and operations of effective CM programs because of their unique ability to identify control points and effectively designed controls. They also are experts at interpreting risk and controls information from the results of CM programs.

5.2.2 – System Solution Management

The system solution management (SSM) function is similar in concept to the systems development life cycle (SDLC – see Dimension 3, section 3.2.2.4 for SDLC content). The purpose of system solution management is to ensure quality in systems development and deployment. That is, to make sure applications have the appropriate controls, and that errors and other risks have been minimized.

System solution management also has a business purpose. Generally speaking, that purpose is to make sure the system aligns with the business model, strategic plans, and goals of the enterprise.

---

[12] Illustration taken from http://en.wikipedia.org/wiki/Business_activity_monitoring.

Within reasons of budget and other constraints, the SSM should lead to the selection of a solution that fits the business processes as close as possible, and is effective in aligning with the entity's strategies.

5.2.2.1 – Definition of the System Acquisition and Evaluation Life Cycle

There are three stages and nine individual functions in the System Acquisition and Evaluation Life Cycle (SAELC). The phases are simply labeled numerically. Exhibit 5.8 depicts the elements of SAELC. All of the following activities and processes should be fully documented.

5.2.2.1.1 – Initial Phase:

The initial phase begins with a ***business case***. Usually a business unit manager discovers a need for a new application or a change in an existing application, and follows some policy in requesting a change. Entities that have a mature IT governance structure and process will require changes to be submitted for consideration to the IT governance structure (e.g., a change management committee, IT steering committee, BoD subcommittee, or project management office {PMO}) in the form of a business case. In the business case, the proposal will be outlined as to need, supported by either high-level or detailed business, functional, and technical requirements, and documentation provided to describe the proposed solution. Based on P&P criteria, the business case usually provides for ROI or other factors used in decision-making.

EXHIBIT 5.8 – SYSTEM ACQUISITION & EVALUATION LIFE CYCLE

First Phase	***Second Phase***	***Third Phase***
Business Case	System Development	Training
Information Requirements	Quality Control	Transition
Solution Selection	Solution Implementation	
System Design		

Once the appropriate structure receives the business case, it will be evaluated based on general guidelines provided by the BoD. That could involve the amount of investment executive management is willing to make on a single project, or how much of the annual capital budget is remaining compared to the amount requested in the business case. There should also be a strategic alignment evaluation. Is the objective and functionality of the proposal aligned with the strategic goals and objectives of the entity, especially those most recently communicated from the BoD to the IT governance structure?

If the proposal is approved by the IT governance structure, or whatever approval mechanism exists, then the system development process begins. Typically, that beginning is to complete a thorough ***information requirements analysis***. Systems analysts or business analysts would interview end users and the project sponsor to determine the information needs. This step would also include reviewing existing business processes, existing applications (if applicable), and outputs or proposed outputs. The systems analyst should also make sure a security specialist scrutinizes the proposal, and even considerations for BI data that should be captured that might otherwise not be recognized. The process would also capture the business environment requirements, functional requirements, and business process requirements.

Once a requirements document is completed and vetted among all key stakeholders, then the process typically looks at alternative solutions. ***Solution selection*** could be build it or buy it (if the IT staff includes programming capabilities). If it is buy, there are still usually several alternative solutions. Major projects seeking alternative solutions could take the information requirements documents and create a request for proposal (RFP) that asks software vendors to propose based on those requirements. Some due diligence would then be performed to sort through the vendor proposals to make the best choice from among them.

If the entity decides to develop its own solution, then the ***system design*** needs to be developed in detail from the high-level documentation and information requirements developed up to this point. This phase should include a full set of application or system development documentation. The scope of application development is not included in this Dimension.

5.2.2.1.2 – Second Phase:
The second phase takes the system design, or choice of vendor product from a RFP selection, and goes through some due diligence before being implemented.

System or application development involves turning the system design into a fully functional, high quality solution, ready to go through an appropriate testing process, and on to implementation.

The application should be tested alone, which would have been done by the programmer. It should also be tested by the end user and/or the project sponsor for full functionality and errors. Then the application should be tested with other applications it regularly interfaces, usually an accounting or financial module. Then the application should be tested in the accounting cycle as a whole, if there are multiple modules in the cycle. Finally, the application should be tested with the GL and enterprise applications and databases.

An important asset to testing is the use of a simulator or staging area. A staging area replicates the enterprise system in terms of platform, operating system, all relevant applications, and all relevant databases – at the enterprise level or scope. With this tool, an appropriate level of testing can be performed reliably. [See 3.2.2.4.1.7 for more on testing]

The testing need to follow some effective detail test plan. The test cases should include a sufficient number of different permutations of possible scenarios in order to test the scope of possibilities. They should also be developed in such a way to test controls, at least the key controls. That plan sometimes is summarized on a check list complete with dates and signatures to ensure the entire plan was performed, and the performance was acceptable. The results should be documented for anlaysis and for reference for future testing.

5.2.2.1.3 – Last Phase:
The last phase involves the transition from the old way of doing things and the new way; that is, the completion of putting the application or system into operations.

One element that sometimes is either ignored, or treated too lightly, is ***training***. The greater the scope of change, the more the business processes have been changed or affected, the greater the need for training, because the greater the risk for data entry and business processes to not function properly. One way to reduce risk of failures in business processes, and errors in data entry is to provide adequate training when changes to applications and/or business processes change.

Another key success factor in changes to systems is controls over the ***transition*** from the old system to the new one. The IT staff will need to plan for that transition (conversion, implementation) and provide controls and activities concomitant with the level of assessed risk involved with the implementation. For high risk of conversion, there is likely to be a team of experts on site for the initial few hours of operation. There will be other controls, whether it is increased testing, or the choice of transition method. High risk is associated with the degree of the change, the scope of applications and systems affected, and the nature of the change (e.g., a change in the formula for calculating utility charges for a municipal utility is significant risk as all of the revenues and their accuracy are dependent on that calculation).

The transition can follow one of multiple choices for conversion: cutover, parallel, or phased. Cutover refers to turning the old system off and immediately turning the new one on. The risk of problems is high, as all systems could be affected by a failure, and there is likely no going back to the old system without great cost and difficulty. However, some conversions are best suited for cutover. Parallel means the old system and the new system are run simultaneous through some reasonable time frame. The risks of failures are minimized with this approach, but the cost of transition is the highest with this method. The phased approach is sort of a mix of the two. One business unit is chosen to be a "beta" where a cutover approach is used. However, because it is a single business unit, the risk is limited to that one unit. When the new system is operating reliably, then another business unit (or units) phase in by converting using cutover, and that process continues until all units are converted to the new system. This approach has reduced risk compared to a cutover, and reduced cost compared to the parallel.

However, parallel is seldom used in recent years. Small and mid-sized companies tend to favor keeping the system running with data as of a certain cut-over date, and to migrate limited amounts of data, such as GL balances as of month end.

5.2.2.2 – Risks Associated with Financial System Management

There are different risks associated with the approach to systems acquisition, depending on whether the entity develops the system internally or buys the system from a vendor.

5.2.2.2.1 – Customization of Financial and Accounting Information Systems

Anytime an entity writes its own code, the inherent risk (IR) of that process is generally assessed as high. There are, however, principles that can adequately reduce the residual risk by introducing effective mitigating controls (for instance, see 3.2.2.4 that demonstrates how the usage of SDLC principles can serve as mitigating controls for this particular risk). Control activities like effective QC, testing, use of a staging area, and thorough documentation are generally effective in mitigating this risk.

5.2.2.2.2 – Purchase of Commercial Financial and Accounting Information Systems

The purchase of commercial systems has less inherent risk IF the vendor is a reliable vendor. The current version being used should be one that is fairly recent. Sound vendor management should be in place as well. That is, it is possible for the purchase of a commercial package to lead to major control problems, errors, and other negative impacts on the processing of financial and accounting information and transactions. For example, if an entity purchases version 1.0 from a new software manufacturer, the IR is probably as high as it can be assessed. In addition, the likelihood of bugs, errors, and/or problems is probably 100 percent.

A reliable vendor would be one that has a respectable portion of the market share, has been in the software manufacturing business for a relatively long time (for that type of software), regularly updates it software, and has a good reputation for the support of its products. The more entities that use a COTS package and/or the longer the software has been around, the more likely there is sufficient controls, and a reduction in the risks associated with processing.

Generally speaking, purchasing COTS is less expensive than developing in-house, customized solutions.

Both approaches can have IR mitigated, with the right controls or circumstances, to an acceptable level of residual risk.

5.2.3 – Application Integration Management

If allowed to follow a natural ad hoc evolution, an entity will purchase and/or build various systems and applications that essentially operate in virtual silos. That is, the systems will not automatically and effectively interface or integrate with all of the other systems and applications. If the application integration is to be effective and efficient, there must necessarily be planning, P&P, and due diligence to ensure that all new applications follow an enterprise integration framework.

That framework would begin with a selected infrastructure, a choice of platform(s) and operating system(s), and the specific methodology for integrating all applications within the infrastructure. It would include a framework or model for ongoing integration of applications across time.

Application integration occurs when two different applications (from two different systems) need to share information or combine information in order to complete a business process or business report. For instance, when processing a sales order or quote, the business process may require information from both the accounting system data and the customer relationships management (CRM) system data. The same is true in generating a business report for sales history, even if it is an inquiry.

5.2.3.1 – Understanding the Benefits of Application Integration versus Disparate Applications and Databases

There are a number of benefits to using an enterprise application integration framework. One is the reduced risk associated with data transfers. Typically, disparate systems will require data transfers from one or more systems into financial reporting or accounting systems (e.g., transfer of revenue from a disparate sales system to the GL system; the same for other accounting cycles where the cycle uses a disparate application). Often these disparate systems then transfer the GL data to yet another disparate system, financial reporting. Each data transfer has a relatively high IR for risk of data integrity, and completeness and accuracy assertions.

There is also an efficiency aspect. The more the applications are fully integrated, the automated transactions and posting to affected systems will occur, and that naturally leads to less time spent performing all of the data transfers and communications.

That integration also leads to increased effectiveness – specifically the reduction of errors, problems, and IT risks. The fewer times data is handled, the fewer errors there should be.

5.2.3.1.1 – Integration Among Basic Financial Accounting Modules

Application integration is found in many of the COTS basic financial accounting systems such as Microsoft Dymanics, Sage MAS90, Intacct, and NetSuite. That is, the system has applications for all of the accounting cycles (purchasing, payroll, sales, disbursements, and inventory), journal entries, GL, and financial reporting. Furthermore, all of the transactions are basically interfaced with the relevant applications.

If the entity does not use an enterprise COTS financial accounting system, then it will need an application integration plan to make sure the same objectives can be achieved. That is true whether the entity writes its own code or uses a combination of commercial and proprietary applications.

There are also risks associated with non-integrated financial systems. Processing and data can be inefficient due to duplication of them. Reporting errors are more likely in non-integrated systems. Data from one system sometimes is rekeyed into another system, causing inefficiencies and increasing the risk of data errors.

5.2.3.1.2 – Other Related Systems

Other relevant systems should also be included in an application integration plan. For manufacturers, that would mean manufacturing resource planning (MRP) systems would need to be included in the enterprise application integration plan. The same is true if the entity uses electronic data interchange (EDI), electronic commerce (e-Commerce), electronic funds transfers (EFT), and other systems related to financial and accounting transactions.

5.3 – DATA ANALYSIS & REPORTING TECHNIQUES

The processes described in data consolidation, data cleaning, data transformation, and data reduction are the steps necessary for data preparation that leads to effective data mining and BI. It is estimated that 80 percent of the effort to build an effective BI or data mining system is expended in data preparation.[13] However, before data preparation begins, there needs to be an understanding of the infrastructure.

[13] Turban, Sharda, Delen, and King. *Business Intelligence: A Managerial Approach*, 2e. 2011. Pearson: Boston, MA. Page 150. The data preparation segments (5.3.2 – 5.3.5) are based on the same book, pages 150-152.

5.3.1 – Infrastructure / Platforms Typically Employed

The choice of infrastructure is important in developing a database system for data analysis and reporting. Sometimes, an existing platform is suitable, and sometimes the entity has to develop an effective solution to integrate the data warehouse, sources of data, and analytical and reporting tools. Typical solutions include ERP and data warehouse systems. When one of these platforms is not present, a data analysis / reporting portal may be possible where similar ease of access and use would exist.

5.3.1.1 – ERP or Other Enterprise Software as the Source

One infrastructure that could be used is an existing Enterprise Resource Planning (ERP) system. If an enterprise infrastructure exists other than ERP where application integration in particular is in place, then that infrastructure should be equally as useful as ERP. There would be access to selecting and collecting data, and an excellent resource for the data analysis/reporting system/database.

5.3.1.2 – Data Warehouse

Typically, the database used in data analysis and reporting is either in an integrated enterprise system, or data is transferred from operational systems and databases, and other relevant systems and databases to a data warehouse for specialized purposes and usage.

Data warehouses are used for business intelligence (BI), dashboard systems, data mining, decision support systems (DSS), Executive Information Systems (EIS), and Online Analytical Processing (OLAP) "cubes" (i.e. data analysis, "slice and dice" approach).

5.3.1.2.1 – Definition and Purpose

The primary purposes of a DW are to clean, transform, catalog, and make available data for strategic, analytical, and other purposes for management and business professionals. Those purposes include data mining, online analytical processing, market research, and decision-making. Other essential components of a DW system are to retrieve data, analyze data, extract/transform/load (ETL) data, and to provide for adequate management of a data dictionary. DW also includes business intelligence tools to make effectual use of the data.

5.3.1.2.2 – Data Structure

There are basically two kinds of structure for data in a DW: dimensional data or normalized data.

Bill Inmon first created the normalized data approach. Following its title, this approach normalizes data for a DW. This approach is also called "snowflake". Tables are grouped together by subject areas (e.g., customers, products, employees, purchases). The result, is dozens of tables linked by the foreign/primary keys. The addition of data from operational systems to a snowflake DW is fairly straightforward.

The disadvantages are: (1) it can be difficult for users to join data from different sources to obtain more meaningful information, and (2) it can be difficult for users to access the information without thorough knowledge of the data sources and the DW data structure.

Ralph Kimball is credited with creating dimensional data approach, which is also called "star". In the star format, transactional data is designed and defined as facts (generally, numeric data) or dimensions (reference information that adds meaning to the facts). For example, a sale transaction has quantities sold and dollar amounts (i.e. "facts"). It also includes the date of sale, region in which it was sold, the sales representative who made the sale, the category of inventory or service, and a variety of other relevant data that describes the numeric data (i.e. dimensions).

Generally, the dimensional approach is considered the easier of the two for users to grasp conceptually, and easier to use. Data retrieval tends to be more efficient in dimensional data (partly because it has been de-normalized, reducing the number of files needed to extract a set of data). Business users like the dimension approach because of the ability to easily "slice and dice" the data; e.g., sales by region, sales by time period, sales by sales rep, sales by sales rep and time frame, etc. In addition, use of dimensions generally allows for a more efficient management of GL accounts. ERP systems are moving towards the dimensional approach for data analysis and reporting.

The disadvantages of dimensional data are the fact: (1) loading the data from different systems and databases is complicated to get it into dimensional form, and (2) it is difficult to modify the DW structure if the entity changes the way it does business processes or captures data. Also, there is a tendency for larger entities to struggle with the "one way" dimensions that have to be defined (e.g., everyone must refer to and use city, state, and zip code as CSZ, and it must be one field, not three).

These data structures are not mutually exclusive. Star data structures are sometimes subjected to some normalization. There are also other approaches than these two.

5.3.1.2.3 – Extract, Transform, Load (ETL)

Because DW data is a coherent collage of data from a variety of databases, there is necessarily a sophisticated and structured approach to gathering and importing data into the DW database. That process is referred to as ETL – extract, transform, and load.

The extract refers to extracting data from the various data sources outside of the DW. Transform refers to the transformation of that data into usable form for the purposes of the DW (e.g., data analytics, data mining, or other business intelligence purposes). Load refers to loading the transformed data into the DW database.

Usually the DW database is cumulative data over several years. However, the timing of the updates varies; it could be updated frequently, example daily, or infrequently, example monthly. Eventually, some data will need to be overwritten or deleted in the DW database.

ETL presents a lot of risks. As said before, anytime data is transferred from one system to another, there is a relatively high IR. Add to that the transform step where data is being manipulated. Also, rules are being applied to data in the load step. So there are numerous aspects of ETL that lead to high risk for the ETL process. Therefore there is a fairly substantial need for controls to mitigate these risks.

The CITP is one professional who can assist in identifying those risks, developing effective controls and procedures to mitigate that risk, and analyze the resulting database for data quality and integrity.

5.3.1.2.4 – Data Marts

Data marts are subsets of the DW database with a specific purpose in mind. Often the purpose is related to the business user, especially business unit managers, and they become the "owner". Data marts are created for reasons such as: easy access to frequently needed data, collective view of a group of users, to improve end-user response time, to offload DW data to a separate computer for greater efficiency, security (to separate an authorized data subset), expediency, and politics.

5.3.2 – Data Preparation

Before effective business intelligence or data mining can happen, data from various sources must be consolidated. That consolidation process includes at least three steps: collect the data, select the data, and integrate the data.

This four-step data preparation is needful because real-world data are generally incomplete, contain errors, and have inconsistencies. All of these have to be addressed before the data is reliable enough to use in data mining or BI.

Data preparation is associated with data quality and therefore should be subject to the timeliness, format, and user-oriented content concepts described in the data integrity section above (see 5.1.1.3).

5.3.2.1 – Data Consolidation

Sources of data must first be identified. The principles of data consolidation recommend that the sources be documented in the data mining or BI system by mapping the various data sources to the end result database, usually a data warehouse. Then the data can be collected from those various sources.

5.3.2.1.1 – Data Mapping and Collection

The data identification and mapping would necessarily need to be based on a thorough understanding of the enterprise data structure and data flows, hopefully from established documentation.

Data flows can occur within a system, among systems, and even include manual flows of data offline. All of these should be examined in order to reflect the full data flow through the entity accurately.

5.3.2.1.2 – Data Selection

Depending on the needs of the end system (data warehouse, data mining, or BI system), the next step is to select the needed records and variables from the sources identified in step one (mapping and collection). Those records or variables not needed will be ignored, automatically filtered out of the selection process.

5.3.2.1.3 – Data Integration

Using the understanding of the data from the mapping process, the data selected is then integrated. Records and variables coming from various data sources are integrated into the target database.

5.3.2.2 – Data Cleaning

In the second phase, data is "scrubbed" or cleaned. This cleaning is necessary because data tends to have missing values, outliers, and inconsistencies in operational databases.

5.3.2.2.1 – Impute Missing Values

When values are missing, they are either intentionally ignored or an imputed value must be determined upon integration. Imputed values are based on the most probable value. Sometimes missing values are a reflection of reality and thus should be null.

The formula or process used to impute values needs to be predetermined, logical, documented, and repeatable. The system should also track the fact a missing value was assigned an imputed value. This transparency for assigning imputed values is critical to data integrity, and to relying on information being generated.

5.3.2.2.2 – Reduce Noise in Data

Noisy data, outliers and errors, have to be corrected as well. Again, an analyst or BI expert would need to determine the most acceptable values to replace, or smooth out, outliers and errors.

5.3.2.2.3 – Eliminate Inconsistencies

Using domain knowledge, or the assistance of an expert, inconsistencies have to be fixed. Inconsistencies include unusual values in for a variable (column, field).

5.3.2.3 – Data Transformation

Data transformation then takes the clean data and transforms it into a more usable form for data mining and/or BI.

5.3.2.3.1 – Normalize Data

The first transformation is to normalize the data. By normalizing data[14], all variables (columns, fields) will be treated equally by data analyses.

5.3.2.3.2 – Discretize / Aggregate Data

It may also be best to discretize certain data. Discretize means to convert numeric values to categorical values (high, medium, low). Data might also need to be aggregated. For instance, instead of using 50 states, they might be aggregated into just four regions. Data that is subject to either of these activities are because of the intended use of that data in the data warehouse, usually to simplify reporting and usage of the data.

---

[14] Normalized data means to transform all values in a column (variable, field) to some number between 0 (equivalent to the lowest value) and 1 (equivalent to the highest value). Another way of thinking of it is that the new value represents the relative position, as a percentage, of where that value falls along all possible values. The reason to normalize data is to prevent columns with large values from getting too much weight in data analyses (e.g., purchases of fixed assets over purchases of office supplies).

It is also fairly common for data to be kept in detail, then lightly summarized in a separate file, and highly summarized in yet a third file. That way different users can view the data in different levels of aggregation without waiting for the system to do the aggregation, and it allows for quick and efficient drill down from the highly summarized view/report.

5.3.2.3.3 – Construct New Attributes

Sometimes it is efficient for new attributes (variables, columns, fields) to be created to increase information content while reducing the complexity of relationships in the data. That is, those relationships that are not directly identified by the data have new attributes created to provide values to describe those relationships.

5.3.2.4 – Data Reduction

While one goal of DW data is to accumulate a vast array of data, too much data can be unmanageable, and make the understanding and use of the database too complicated. Therefore, often DW developers actually reduce the volume of data being loaded into the DW database.

5.3.2.4.1 – Reduce the Number of Variables

Often DW developers actually reduce the number of fields (variables) to a more manageable number. Domain experts and statistical results can help facilitate an effective number of variables.

5.3.2.4.2 – Reduce the Number of Records

The same principle applies to the number of records being loaded. Too many records would decrease the speed of using the DW. Once again, domain experts or stats might be used to determine if some of the records could be eliminated without losing significant information.

5.3.2.4.3 – Balance Skewed Data

Typically, balanced databases tend to produce better prediction models than unbalanced ones. When data is skewed, the distribution of the values do not follow normally distributive properties statistically. If data in data sources are skewed, a stratified sampling would probably lead to a more balanced database than random sampling. Another approach would be to oversample the less represented data values, or under sampling the more represented data values.

Reviewing the scope of necessary efforts in data preparation above explains why probably 80 percent of the average data analysis and reporting systems is involved with data preparation.

5.3.3 – Available Functions, Tools, and Approaches

Once data has been extracted, transformed, and loaded into the data analysis and reporting database (DARB), it is time to use tools and techniques to make effectual use of the information it can produce.

5.3.3.1 – Functions

There are three key functions to the data analysis and reporting database: extraction, data mining, and querying.

5.3.3.1.1 – Extraction

One basic function is extraction. That is, users can extract data from the DARB to be used for analysis or reporting. The result is similar to a data mart except it is user-defined, ad hoc, and on demand. Thus when business professionals or managers find an emerging need for a particular set of data that is in DARB, that person can extract the relevant data and perform the necessary process.

5.3.3.1.2 – Data Mining

Data mining is a process of examining large data sets for strategic purposes of learning something previously unknown from the data itself. Data mining application can be seen as two broad types: hypothesis testing and knowledge discovery (a.k.a. pattern discovery). The target objective can be to determine profiles of certain people or entities, better marketing, knowledge discovery, or fraud detection. For instance, banks apply data mining to check effectiveness of loan and credit card application decisions, insurance companies apply data mining for accident prevention and premium pricing, Amazon.com used data mining to determine inventory policy, and hotels use data mining to utilize its capacity. Customer relationship management is frequently the goal of a data mining system.

Data mining models generally follow one of several DM methodologies: memory-based reasoning, cluster detection, decision trees, market-based analysis, and link analysis. Even artificial intelligence (AI) tools are being used for data mining; tools such as neural networks, and genetic algorithms.

The memory-based reasoning (MBR) methodology works well for matching and fraud detection. The application of MBR is to assign to a new observation a pre-classified example (past transactions where results are known and thus can be accurately classified). Then a distance metric is used to classify new observations – that is, identify the highest number of matching fields to the pre-classified examples to predict the outcome of the new observation.

The cluster methodology is based on classical statistical clustering algorithms, and is useful for predictions, such as timely loan repayment. In clustering, the average characteristics of pre-classified examples of the same outcome are used as measures for a new observation. The accumulated distance of attributes from the new observation to the body of each outcome's attributes provides for a prediction of the outcome of the new observation. Usually, the values of all attributes are statistically normalized (0 to 1 values) for effectiveness.

Decision tree algorithms can be developed to automatically generate a set of business process rules. The most differentiating attribute of the pre-classified examples is used to build a decision rule (e.g., for banking loan decision, if credit history is "good", outcome is "pay on time" 89% of time – if credit history is "none", outcome is "pay late" 75% of time – if credit history is "poor" and income is < $30,000, outcome is "default" 80% of time). If the first "branch" of the decision tree is not satisfactorily high enough in prediction power, the next branch is examined.

Market-based analysis is the least structured form of data mining and involves what is known as shopping basket analysis in the retail outlets and food industry. The intent of this methodology is to identify products that tend to be purchased together.

The link analysis methodology is sometimes applied in the insurance industry to identify fraudulent claims. Tools such as Analyst's Notebook, Netmap, and Watson construct links to various objects to identify associations that might otherwise go unnoticed. The latest generation of link analysis tools provides not only graphical images of the links but also some interpretation of the links.

5.3.3.1.3 – Querying

Querying refers to structured query language (SQL) and similar tools that have the ability to filter data into meaningful information. Actually, SQL can insert data, query data, update data, and delete data. For data analytics and reporting, however, generally the query function is used.

In querying, data is filtered using the SELECT command to choose attributes (fields, columns). Other commands choose the file (FROM) or records (WHERE), and provide a variety of other functions to facilitate the generation of customized information.

With Microsoft SQL Server Analysis Services, there is a special querying language, data mining extensions (DMX), that is for data mining models. It works much like SQL and databases, using a data definition language (DDL) and data manipulation language (DML). However, in the case of DMX, the functionalities are built specifically for data mining purposes. Thus there are special commands in DMX to build prediction models and other data mining models.

5.3.3.2 – Understanding the Types of Tools Available

The tools needed for an effective data analytic and reporting system cover a range of functions (see Exhibit 5.9). Some tools serve multiple purposes, and most have been discussed above.

5.3.3.2.1 – Data Management

Chronologically, the first set of applicable tools would be the data management tools. These tools would be used to integrate the operational data and other relevant data into the data analytic and reporting system (e.g., ETL). It would also be the tools that allow for ongoing management of that database for effective use (e.g., data marts).

5.3.3.2.2 – Reporting

Reporting tools can be divided into general purpose, visualization, and strategy and performance management. The general-purpose tools would include OLAP, DSS, EIS, and dashboards. OLAP provides "slice and dice" reporting of multi-dimensional data that can be very beneficial. DSS reports assist managers in making more effective or efficient decisions. EIS systems provide executive managers highly summarized data in succinct form as relevant information. Dashboards also are used frequently to report data, especially live, dynamic results of certain critical information.

EXHIBIT 5.9 – BI TOOLS[15]	
Data Management	DBMS ETL DW and Data Marts
Reporting: General Purpose	OLAP EIS DSS Dashboards
Reporting: Visualization	OLAP EIS Dashboards
Reporting: Strategic and Performance Management	BPM Dashboards Balanced Scorecards
Business Intelligence	Data Mining Other mining (web, text) Link Mapping (e.g., Netmap)

The visual tools are EIS, OLAP, and dashboards (some of same tools as general reporting). OLAP uses the cube methodology and the results are natural subjects for visualization (e.g., sales by territory, sales by period of time, sales by category and time, as bar graphs or line graphs). Typically, EIS summarize a specified area of data into a single visual for executives (sometimes actually a dashboard). Dashboards are particularly suited for visualization. When reports are generated to compare actual results to budgets or predictions, that comparison can easily be reported with visual results. For example, if results are on target or within expected parameters, the cell or figures are often colored green. If results are slightly off target, slightly behind expectations, the result is shown in yellow (i.e. "caution"). In addition, if results are behind by some designated degree, the result is shown in red (i.e. "alarm").

The strategy and performance management reporting tools include Business Performance Management (BPM, similar to BAM in 5.2.1.2.1), dashboards, and balanced scorecards. BPM is a special tool specifically for the purpose of business performance management. Dashboards provide the kind of information that can measure performance (e.g., using the color scheme mentioned above) or strategic information as well. Balanced scorecards have been around in manual and technology form for many years, and provide a holistic evaluation of the entity's performance.

5.3.3.2.3 – Business Intelligence

The BI tools include data mining, other mining, and link mapping as examples. The BI tool most applicable in a situation is often a data mining tool. Web and text mining are becoming more popular recently as other mining tools. The link analysis tool (see 5.3.3.1.2) provides mapping of relationships among data and can be useful for certain situations (e.g., fraud detection, espionage).

---

[15] Partially taken from Turban, Sharda, Delen, King. "Business Intelligence: A Managerial Approach", 2e. 2011. Pearson: Boston. p. 32.

5.3.3.3 – Using Reporting Tools to Generate Information for Management and Business Users

Often an entity will deploy an enterprise system, especially COTS such as Oracle or SAP, and find many gaps in its needs for reporting. Report writers became valuable to fill that gap, and meet the need to have a richer body of reports available, and they soon became valuable as business intelligence applications as well. Some of the more popular ones are Crystal Reports, Cognos, and Hyperion.

5.3.3.4 – Real-Time Data Analysis

As mentioned above, operational decisions and other tactical needs have led to real-time data warehousing (RDW), or Active Data Warehousing (ADW). This type of system expands and supplements traditional DW and allows employees, vendors, and customers access to real-time information for decision-making. RDW can improve customer relations, supply chain management (SCM), logistics, and other aspects of the business.

As data is generated in the OLTP system, data is moved almost at once into the DW instead of being moved at the end of the day or end of the week. This allows, for all practical purposes, instant updates to the DW and replaces the intermediate transfer process, and possibly reduces the total time and resources involved. Then immediate and historical data are both available for strategic and tactical purposes.

5.3.4 – Tool Selection Process

Many factors go into a decision in selecting a tool for various functions of the BI system, data analytics and reporting system. That selection process probably begins with the infrastructure choice mentioned in 5.3.1 – will the entity try to get by using its ERP or enterprise system, or develop a more sophisticated and useful DW type system?

5.3.4.1 – Understanding Which Analyses and Reporting Tools Are Best

Using exhibit 5.9, and the discussion following, it can be seen that the differences between the tools may be subtle but obviously, a best fit is the objective. If the entity owns one of the reporting tools in 5.3.3.3 already (e.g., Crystal Reports), then it is likely Crystal Reports could serve much of its BI reporting needs as well. If the entity can develop a robust dashboard system, it could possibly serve as general reporting, visual reporting, EIS, strategy management, and performance management. These types of mental thought processes should enable the entity to make efficient use of its resources and still build a sophisticated, effective BI system.

5.4 – BUSINESS PERFORMANCE MANAGEMENT

Business Performance Management (BPM) more or less combines aspects of DSS, EIS, and BI into an integrated set of processes, methodologies, metrics, and tools designed to measure and manage the entity's overall financial and operational performance. BPM is an effective tool to align plans, objectives, and strategies with ongoing operations. The monitoring and measuring performed by BPM provides the means to ensure strategic success.

BPM has the following components at a minimum: (1) a set of integrated management and analytical processes supported by technology that addresses operational and financial activities and goals, (2) tools to assist in defining, measuring, and managing performance against goals, and (3) a system to plan, report, model, analyze, and monitor key performance indicators (KPIs) which are linked to strategy.[16]

5.4.1 – Budget & Profitability Management

In all entities, resources are limited. Those scarce resources need to be managed by aligning resources with strategic goal, objectives, and plans. Objects of financial need should be assessed a level of strategic value and funded accordingly – with the higher strategic needs being financed first and more fully.

Almost all entities conduct the process via a budget process. Budgeting naturally leads to funding of tactical operations. Thus tactical resource planning is a part of BPM, and a key part of budgeting in particular.

The budget and profitability management process uses a rational and structured approach that begins with financial goals and budgeting tactics to meet some profitability threshold. Thus both revenue generating tactics and cost control tactics become a part of the solution of this process.

5.4.1.1 – Types of Systems-Aided Budget or Cost Management Processes

Systems can aid in measuring budget or cost management. Almost all financial software applications commercially available have budget and cost management functions. There are also special tools, such as sophisticated budgeting systems, or specialized cost management systems.

5.4.1.2 – Examples of Performance Management Software

Examples of COTS financial systems with performance management functions include Microsoft Dynamics, Sage products (such as Peachtree and MAS 90), Interacct, NetSuite, and others.

5.4.1.2.1 – Cost or Revenue Reporting Automation

Accounting applications usually provide for standard reports for costs and revenues. Revenues are usually fairly sophisticated, and the insurance revenues shown in the dashboard of Exhibit 5.10 show the kind of information that is available for dashboards and BPM applications.

5.4.1.2.2 – Analysis by Job or Process

Job costing has been an effective measure of tracking revenues and costs of specific jobs in certain industries, such as construction. Anything that is a discrete job, with sufficient level of costs or activities, is a good subject for job costing.

ABC took that process in reverse and developed drivers of the cost and suggested measuring them, and focusing on them for potential cost reduction. Therefore, tracking and analyzing costs by process can potentially provide better information and process improvement than simply tracing actual versus budgeted costs.

---

[16] Taken from Turban, Sharda, Delen, King. "Business Intelligence: A Managerial Approach", 2e. 2011. Pearson: Boston. p. 85.

5.4.1.2.3 – Management Information Dashboards

Dashboards provide visual displays of information that makes the assimilation of that information, and the various nuances of it, easy and quick. The particular visual aid is tailored to the information being presented and can be color coded, as described throughout herein, or a needle on a dial with a shaded area of expected results, and the placement of the needle instantly provides whether the metric is on target, less than expected, or more than expected – and by how much. Bar graphs, pie charts, pyramids, and a variety of objects can be used; the key is to use one that provides the best visual for instant understanding.

Dashboards are not limited to real-time information, but can also work with static information. Dashboards can be online or offline. Most dashboards allow drill down to occur so that if a user sees some displayed information that needs investigating, a click on that object will drill down into the details that make up the dashboard object (e.g., bring up a list of transactions, a report, or a list from which the dashboard summarized the object displayed).

Some sample dashboards for an insurance company are shown in Exhibit 5.10 below.

EXHIBIT 5.10 – SAMPLE DASHBOARDS: INSURANCE COMPANY[17]

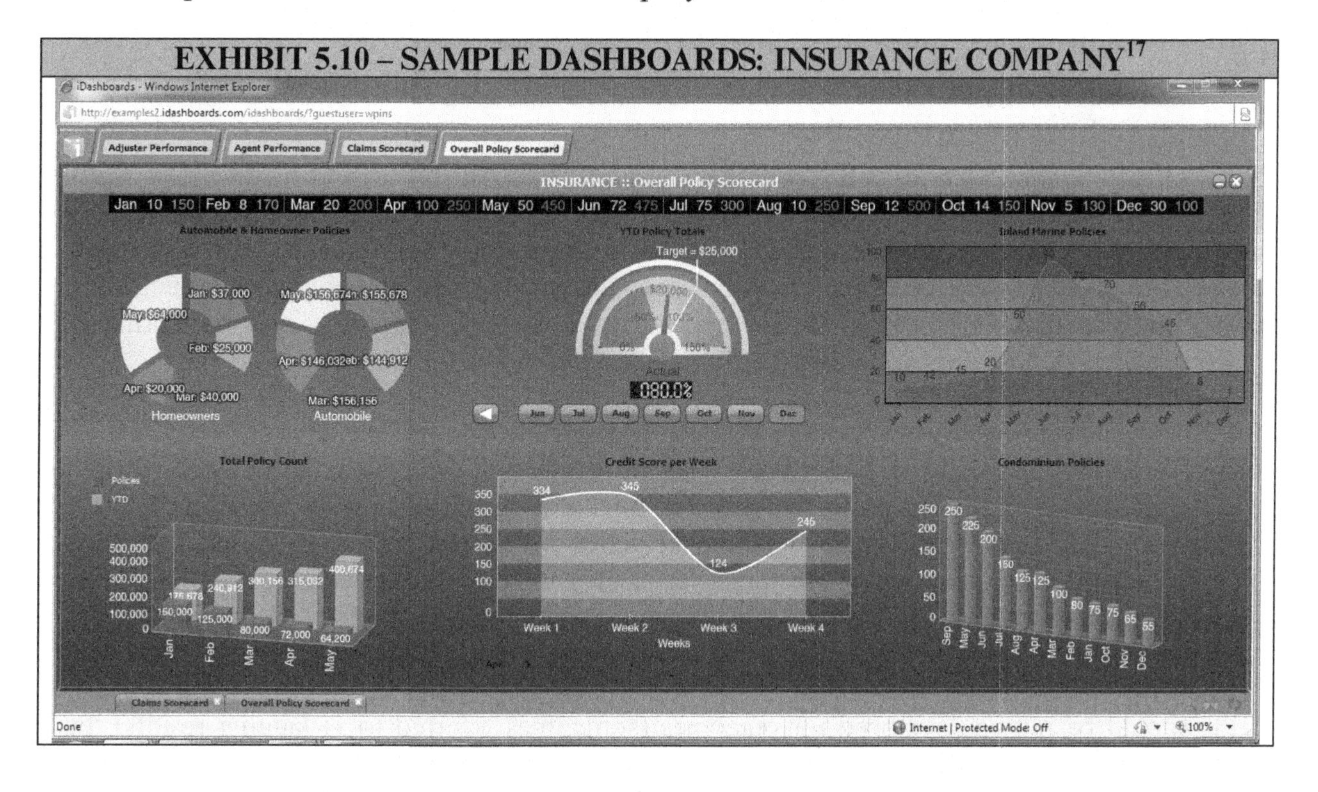

[17] Taken from www.dashboardspy.com, last accessed July 1, 2011.

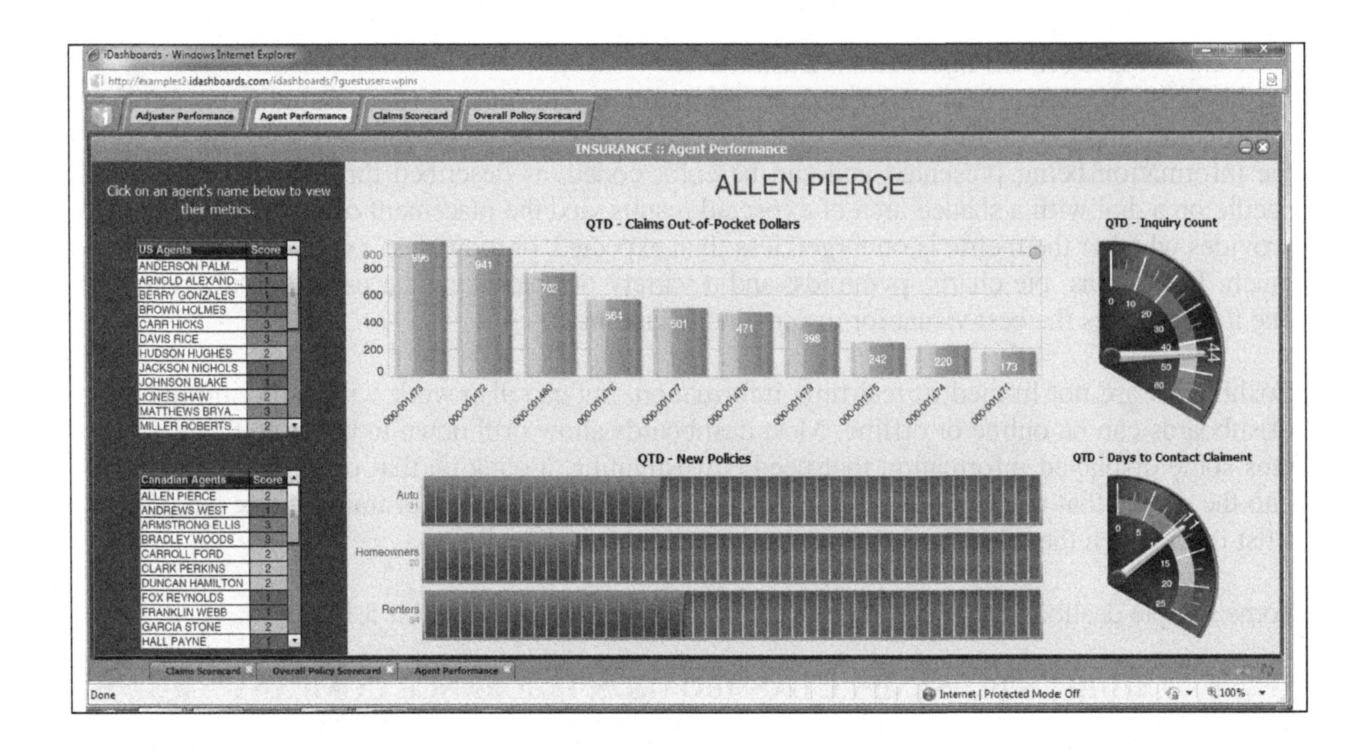

5.4.2 – Performance Metrics and Reporting

Care should be taken to not be caught up with the process of developing and using metrics and lose sight of the primary purpose, which is strategic alignment. Therefore, the term KPI means the performance indicator being measured has been analyzed to ensure it is aligned strategically; it is "key" to strategic success. A KPI represents a strategic objective, and measuring its performance is done against a strategic goal.

5.4.2.1 – Key Performance Indicators (KPIs) and Metrics

Effective KPIs will usually be multidimensional in nature. For example, a KPI might include a specific goal (e.g., 5 percent profit margin), but also a target range (e.g., 5 percent or more is "good" or green, 3.5-4.99 percent is "caution" or yellow, 0-3.49 percent "bad" or red, and a loss "terrible" or black). If that goal is for three years, then there should be some past, present, and future results. For instance, in year two, there would be the actual results of year 1 (e.g., 4.7%), and the current year results (e.g., 4.6%), and some prediction model result for year 3 (e.g., 4.5%).

KPIs should be not be developed for outcomes (sometimes referred to as lagging results), but also for driver KPIs (sometimes referred to as leading indicators). Much like the drivers in activity-based costing (ABC), where drivers were related to the processes or factors that drive the costs, leading indicators drive the results being measured as KPIs. For instance, the number of sales meetings scheduled, or the number of prospects might have a linear relationship to the number of new customers. If new customers are a KPI, then number of sales meetings scheduled or number of prospects should be a driver – a leading indicator.

Similarly, an effective BPM methodology would be holistic in all that KPIs measure. The Balanced Scorecard (BSC) became popular for that very reason – the aspects other than financial it was able to measure, and juxtapose four key areas for a holistic measure of how the entity is performing. For that reason, scorecards are common in BPM systems.

5.4.2.2 – Systems-Aided Alignment of Measures/Metrics to Organizational Objectives

As KPIs are developed, specific targets are established and performance ranges are determined (e.g., what is good, weak, and poor performance). There are tools that enable the entity to establish organizational objectives in the tool, and then align measures and metrics against them using the tool.

5.4.2.3 – Financial Measures Through Financial System Outputs

The majority of performance measures are financial in nature, and therefore come from financial systems. A financial budget provides a good example. The traditional budget reports can be designed to include budgeted figures, actual figures, and encumbrances to provide a holistic set of financial measures on how each line item, and the various components of financial operations, are performing.

5.4.2.4 – Customer-Related Measures Through Financial System Outputs

Financial system outputs provide some measures of customer metrics. Accounts receivable and sales data can measure customer retention, a KPI in most businesses. Likewise, accounts past due can indicate either poor processes in authorizing customers or customer dissatisfaction.

5.4.2.5 – Monitoring

Information overload can drown out effective monitoring. Therefore, it is imperative that entities employing BPM not only have monitoring, but also develop a system of monitoring with strategic care. Measures to monitor should answer the questions: what do we monitor, why do we monitor it, and how do we monitor it? Monitoring is naturally tied to response as well, timely and effective responses to certain deviations in performance.

Effective monitoring should include more than actual versus budgeted or expected results. It should be able to identify and measure underlying assumptions and processes, identify cause and effect relationships, and the overall validity of the strategy. Other factors would include things such as market demands, availability of parts, and other facts related to assumptions used in the development of the strategy.

Advanced Reading Recommendations:

Laudon, Kenneth C.; Laudon, Jane P. "Management Information Systems: Managing the Digital Firm", 11e. 2009. Prentice Hall: Upper Saddle River, NJ.
Moeller, Robert R. "IT Audit, Control, and Security". 2010. Wiley: Hoboken, NJ.
Turban, E.; Sharda, R.; Aronson, J.; King, D. "Business Intelligence: A Managerial Approach", 2nd edition. 2010. Prentice Hall: Upper Saddle River, NJ.

GLOSSARY:

Artificial Intelligence
AI is an area of computer science study that involves automated reasoning and problem solving, emulating human intelligence.

Attribute
A characteristic of something in a data file. For example, the part number of an inventory item.
Also referred to as a field, or a column in relational databases.

Balanced Scorecard
BSC is a holistic performance measuring and managing methodology combining financial, customer, internal processes, and learning/growth objectives into a single report.

Business Activity Monitoring
BAM is software that assists management in monitoring business activities, especially automated processes. It refers to aggregating, analyzing, and presenting business process performance.

Business Intelligence
BI is a structure and process that combines information architecture, databases, analytical tools, reporting tools, and other applications to gather and communicate business information for strategic and tactical purposes.

Business Performance Management
A BPM is a comprehensive structure and process that measures and analyzes enterprise performance, operational and financial, to achieve strategic advantages.

Business Process Management
Business Process Management (BPrM) is a holistic management approach to managing business processes at the enterprise level to promote efficiency and effectiveness, while stressing improvements, innovation, and integration with technology.
[**NOTE**: *To avoid confusion, business process management is labeled BPrM to distinguish it from business performance management, both of which are referred to as BPM in their disciplines.*]

Commercial Off-the-Shelf Software
COTS is a software that is published and made commercially available to the general public.

Conceptual Schema
The schema or view of information requirements before it is converted into an actual database. It is a composite view of all user views / schemas. Also referred to as a logical view.
See also user schema and physical schema.

Critical Success Factors
A CSF is a comprehensive structure and process that measures and analyzes enterprise performance, operational and financial, to achieve strategic advantages.

Dashboard
A visual presentation of information that allows for quick assimilation of the facts, and understanding of the significance or importance of the information.

Data
Raw facts such as numbers, letters, or special characters. Apart from outside manipulation, data is virtually meaningless.

Data Mart
A cogent subset of data warehouse database that is useful to one or more users of the entity, or its customers or vendors for reporting or analyzing information.

Data Mining
Data processing using large data sets and sophisticated data search capabilities and statistical tools to discover patterns or correlations, or to make predictions based on historical data.
Source: Google dictionary

Data Warehouse
A data repository of historical and possibly current data that has been cleansed, transformed, and loaded into the repository in a standardized format for business intelligence gathering, data mining, analytics, and other similar purposes.

Database
A closely related collection of data files where the data is shared among users.

Database Management System
A DBMS is a system of software for creating, updating, and querying a database.

Decision Support System
A DSS is a system of applications, data, and usually dashboard that supports managers, often modeling data or problems to facilitate effective decisions.

Electronic Commerce
Electronic business applications or processes that facilitate commercial transactions. Electronic commerce can involve electronic funds transfer, supply chain management, e-marketing, online marketing, online transaction processing, electronic data interchange (EDI), automated inventory management systems, and automated data collection systems.
Source: Wikipedia; http://en.wikipedia.org/wiki/Electronic_commerce

Enterprise Resource Planning
ERP integrates internal and external systems across the entire organization, integrating financial, accounting, manufacturing, sales, service, customer relationship management, and supply chain management systems.

Entity-Relationship Model
An ER is a data model that focuses on the relationship between two data files and how the records of one file relate to the other. The result of documenting the relationship is called an ER diagram.

Extract, Transform, and Load
ETL is a database process especially applied to data warehouses that involves: extracting data from outside sources, transforming data to fit organizational needs, and loading the data into the target database or data warehouse.
Source: Wikipedia; http://en.wikipedia.org/wiki/Extract_transform_load

Field
See attribute. Also referred to as a column in relational databases.

File
A closely related set of records. A full set of all instances of the thing being tracked in the database.
Also called a table in relational databases.

Information Lifecycle Management
An ILM is the structure and processes associated with managing information from creation or capture through disposition or destruction.

Key Field
A field that uniquely identifies records within the file. The key for a particular file is called a ***primary key***. The presence of a primary key in another file is referred to as a ***foreign key***.

Key Performance Indicator
A KPI is a type of performance measurement where the object and target metric has been developed strategically. KPIs define and measure progress toward organizational goals.

Neural Network
Computer technology that mimics the human brain – processing information, solving problems, and making predictions.

Normal Form
A structured process of breaking down a transaction into separate files in order to eliminate certain data anomalies.

- 1NF: First normal form – the first step in normal form process that eliminates repeating groups of data.
- 2NF: Second normal form – the second step in normal form process that eliminates partial dependencies, where some fields are dependent on only part of a concatenated key field.
- 3NF: Third normal form – the third step in normal form process that eliminates transitive dependencies, where some field or fields are dependent on a non-key attribute.

There are more normal forms but generally, databases are normalized only up to 3NF.
NOTE: *Normalization and normal form is different from the statistical process known as normalized data.*

Normalized Data (statistically)
The statistical process of converting all of the values for an attribute to a number between 0 and 1; or to give a percentage or ratio of a particular value to the range of possible values for the attribute.
NOTE: *Statistically normalized data is different from the data structure process known as normalization.*

Online Analytical Processing
OLAP is an approach to analyzing and querying multi-dimensional data, and is a part of the business intelligence discipline.

Online Transactional Processing
OLTP is a system that initiates, records, and processes transactions such as accounting and finance. OLTP records daily transactions for the organization to capture and report financial results.

Physical Schema
The schema or view of information requirements that is an actual database. Also referred to as an internal view.
See also conceptual schema and user schema.

Real-Time Data Warehouse
A Real-Time Data Warehouse captures and provides data in more or less real time.

Record
A closely related set of fields (attributes, columns) that constitute an instance of the thing being tracked by the data file.
Also called a tuple, or a row in relational databases.

Relational Database
A database whose records are organized into tables with columns and rows making it easy for users to understand and work with this data framework. Tables are normalized and related to each other through related attribute/column values.

Snowflake Data Schema
So called because an ER diagram looks like a snowflake. Snowflake is the data structure for data warehouse databases that uses normalized data, usually to 3NF. Bill Inmon is credited with the snowflake design.

Star Data Schema
Star is the data structure for data warehouse databases that uses dimensional data to amplify factual data (quantifiable values). Ralph Kimball is credited with the star design.

Structured Query Language
An SQL is a database function that allows users the ability to perform various database functions for a command line, such as adding, deleting, and changing data. Its most popular use, however, is querying where users can extract a list of information ad hoc using English-like commands.

User Schema
The schema or view of information requirements related to a specific user or group of users, before it is converted into a logical view or database. Also referred to as an external view.
See also conceptual schema and physical schema.

CASE & STUDY QUESTIONS:

Expedia Inc. is the parent company to some of the world's leading travel companies, providing travel products and services to leisure and corporate travelers in the U.S. and around the world. It owns and operates a diversified portfolio of recognizable brands including expedia.com, hotels.com, hotwire.com, and others. The offerings consist of airline flight, hotel stays, car rentals, destination services, cruises, and packaged travel. It acts as an agent in the transaction, passing reservations booked by its travelers to the relevant airline, hotel, car rental company, or cruise line. Together, these factors make Expedia the largest travel company in the U.S., and the fourth largest in the world. Its mission is to become the largest and most profitable seller of travel in the world, by helping everyone everywhere plan and purchase everything in travel.

Customer satisfaction is an important aspect in Expedia's overall mission, strategy, and services. Because most of its business is conducted online, the customer's shopping experience directly impacts Expedia's revenues. The online shopping experience can make or break an online business. It is also important that the customer's shopping experience be accompanied by a favorable trip experience. Because the customer experience is so important, all customer issues need to be tracked, monitored, and resolved as quickly as possible. Unfortunately, in the beginning of the business, Expedia lacked the ability to see the need to capture information about all aspects of customer satisfaction fully. It had no uniform or comprehensive way to measure satisfaction, of analyzing the drivers of satisfaction, or of determining the impact of satisfaction on the company's profitability or overall business objectives.

The customer satisfaction group knew that it had lots of data. In all, there were 20 disparate databases with 20 different owners. Originally, the group charged on its business analysts with the task of pulling together and aggregating the data from these various sources into a number of key measures for satisfaction. The business analyst spent 2 to 3 weeks every month pulling and aggregating data, leaving little time for the task of analysis. Eventually, the group realized that it was not enough to aggregate the data. The data needed to be viewed in the context of strategic goals, and individuals had to take ownership of the results.

To tackle the problem, the group decided to refine its vision and system. It began with a detailed analysis of the fundamental drivers of the department's performance and the link between this performance and Expedia's overall goals. Next, the group converted these drivers and links into an output with a perspective of financial and non-financial information including financial, customer, and internal growth. The process involved the following steps:

1. ***Deciding how to measure satisfaction***. This required the group to determine which measures in the 20 databases would be useful for demonstrating a customer's level of satisfaction.
2. ***Setting the right performance targets***. This required the group to determine whether KPI targets had short-term or long-term payoffs. Just because a customer was satisfied with his or her online experience does not mean that the customer was satisfied with the vendor providing the travel service.
3. ***Putting data into context***. The group had to tie the data to ongoing customer satisfaction projects.

The various real-time data sources were fed into a main database called the Decision Support Factory (DSF). In the case of the customer satisfaction group, these include customer surveys, CRM systems, interactive voice response systems, and other customer-service systems. The data in DSF are loaded on a daily basis into several subsets of data (based on topic) and multidimensional cubes. Users can access the data in a variety of ways that are relevant to their particular business needs.

Ultimately, the customer satisfaction group came up with 10 to 12 objectives that linked directly to Expedia's corporate initiatives. These objectives were, in turn, linked to more than 200 KPIs within the customer satisfaction group. KPI owners can build, manage, and consume their own scorecards, and managers and executives have a transparent view of how well actions are aligning with the strategy. The scorecard also provides the customer satisfaction group with the ability to drill down into the data underlying any of the trends or patterns observed. In the past, all of this would have taken weeks or months to do, if it was done at all. With the scorecard, the customer service group can immediately see how well it is doing with respect to the KPIs, which in turn, are reflected in the group's objectives and the company's objectives.

Source: Based on Microsoft, "Expedia: Scorecard Solution Helps Online Travel Company Measure the Road to Greatness", April 12, 2006.
http://download.microsoft.com/documents/customerevidence/22483_Expedia_Case_Study.doc

1. Based on the information provided in this case, which of the following best describes the subsets of data from the DSF?
   (A) KPIs
   (B) Data Marts
   (C) Balanced Scorecards
   (D) Business Activity Management

Key: B
Section Name: Data Marts (5.2.1.2.5)
Bloom's Taxonomy category: 1. Knowledge, 2. Comprehension
Reference: Business Intelligence: A Managerial Approach, pages 33, 100-102.
Solution:
Stem (B): *A subset of data from a BI type database whose purpose is designed to assist users in analyzing the data is called a data mart.*
Option (A): KPIs are key performance indicators that are not data in a database.
Option (C): Balanced Scorecards use data from a database, but the context was a subset of data with a design intent, which is a data mart. Scorecards are a presentation of data.
Option (D): BAM is a system that monitors business processes. The DSF is capturing customer satisfaction data.

2. In the same section of the case, there is data being pulled as multidimensional cubes. Which of the following is the best purpose of this kind of data?
   (A) Build OLAP
   (B) Build balanced scorecards
   (C) Build SQL query
   (D) Build User Schema

Key: A
Section Name: Reporting (5.3.3.2.2)
Bloom's Taxonomy category: 1. Knowledge, 2. Comprehension
Reference: Business Intelligence: A Managerial Approach, pages 57-59, 100-102.
Solution:

Stem (A): *Multidimensional cubes are peculiar to Online Analytical Processing (OLAP) processing and reporting.*

Option (B): Balanced Scorecards are multi-perspective reports that are not dependent on the form of data

Option (C): SQL query is a filtering exercise to extract data, and is not dependent on the form of the data

Option (D): User schema is a view of data from the user's perspective and not associated with data structure

3. Based on the case above, which of the following best identifies the DSF system?
   (A) BAM
   (B) BPrM
   (C) BPM
   (D) RDW

Key: D
Section Name: Real-Time Data Analysis (5.3.3.4)
Bloom's Taxonomy category: 1. Knowledge, 2. Comprehension
Reference: Business Intelligence: A Managerial Approach, pages 65-69, 100-102.
Solution:

Stem (D): *The DSF described in the case is a data warehouse, and appears to be updated in real time or near real time, making it a Real-time Data Warehouse*

Option (A): Business Activity Management (BAM) systems focus on monitoring business processes, not capturing enterprise data

Option (B): Business Process Management (BPrM) systems focus on improving business processes, not capturing enterprise data

Option (C): Business Performance Management (BPM) systems use enterprise data to analyze and report on performance, but are not the data source

4. When Expedia refined its customer satisfaction system, it wanted to put the newly defined drivers and linked results into a report for financial, customer satisfaction, and internal growth. What would you recommend as the best approach to accomplish this need?
   (A) Balanced Scorecard
   (B) Dashboard
   (C) EIS
   (D) BPM

Key: A

Section Name: Reporting (5.3.3.2.2)
Bloom's Taxonomy category: 1. Knowledge, 2. Comprehension, 3. Application, and 4. Analysis
Reference: Business Intelligence: A Managerial Approach, pages 100-102, 103-104.
Solution:

Stem (A): *Balanced scorecards (BSC) present financial, customer, learning/growth, and internal processes information in a succinct form to give management a balanced view of how the enterprise is performing*

Option (B): Dashboards are visual representations of data, especially tactical and operational information. This request was for financial, learning and customer satisfaction.

Option (C): Executive Information Systems (EIS) provide a similar visual product (succinct, one screen), but is usually strategic information. Only BSC includes the three aspects mentioned.

Option (D): Business Performance Management (BPM) reports are the broad term for BSC, EIS, dashboards, and all other reporting

5. In the case, there was an initial attempt to build a system to meet the needs to analyze and report on customer satisfaction. Which of the following is the best reason why that original system failed to satisfactorily meet Expedia's needs?
   (A) Lack of data, insufficient data, to meet their needs
   (B) Inexperienced business analyst who could not develop the design
   (C) A failure to aggregate data from the 20 different databases
   (D) A failure to view the data in context of strategic goals

Key: D
Section Name: Initial Phase of Systems Solution Management (5.2.2.1.1), Performance Management (introduction) (5.4.2), KPIs and Metrics (5.4.2.4)
Bloom's Taxonomy category: 2. Comprehension, 3. Application, 4. Analysis, 6. Evaluation
Reference: Business Intelligence: A Managerial Approach, pages 100-102.
Solution:

Stem (D): *According to the case, the customer satisfaction group eventually realized that it was not enough to aggregate data, that the data needed to be viewed in the context of strategic goals. This conclusion is consistent with BPM and KPI principles.*

Option (A): The case demonstrates that was more than adequate data, 20 different databases, and the same data that was eventually used in the BPM/Data Warehouse solution

Option (B): The business analyst appears to have not only done what was asked, but did a good job of it

Option (C): The case demonstrates the 20 databases were aggregated successfully in the original system, but it was not enough to just aggregate that data

Printed in the United States
By Bookmasters